AF702808

The Challenge of Religious Discrimination at the Dawn of the New Millennium

The Challenge of Religious Discrimination at the Dawn of the New Millennium

Edited by Nazila Ghanea

Martinus Nijhoff Publishers
Leiden/Boston
2003

A C.I.P. Catalogue record for this book is available from the Library of Congress.

Printed on acid-free paper.

ISBN 90 04 13641-x
© 2004 Koninklijke Brill NV, Leiden, The Netherlands.
http://www.brill.nl

Typeset by *jules guldenmund layout & text*, The Hague.

Koninklijke Brill NV incorporates the imprint Martinus Nijhoff Publishers.

All rights reserved. No part of this publication may be reproduced, stored in a retrieval system, or transmitted in any form or by any means, electronic, mechanical, photocopying, microfilming, recording or otherwise, without written permission from the Publisher.

Authorization to photocopy items for internal or personal use is granted by Brill Academic Publishers provided that the appropriate fees are paid directly to The Copyright Clearance Center, 222 Rosewood Drive, Suite 910, Danvers MA 01923, USA. Fees are subject to change.

Printed and bound in The Netherlands.

Table of Contents

Acknowledgements

Nazila Ghanea

> Religion is intended to be the cause of unity, love and fellowship and not discord, enmity and estrangement

`Abdu'l-Bahá

The idea for this edited collection emerged from the theme of the Spring 2001 Human Rights Seminar Series held at the University of London, Institute of Commonwealth Studies. This series focused on the subject of 'Religious Discrimination: 2 Decades after the UN Religious Discrimination Declaration'. Academics, NGO and interfaith activists and government representatives contributed to that series.

A number of those contributors have submitted chapters to this edited collection. However, other contributions were invited in order to add to the breadth and balance included in this collection. Warm thanks are therefore extended first of all to the authors of the chapters and of the Introduction to this collection—for their valuable insights and input; to the contributors to the seminar series for their support of this initiative; and to the Institute of Commonwealth Studies and to the UK Bahá'í community respectively—for hosting and co-sponsoring the original seminar series. Thanks also go to Lynda Warrington for her editorial work and to Lindy Melman and Rippy

Dusseldorp Saran at Martinus Nijhoff Publishers for their kind assistance during the publication process.

Any proceeds from this publication will be contributed to the fund of the UN Special Rapporteur on Freedom of Religion or Belief, in order to support the furthering of the principles set out in the UN Declaration on the Elimination of All Forms of Intolerance and Discrimination Based on Religion or Belief. The collection is dedicated to all efforts to eradicate discrimination based on religion or belief.

Introduction

Kevin Boyle

Professor, Human Rights Centre, University of Essex

This collection of essays was assembled before "9/11" and all that has followed from those epochal events including military interventions by Western Christian states in two Islamic countries—Afghanistan and Iraq, leading to the overthrow of their governments. But the themes and issues that are explored in this book—religion, human rights, politics and society—could not be more relevant to the post 11 September world.

The collection was intended to mark the 20th anniversary of a milestone in international normative accommodation over the recognition and defence of the rights to freedom of thought, conscience, religion and belief. On 25 November 1981 after many years of effort, the United Nations General Assembly adopted, without a vote, the Declaration on the Elimination of all Forms of Intolerance and Discrimination based on Religion or Belief. The Declaration is not legally binding but builds on the commitments of the International Bill of Human Rights which are. It espouses freedom of religion as an individual human right and calls on states to guarantee its individual and communal dimensions. At the same time the Declaration extends protection to atheistic and agnostic beliefs and indeed the right to hold no beliefs. But the central significance of the Declaration is to confirm the injunction of the UN Charter to the peoples of the world, 'to practice tolerance and to live together as in peace with one and other as good neighbours'. In a world characterised by an immense diversity as well as rivalry of beliefs, the international community and the states and peoples that comprise it, must defend the rights of the holders of all beliefs, majority or minority, religious or other than religious, from disadvantage and discrimination. At the same time international human rights law must remain neutral between the competing claims to truth of all religions and ideologies. A position of neutrality however is not the same as one of indifference. There is no incompatibility between respect for the phenomenon of human spirituality and acknowledgment of multiple understandings of that spirituality.

This vision of accommodation and mutual respect in matter of faith and conviction espoused by the 1981 Declaration is a tall order for the contemporary world. It may even be judged in the light of the deep gulf now exposed between Islam and the West as impossible, not to mention the many conflicts in other regions in which the religious differences between communities can appear insurmountable. But it remains the only path to pursue if the goals of human security and world peace are to be achieved in this 21st century.

The 20th anniversary of the Declaration in 2001 passed without much notice outside the circles of those interested in and working for universal religious freedom. It was not overlooked because of 11 September. It was overlooked because questions of freedom of conscience, and religion including the abysmal data on persecution and discrimination of these freedoms have not traditionally attracted much interest as human rights concerns in the Western societies that have tended to define international human rights priorities. Lack of interest in other parts of the world, speaks volumes as to the limited impact of international human rights standards on established systems of religious (or in the case of China), irreligious power.

One positive effect of the religiously motivated terrorism that resulted in the atrocities of 11 September may be that the neglect and by and large general ignorance of religious freedom issues can be reversed. The marginalisation of religious belief, despite its being the central constituent of individual and communal identity and of the deepest personal significance to the majority of human kind, is a lamentable failing in the conduct of international affairs. Patterns of religious discrimination and persecution have been too often ignored, fostering frustration and inter-communal violence. At the same time religious militancy and extremism engendered by majorities and minorities, represents a huge challenge in many countries developed and developing. As a result of rapid worldwide urbanisation, international migration, refugee flows and the revolution in communications, communities with different religious beliefs practices and cultures, including secularism, can no longer exist in remoteness one from the other. All must live irreversibly side-by-side for the future. But the collapse of distance and the growing awareness of human interdependence have yet to lead to the dispelling of ignorance about the other particularly in matters of religion and belief. Countering ignorance, myths and stereotypes, encouraging mutual respect for and acceptance of religious diversity must become an essential requirement of educational programmes in all countries.

The starting point of educational thinking might well be the 1981 Declaration. Its origins and content are examined in detail in *Nazila Ghanea's* chapter, which also considers its significance alongside other sources of legal obligation to uphold freedom of religion or belief. The modest achievements to date by the international community to encourage the Declaration's observance by States is considered in *Carolyn Evans* assessment of the work of the United Nations Special Rapporteur on the promotion and protection of freedom of religion or belief. Despite the derisory resources allocated to him, Evans offers a positive verdict on what he has been able to achieve with an inevitably fraught and sensitive mandate. The authority to undertake country visits has added a considerable value to the role of the Special Rapporteur. Such visits increase the prospects of the longer-term alleviation of the plight of victims in countries where these freedoms are at risk or are seriously violated. But at the same time in situ reports deepen international understanding of the often complex social factors that sustain religious discrimination and persecution. Thus discrimination and violence against believers often emanates not from the state but from other religious communities, movements or churches. While noting the attention that the Special Rapporteur has given to the question of women and religion, Carolyn Evan's would like to see for the future greater depth of treatment of other sensitive and complex issues, including the subject that now preoccupies the world, that of religious extremism or fundamentalism. The Special Rapporteur has long championed the link between building tolerance and education for and about religion. The chapter reports briefly on the significant first step taken to engage States on the need to tackle this vital subject, the Madrid Consultative Conference held in November 2001.[1]

A central concern of the Special Rapporteur has been to give voice however limited to those who experience intolerance and persecution because of their religious beliefs. His annual reports document the complaints of what can only be a sample of the individuals who are not only denied freedom to practice their religion but in too many cases are assaulted or killed because of

1. Final Document of the International Consultative Conference on School Education in Relation with Freedom of Religion or Belief, Tolerance and Non- Discrimination, www.unhchr.ch

their faith. *Mohammed Eltayeb,* drawing on his important research on religious persecution, offers a useful typology for the study of religious persecution.[2] He defines religious persecution as gross violation of the right to freedom of thought, conscience, religion or belief, that emanates from systematic and active state policy and action to harass, intimidate and punish individuals and religious groups, so as to infringe or threaten their right to life, personal integrity or personal security. His focus here is on one type of religious persecution, intra-religious persecution. That concept addresses the persecution of communities within the same religion in contrast to inter-religious persecution directed at believers of other religions. His examples are all drawn from present day Islam, the Ahmadiyya in Pakistan, the Shi'is of Saudi Arabia and the Republican Brotherhood in Sudan. His central thesis is that these cases and other examples of apparent doctrinal disputes in other religions should not be approached as exclusively religiously grounded. Rather such conflicts and their descent into gross human rights violations reflect a range of economic, social and political factors that have exacerbated religious tensions. (The implausibility of insisting that the decades of sectarian conflict in Northern Ireland was not about religion or was exclusively about religion comes to mind). It is also argued that intervention through analysis or human rights advocacy will prove more effective if it brings out the broader context of the dispute as the basis for dialogue and resolution. A human rights approach cannot engage with the theological dimensions of particular controversies. But in common with other contributors, Eltayeb insists that neither can human rights be set apart in some secular space distant from religion if contemporary human rights values are to become integral to the religious culture that is Islam.

The volume includes a number of chapters reflecting on aspects of freedom of religion and belief in the United Kingdom and the Netherlands. Both countries are mature democracies where there has been an historical experience of religious conflict (most recently in the United Kingdom in Northern Ireland) but which are also societies that have long developed a culture of tolerance and openness to religious diversity. In both countries the new challenges to what had become complacency over religious discrimination have emerged from the arrival and settlement of significant numbers of immigrants especially Muslims. Both societies have combined policies of balancing integration of immigrants with autonomy and freedom in matters of religion and culture. In both countries the question as to how that balance is to be pursued for the future is a subject of intense debate. The context is the experience shared with all of Western Europe; more and more vocal resistance to immigration and to

2. M.S.M. Eltayeb, *A Human Rights Approach to Combating Religious Persecution: Cases from Pakistan, Saudi Arabia and Sudan* (Antwerpen, Groningen, Oxford: Hart Intersentia, 2001).

acceptance of refugees and asylum seekers, a serious growth of racism, discrimination and violence directed at religious and racial minorities emanating from the majority populations and hesitant, confused debate over the implications of a multi cultural future. The events of 11 September and their aftermath have manifestly increased tensions. No one can doubt that 'Islamophobia' is widespread throughout Europe.

Cornelis de Jong takes as his point of departure the murder of Pim Fortuyn, the Dutch populist politician who had described Islam as a 'backward religion' and who campaigned on a platform of removing the constitutional prohibition on religious and racial discrimination. This chapter is a valuable and in-depth reflection of the enormous impact of that murder on Dutch politics and the challenges shared by all European societies as to how to assure the majority population that just accommodation to the religious freedoms of minorities, including on dress for example, can be combined with a shared identity of citizenship. He notes perceptively that in part Fortuyn had been successful and may have even believed that the manifest social change in the Netherlands wrought by economic globalisation was a result of immigration. But negative reactions to tumultuous global change are not confined to Dutch people. It is also often identified as a key element in explaining the emergence of militant religious extremism, including Islamic extremism. De Jong argues for a much greater investment by the Government in encouraging dialogue between Muslim and non-Muslim citizens. A dialogue should address the issues of difference for example the questions of treatment of women and attitudes towards homosexuals where the majority community can insist on the need for national secular standards on non-discrimination be upheld.

Tariq Madood compliments that chapter with an examination of British Muslims and British secular multiculturalism. He provides an account of how the development of the anti racism movement with its various concepts of equality and support for blackness as constituent of political identity sidelined Muslims for whom the most powerful pole of identity is religion. Taking that identity seriously is essential if a true multicultural society where at least half of the 'black' population is Muslim is to be achieved and where political participation by Muslims is to be welcomed. A religious strand to multicultural democracy is also a theme pursued by *Michael Ipgrave*. He notes that despite the radical decline in religious observance, Britain is not only formally a Christian state but has had an established Church since the Middle Ages. He traces the origins of the title famously given to Henry VIII by Pope Leo X of 'Fidei Defensor', a title maintained by that King after he had broken with Rome and by British monarchs since. Prince Charles the likely next monarch aroused controversy in 1994 when he announced that he intended to be the Defender of Faith, rather than Defender of *the* Faith, that is Anglicanism, the established church in Britain. Ipgrave reflects on the possibility that the reinterpretation of establishment so as to encompass the religious plurality of contemporary Britain, including Islam, could be a more constructive development than the dis-establishment and formal separation of Church and State. How such arrangements might comport with the jurisprudence of the European Court of Human Rights on freedom or conscience and religion could be an interesting speculation. In his analysis of that jurisprudence, *Malcolm Evans* rightly questions the decision in the *Refah Party* Case, in which a chamber of the Court held that it was not in conflict with the European Convention on Human Rights for Turkey to have suppressed what was the majority political party in power because of its espousal of Islamic ideals. The full Court has since unanimously upheld that decision.[3] The ruling means that it is incompatible with the democratic values that underpin the Convention to implement Islamic law. The implications of this judgement for a Europe where the Roman Catholic Church is lobbying for a reference to God, meaning the Christian God, in the proposed new Constitution for the European Union requires urgent reflection. Such reflection must begin as suggested in *Nazila Ghanea's* second chapter, 'Faith in Human Rights, Human Rights in Faith', with a great deal of more honesty and a great deal more in depth thinking about the relationship between law and religion. She explores the need for a rapprochement between religion and human rights and a collaboration that can advance the universal acceptance of human rights principles and codes internalised as moral commitments rather than as external and contested legal obligation.

Paul Weller examines recent research data on religious discrimination in England and Wales, bringing out well the new problems of distinguishing discrimination based on religious belief from the experience of ethnic or colour based discrimination. One finding in the research underscores a point already emphasised in this introduction –ignorance of the other was one of the most frequently cited reasons for unfair discriminatory or offensive behaviour towards minority religions. He cites a Jewish respondent for example whose neighbour was 'shocked' to find out that Jews do not celebrate Christmas or Jesus. Or another example, the comment "what is wrong with your head" used to a Sikh man. Tackling religious discrimination requires legislative action and the chapter by *Peter Cumper* examines in a British context the positive protections that will result from the implementation of Council Directive 2000/78/EC, that outlaws throughout the European Union workplace discrimination on grounds of sex, race, age, religion or disability. He notes wryly that the Directive's coming into force will not affect the most evident example of institutionalised religious discrimination in Britain, the fact that succession to the

3. Refah Partisi and Others v. Turkey judgment of Grand Chamber of 13 February 2003.

crown is confined by law to those of the Protestant Christian faith. Nor will it change the position that the English law of blasphemy extends to the protection of the Christian faith only.

As we await the coming trial of strength between Islamic and Christian influenced conceptions of democracy in the rebuilding of Iraq, it is clear that religion is back. To repeat: all of the themes and the issues discussed in these essays are now at the centre of global political debate.

Chapter 1

The 1981 UN Declaration on the Elimination of All Forms of Intolerance and of Discrimination Based on Religion or Belief: Some Observations

Nazila Ghanea

*Lecturer in Human Rights and International Law and MA Convenor, University of London, Institute of Commonwealth Studies.**

The UN Declaration on the Elimination of All Forms of Intolerance and of Discrimination Based on Religion or Belief (henceforth 'Religious Discrimination Declaration' or the 'Declaration') is clearly the 'most important international instrument regarding religious rights and prohibition of intolerance or discrimination based on religion or belief'.[1] However, it seems

* Thanks are extended to Olivia Ball for her comments on an earlier draft of this chapter.

1. N. Lerner, 'Religious Human Rights Under The United Nations' in J.D. van der Vyver and J. Witte Jr, (eds.), *Religious Human Rights in Global Perspective, Legal Perspectives*, p. 114 (The Hague: Martinus Nijhoff Publishers, 1996).

that even 22 years on, little political will exists to bring this Declaration to fruition as a binding legal instrument.[2]

The Declaration, as the name suggests, does not consist of a positive rendition of freedoms regarding religion or belief. From the outset, it is set in the wider context of the elimination of discrimination and intolerance as a whole. Its tone is therefore less forthcoming, and more in line with the International Convention on the Elimination of All Forms of Racial Discrimination (henceforth 'ICERD')[3] and the Convention on the Elimination of All Forms of Discrimination against Women (henceforth 'CEDAW'),[4] rather than the more positive elaboration of rights in the United Nations Convention on the Rights of the Child (henceforth 'CRC').[5] The language is set towards preventing and eliminating discrimination rather than protecting and defending particular associated freedoms. The Religious Discrimination Declaration is largely silent on specific preventive and combative measures to be taken by States in combating discrimination based on religion or belief.[6] It also makes no mention of redress, equality before the law or effective remedies for violations suffered.

This makes the Declaration much weaker in fact than ICERD. Whilst Article 1(4) of ICERD explicitly recognises the possibility of positive discrimination towards the advancement of disadvantaged racial or ethnic groups requiring such assistance, no such recognition is mentioned in the Religious Discrimination Declaration. ICERD also spells out in some detail what measures should be taken by States in condemning racial discrimination.[7] Furthermore, unlike the Religious Discrimination Declaration, ICERD prohibits propaganda based on such ideas of racial superiority and it also prohibits incitement of racial discrimination.[8] ICERD also ensures equality before the

---

2. However, this does not mean that the Declaration has no legal effect. As Sullivan has argued, 'Because it [the Declaration] is enunciated in normative terms, elevating the rights and freedoms in question to normative status, the Declaration has a certain legal effect ... That the United Nations General Assembly intended that it be normative and not merely hortatory is apparent from its Articles 4 and 7'. D.J. Sullivan, 'Advancing the Freedom of Religion or Belief through the UN Declaration on the Elimination of Religious Intolerance' *The American Journal of International Law* 82 p. 488 (1988).
3. International Convention on the Elimination of All Forms of Racial Discrimination (1965), which came into force in 1969. This Convention was adopted through General Assembly Resolution 2106 A(XX) of 21 December 1965.
4. Convention on the Elimination of All Forms of Discrimination against Women (1979).
5. United Nations Convention on the Rights of the Child (1989).
6. An exception to this is Article 4's specific reference to States taking 'effective measures to prevent and eliminate discrimination on the grounds of religion or belief'. However, no measures are proposed or outlined, so the provision remains very vague.
7. *Supra* note 3 Article 2(1).
8. *Supra* note 3 Article 4. See section on 'Omissions in the Declaration, Incitement to Religious Hatred' later in this chapter for more discussion on this matter of incitement.

law in the enjoyment of a broad range of rights[9] and the need for particular remedies, reparation or satisfaction in the case of any damage suffered from racial discrimination.[10] The Religious Discrimination Declaration does not.

Adoption History

Attention will now be given to the complex adoption history of this Declaration. The General Assembly (henceforth 'GA') had been concerned both with racial *and* religious hatred. This had followed resolution 1510 (XV) of the GA of 12 December 1960, which had condemned 'all manifestations and practices of racial, religious, and national hatred in the political, economic, social, educational and cultural spheres of the life of society' as violations of the UN Charter and the Universal Declaration of Human Rights (henceforth 'UDHR'). However, an enduring rupture occurred between the international concern with race and religion when the drafting of a legal instrument on racial discrimination came to be prioritized over that on religion. This led to the adoption of the Declaration on the Elimination of All Forms of Racial Discrimination in 1963[11] and the adoption of the ICERD in 1966. Next, the GA had requested both a draft declaration and a draft convention on religious intolerance. The slow pace of progress drove the GA in 1972 to give priority to the formulation of a Draft Declaration on Religious Discrimination. Discussion on a Convention was thus postponed indefinitely.

It took nine further years and much lobbying, until 10 March 1981, for the UN Commission on Human Rights to complete a draft.[12] This draft was adopted by a vote of 33 to 0, with 5 abstentions at the Commission on Human Rights and a vote of 45 to 0, with 6 abstentions, at the Economic and Social Council (henceforth 'ECOSOC'). The Third Committee of the GA adopted

9. *Supra* note 3 Article 5.

10. *Supra* note 3 Article 6.

11. This Declaration was adopted through General Assembly Resolution 1904 (XVIII) of 20 November 1963.

12. General Assembly Resolution 1781 (UN Doc A/5217) of 1962 requested the preparation of a draft declaration and a draft convention on the elimination of religious intolerance. In 1964 a preliminary draft declaration was submitted by the Sub-Commission to the Commission on Human Rights. Thereafter, a working group formed by the Commission considered a number of the articles. The Sub-Commission presented a preliminary draft convention to the Commission in 1965, and this was considered at the Commission over the following two years. The Commission's draft convention was transmitted to the GA in 1967, but in 1972 the GA decided to prioritise attention to the completion of a draft declaration. The Commission worked on this from 1974 to 1981, when a text for the Declaration was completed and transmitted to the GA.

the revised text of the draft Declaration by consensus on 9 November 1981. The GA itself then finally adopted the Declaration without a vote at its 73rd plenary meeting of 25 November 1981.

Even the discussion of the title of the Draft Declaration had not escaped discord. It was originally entitled 'Declaration on the Elimination of All Forms of Religious Intolerance', but in 1973 the words 'discrimination' and 'belief' were added, leading to the present formulation of the Declaration's title. All in all, it is highly evident that the 19 years taken to draft and adopt this Declaration 'indicates the sensitivity and complexity of the issue of freedom of religion or belief',[13] and also that the very adoption of the Declaration can itself be seen as 'a victory taking into account the surrounding gloomy political circumstances and the delicacy of the subject-matter'.[14] The following section will allow an analysis of the content of the Declaration.

The text of the Declaration

Preamble

The preamble of an international instrument is always of significance in contextualising that instrument and highlighting its key aims. Whilst the preambular section is not an operative part of the instrument, it is of significance in setting the tone of the instrument as a whole. The preamble places the instrument within a broader normative architecture and plays a role in the interpretation of the Declaration.

In this Declaration, the Preamble contains six main elements. Firstly, it draws attention to non-discrimination and equality as the primary prerequisites to the elimination of intolerance based on religion or belief. Secondly, it warns of the great suffering and wars that have resulted from the infringement of human rights, particularly of 'thought, conscience, religion or whatever belief'. The preamble states that this has especially been the case when such religion or belief has been used as the basis of 'a means of foreign interference in the internal affairs of other States' and that this has led to 'kindling hatred between peoples and nations'. Thirdly, the Preamble offers what amounts to a description (rather than definition) of 'religion or belief'.[15] It states:

13. B. Tahzib, *Freedom of Religion or Belief: Ensuring Effective International Legal Protection* p. 165 (The Hague: Martinus Nijhoff, 1996).

14. *Ibid.*

15. For a discussion on the merits of there being no definition offered of religion or belief in the Declaration see: Sullivan, *supra* note 2 pp. 491-492.

'Considering that religion or belief, for anyone who professes either, is one of the fundamental elements in his conception of life', then it is for this reason that it 'should be fully respected and guaranteed'. It furthermore encourages the promotion of understanding, tolerance and respect in relation to religion or belief, in order to ensure that they are not (ab)used 'for ends inconsistent with the Charter, other relevant instruments of the United Nations and the purposes and principles of the present Declaration'. Fifthly, this sentiment is expanded in a statement of conviction that freedom of religion or belief '*should*' 'contribute to the attainment of the goals of world peace, social justice and friendship among peoples and to the elimination of ideologies or practices of colonialism and racial discrimination'. Finally, the Declaration is contextualised within wider developments concerning the elimination of various forms of intolerance and discrimination. Resolve is echoed for the adoption of 'all necessary measures' for 'the speedy elimination of such intolerance in all its forms and manifestations and to prevent and combat discrimination on the grounds of religion of belief'. Overall, these themes attempt to justify the pressing need for this Declaration. However, it is unfortunate that more positive reasons for the contribution that religion or belief has made to society at large have not been put forward. In fact, the tone of the Preamble is quite defensive in implying a fear of religion or belief vis-à-vis wars, suffering, foreign interference, hatred and challenges to the territorial integrity of states.

The Operative Articles

Article 1

The opening Article 1(1) is largely analogous to Article 18(1) of the UDHR. Article 1(1) states:

> Everyone shall have the right to freedom of thought, conscience and religion. This right shall include freedom to have a religion or whatever belief of his choice, and freedom, either individually or in community with others, and in public or private, to manifest his religion or belief in worship, observance, practice and teaching.

The word 'everyone' in Article 1 makes its application to non-nationals and non-permanent residents clear. Since no minimum age is indicated, it also applies irrespective of age. The second sentence clarifies the dimensions of the application of the article. Individual belief, as well as the external manifestation of belief, is covered. Examples of the areas where manifestation of belief are covered need to be understood in the light of Article 6 of the Declaration.

There are some very minor differences between this Article and the UDHR's Article 18. The words 'individually or in community with others' replace the UDHR's words 'either alone or in community with others'; and manifestation is expressed in the same components as the UDHR 'worship, observance, practice and teaching' but in a different order.

The major difference from the UDHR's Article 18(1) is the exclusion of the phrase 'this right includes freedom to change his religion or belief' after the opening sentence of Article 1(1). In fact, Article 1(1) does not even include reference to everyone having the right 'to have or to adopt' a religion or belief of his choice, as stated in Article 18(1) of the International Covenant on Civil and Political Rights (henceforth 'ICCPR'). Nevertheless, Article 1(2)'s prohibition of 'coercion which would impair his freedom to have a religion or belief of his choice' goes some way towards compensating for this omission—though, here too, the ICCPR Article 18(2)'s reference to have 'or to adopt' a religion or belief of his choice is left out. Islamic states were not prepared to allow such an inclusion and, since these states, 'held the key to passage of the resolution'[16] through the GA, the position finally had to be accepted by other states. The Human Rights Committee, however, has since asserted that 'the freedom to 'have or to adopt' a religion or belief necessarily entails the freedom to choose a religion or belief, including the right to replace one's current religion or belief with another or to adopt atheistic views, as well as the right to retain one's religion or belief.'[17] It will be discussed later how Article 8 of this Declaration can be considered the 'saving clause'[18] or 'safety clause'[19] with regard to this omission and diminution in international standards.

Article 1(3) is identical in language to the provision of the ICCPR's Article 18(3) and sets out the only acceptable limitations to manifestation of religion or belief as those that are 'prescribed by law' *and* 'necessary to protect public safety, order, health or morals or the fundamental rights and freedoms of others'.[20] Article 1(3) of this Declaration can also be contrasted with Article 29(2) of the UDHR, which also provides limitations. One should, however, be wary of over-extending restrictions in a sphere as sensitive as religion or belief. Restrictions themselves need to be interpreted restrictively.[21] The Human

---

16. Tahzib, *supra* note 13 p. 168.

17. UN Doc.CCPR/C/21/Rev.1/Add.4 General Comment 22, Human Rights Committee, on Article 18 of the ICCPR, The right to freedom of thought, conscience and religion, 48th session, 30/7/93.

18. Tahzib, *supra* note 13 p. 167.

19. C.D. de Jong, *The Freedom of Thought, Conscience and Religion or Belief in the United Nations (1946-1992)* p. 48 (Antwerpen: Intersentia, 2000).

20. Furthermore, Article 4(2) of the ICCPR is explicit in *not* allowing derogation from freedom of thought, conscience and religion in time of public emergency, as provided for under Article 4(1) of the ICCPR.

21. It is in this vein that Sullivan explores the term '*fundamental* rights and freedoms of others' and what this may include and exclude. See: Sullivan, *supra* note 2 pp. 496-498.

Rights Committee stressed in its General Comment regarding the ICCPR Article 18(3) that,

> Article 18(3) should be interpreted in strict terms: restrictions are not allowed on grounds different from those specified in the paragraph, even if they would be allowed in respect of other rights protected, such as national security. Limitations may be applied only for their specific purposes and must be directly related and proportionate to the specific need on which they are predicted. They should not involve discriminatory purposes or be applied in a discriminatory manner. The freedom from coercion to have or adopt a religion or belief and the liberty of parents and guardians to ensure religious and moral education cannot be restricted.[22]

What goes unsaid here, but is clear from its implications, is that no limitations are acceptable to 'having' a religion or belief and that this (i.e. the *forum internum*) is absolute; only 'manifesting' that religion or belief in 'worship, observance, practice and teaching' (i.e. the *forum externum*) can be restricted. De Jong goes further in elaborating how, 'In reality, not all of these manifestations are equally protected.'[23] He highlights the elements required in dissemination of one's religion or belief and analyses this as the weak point of 'manifestation'.[24] However, the burden of proof is on States to demonstrate that, 'a limitation imposed complies with the requirements of paragraph 3'.[25] However, even *with* an acknowledgement of the need to interpret limitations restrictively, many questions remain about the understanding and application of such limitations. What remains is still a legal and political minefield. Which rights exactly are to be deemed 'necessary to protect public safety, order, health or moral' of others, in what circumstances and through what means? How can a restrictive interpretation of these clauses facilitate a vigorous, positive and vibrant environment of interchange between various religions or beliefs? De Jong proposes that, 'the only important limitation ground ... is the protection of fundamental human rights and freedoms of others.'[26] Whilst this may be contested by States, its objective is much clearer and it circumvents much of the potential for political manipulation. Therefore, this Article establishes a rather limited introduction to religion or belief entitlements from the outset. However, Sullivan considers the Article central to the Declaration, insomuch as it 'affirms the right to freedom of thought, conscience and belief, and the right to manifest one's religion or belief'.[27]

22. Lerner's understanding of UN Doc.A/48/40, Annex VI, paragraph 2. Lerner, *supra* note 1 p. 97.
23. de Jong, *supra* note 19 p. 168.
24. *Ibid.* pp. 154-168.
25. Tahzib, *supra* note 13 p. 170.
26. de Jong, *supra* note 19 p. 129.
27. Sullivan, *supra* note 2 pp. 490-491.

Article 2

Article 2(1) is very explicit regarding non-discrimination: 'No one shall be subject to discrimination by any State, institution, group of persons or person on the grounds of religion or other beliefs.' Sullivan refers to this Article's upholding of the prohibition of discrimination as, 'the companion principle to the freedom to manifest religion'.[28] However, she also bemoans the fact that the anti-discrimination provisions outlined in this Article are 'less detailed that those found in other declarations addressing discrimination'.[29]

This emphasis on non-discrimination on the basis of religion or belief can be traced back to the UN Charter, the ICCPR and the International Covenant on Economic, Social and Cultural Rights (henceforth 'ICESCR').[30] Article 55(c) of the UN Charter states that the United Nations shall promote 'universal respect for, and observance of, human rights and fundamental freedoms for all without distinction as to ... religion' as part of its pursuit of the conditions of stability and well-being necessary to peaceful and friendly relations among nations. Non-discrimination on the basis of religious belief is also emphasised in the UN Charter's Article 76 in relation to the trusteeship system. The ICCPR forbids distinctions based on religion or belief with respect to rights enshrined in the Covenant, to the protection of minors and to equal protection by the law. In the ICCPR, Article 2(1) forbids distinctions on the basis of religion; Article 24(1) forbids discrimination as to religion and Article 26 covers equality before the law and equal protection of the law without discrimination. Articles 2(4) and 13(1) of the ICESCR also raise the issue of non-discrimination on the basis of religion with respect to the guarantee of the rights in that Covenant and to education, respectively. Article 13(1) of the ICESCR further emphasises the role of education in promoting tolerance and friendship amongst religious groups. Article 13(3) of the ICESCR is identical to Article 18(4) of the ICCPR regarding parental and children's rights to a religious and moral education in conformity with their convictions. It explains, however, that this right depends on the educational establishment conforming to minimum standards. This shall be discussed further when addressing Article 5.

Returning now to the Declaration, Article 2(1) is very interesting in that it explicitly recognises that it is not only the State and the organs of the State that have responsibilities to avoid discrimination on the basis of religion or belief, but also institutions, groups of persons and each person. The responsibility to avoid discrimination therefore relates to both public and private acts and public and private actors.

---

28. *Ibid.* p. 501.

29. *Ibid.* p. 507.

30. International Convention on Economic, Social and Cultural Rights (1966).

Furthermore, Article 2(2) defines the earlier reference to 'intolerance and discrimination based on religion or belief' as 'any distinction, exclusion, restriction or preference based on religion or belief and having as its purpose or as its effect nullification or impairment of the recognition, enjoyment or exercise of human rights and fundamental freedoms on an equal basis'. This is analogous to Article 1(1) of ICERD. ICERD, however, is more elaborate in stating that it is the human rights and fundamental freedoms 'in the political, economic, social, cultural or any other field of public life' that should not be impaired. Nevertheless, this elaboration of the *public* areas in which discrimination should not be tolerated is expanded in Article 4(1) of this Declaration, and is discussed further below. The reference to 'having as its purpose' or as '*its effect*' is very significant in that discrimination that was allegedly not intended nonetheless constitutes a violation of the Declaration. Whilst an expansive notion of 'due diligence' of states regarding protection of the right to religion or belief is not explicitly acknowledged, this Article recognises a broad interpretation of state responsibilities regarding protection of non-discrimination on the basis of religion or belief. However, this commitment is not outlined in terms of proposing specific means and measures for combating the many instances of such discrimination that continue. Since the governmental regulation of non-governmental or private conduct in the field of religion or belief is so very contentious in many jurisdictions, such clarity would be especially pertinent.

Article 3

Article 3 continues Article 2's theme of discrimination on the grounds of religion or belief. It calls this 'an affront to human dignity and a disavowal of the principles of the Charter of the United Nations'. It goes on to state that this 'shall be condemned as a violation of the human rights and fundamental freedoms' as proclaimed in the UDHR and enunciated in the International Covenants as 'an obstacle to friendly and peaceful relations between nations'. This acts as a rejoinder between the Declaration's themes of discrimination and the Preamble's concern with the consequences stemming from the neglect of these rights. The neglect of rights and freedoms, particularly of religion or belief, is highlighted as having been the cause of war and conflict between nations in the past. In that sense, therefore, the Article serves more as a linkage between these themes than the bearer of any new substantive contribution to the Declaration. Tahzib has a point when she comments that, 'Since Article 3 is of an hortatory nature, it would indeed have been preferable to place that provision in the Preamble or, alternatively, as an introductory paragraph to an article.'[31] Article

31. Tahzib, *supra* note 13 p. 174.

3 really serves as the theoretical expansion of the importance of themes already included in Article 2. It adds little more than a theoretical elaboration of the importance of non-discrimination.

Article 4

States are reminded of the extent of their obligations in this Article. Article 4(1)'s reference to State action towards 'effective measures to prevent and eliminate discrimination' based on religion or belief, is to be welcomed. The aim of the Declaration clearly does, and should, go beyond formal equality and aim towards preventative actions to eliminate such discrimination. This enjoyment of human rights and fundamental freedoms, similar to Article 1(1) of ICERD, refers to enjoyment in *all* fields of 'civil, economic, political, social and cultural life'.

Whilst legislation alone will never be sufficient to achieve this, it is clearly part of the package of necessary measures that States need to take. Article 4(2) therefore holds that States shall make 'all efforts to enact or rescind' legislation as necessary to prohibit discrimination, as well as taking other appropriate measures to 'combat intolerance on the grounds of religion or other beliefs'. Attention has been drawn to this inclusion of the State obligation both to prohibit *discrimination* as well as combat *intolerance*[32]—therefore drawing a distinction between preventive action and channels of redress in instances where abuses occur.[33] However, legislation, whilst important, is clearly insufficient. The experience of treaty bodies with state reporting procedures are replete with vivid examples of how excellent legislation can go hand in hand with the most entrenched of abuses (e.g. against the Dalits in India). The focus on the impact of such legislation is therefore crucial. Sullivan's reading of this Article, that it upholds an obligation by states to take positive measures against discrimination based on religion or belief,[34] is therefore especially pertinent.

Article 5

The themes of the best interests of the child, freedoms in line with the development of the child, and the discretion of parents or guardians with respect to

---

32. *Ibid.* p. 174.
33. Sullivan also supports this distinction between 'intolerance' and 'discrimination': 'The view that intolerance describes the emotional, psychological, philosophical and religious attitudes that may prompt acts of discrimination or violations of religious freedoms is persuasive.' Sullivan, *supra* note 2 p. 505.
34. Sullivan, *supra* note 2 p. 503.

children are all included within this Article. These principles resound strongly with the CRC, which post-dates this Declaration by eight years.

Article 5(1) addresses the right of parents to organise family life in accordance with their religion or belief and 'bearing in mind the moral education in which they believe the child should be brought up'. Children's education in relation to religion or belief is to be in accordance with two, sometimes clashing, guiding principles: the wishes of the parents or legal guardians and the best interests of the child. This emphasis on the wishes of the parents or guardians in relation to the religion or belief of the child is somewhat in contrast with Article 14 of the CRC and its stronger child-centred focus. In that Article, the right of the child to 'freedom of thought, conscience and religion' is upheld, and the role of parents or guardians is limited to providing 'direction' to the child in the exercise of this right 'in a manner consistent with the evolving capacities of the child'.

Article 5(2) again emphasises the wishes of the parents or guardians in the education of the child in matters of religion or belief, but the 'best interests of the child' are to be considered the guiding principle in this regard. This recognition of the parents or guardians is also mentioned in Article 13(3) of the ICESCR,[35] and expressed more generally in the CRC's Article 3—where the protection and care necessary for the well-being of the child, as well as legislative and administrative measures, are all to be tempered by consideration of the rights and duties of parents or guardians. The 2001 Madrid Final Document[36] develops this further. Here, the role of 'parents, families, legal guardians and other legally recognized caregivers' is considered 'an essential factor in the education of children in the field of religion or belief'. The best interests principle also finds mention: 'special attention should be paid to encouraging positive attitudes and, in view of the best interest of the child to supporting parents to exercise their rights and fully play their role in education in the field of tolerance and non-discrimination',[37] with regard to existing international provisions in this regard. What is undeveloped in these instru-

35. Article 13(3) of the ICESCR states 'The States Parties to the present Covenant undertake to have respect for the liberty of parents and, when applicable, legal guardians, to choose for their children schools, other than those established by the public authorities, which conform to such minimum educational standards as may be laid down or approved by the State and to ensure the religious and moral education of their children in conformity with their own convictions'.

36. Final Document of the International Consultative Conference on School Education in Relation to Freedom of Religion or Belief, Tolerance and Non-Discrimination, adopted in Madrid, 23-25 November 2001. This document can be found in UN Doc.E/CN.4/2002/73, Commission on Human Rights, 58th session, 14 March 2002, Report submitted by Mr Abdelfattah Amor, Special Rapporteur on freedom of religion or belief.

37. *Ibid.* Operative Paragraph 9.

ments, however, is any differentiation between 'children' from birth to age 18 or their level of maturity. Regarding older children, de Jong interprets the provision of 'the best interests of the child' regarding religious education as follows: 'Since it does not seem to be in the best interests of a child to attend education in or based on a religion or belief against his or her wishes, once he or she has reached a sufficient level of maturity, it would seem possible to make best use of this provision for the benefit of the rights of the child.'[38]

Article 5(3) deals both with non-discrimination against the child in matters of religion or belief as well as ensuring that the child is brought up without discrimination. Non-discrimination on the basis of religion or belief is a well-established norm. Its focus on the child also finds mention in the CRC's Article 2. The child is to be brought up in 'a spirit of understanding, tolerance, friendship among peoples, peace and universal brotherhood, respect for freedom of religion or belief of others, and in full consciousness that his energy and talents should be devoted to the service of his fellow men'. This is certainly important to the feasibility of the notion of non-discrimination as a whole. It is clear that if education in religion or belief which bred discrimination were to be tolerated, the rights of others to religion or belief (or lack thereof) may well be consequently infringed. This is particularly echoed in the Madrid Final Document, which 'Considers that the young generation should be brought up in a spirit of peace, tolerance, mutual understanding and respect for human rights, and especially for the respect of freedom of religion or belief, and that they should be protected against all forms of discrimination and intolerance based on their religion or belief'.[39] In the CRC's Article 29(1)(d) the goal of education of the child is expressed in much broader terms, not just focusing on non-discrimination against others on the basis of religion. Article 13(1) of ICESCR[40] and Article 26(2) of the UDHR[41] outline the purpose of education in similar terms.

---

38. de Jong, *supra* note 19 p. 583.

39. *Supra* note 36 Operative Paragraph 3.

40. Article 13(1) of the ICESCR states 'The States Parties to the present Covenant recognize the right of everyone to education. They agree that education shall be directed to the full development of the human personality and the sense of its dignity, and shall strengthen the respect for human rights and fundamental freedoms. They further agree that education shall enable all persons to participate effectively in a free society, promote understanding, tolerance and friendship among all nations and all racial, ethnic or religious groups, and further the activities of the United Nations for the maintenance of peace'.

41. Article 26(2) of the UDHR states 'Education shall be directed to the full development of the human personality and to the strengthening of respect for human rights and fundamental freedoms. It shall promote understanding, tolerance and friendship among all nations, racial or religious groups, and shall further the activities of the United Nations for the maintenance of peace'.

Article 5(4) addresses the case of a child not under the care of parents or guardians. In such instances, due account is to be taken of the wishes of the parents or guardians in the matter of religion or belief, whilst tempering this with the best interests of the child as the guiding principle. This also finds more elaborate mention in Article 20(3) of the CRC, which speaks more generally of the 'desirability of continuity in a child's upbringing and to the child's ethnic, religious, cultural and linguistic background'.

Article 5(5) addresses a significant limitation on religion or belief which has a particular bearing on children. 'Practices of a religion or beliefs in which a child is brought up must not be injurious to his physical or mental health or to his full development'. This, however, is to be interpreted having taken Article 1(3) into account, which recalls the grounds of limitations on the manifestation of religion or belief as those which are prescribed by law and necessary to protect public safety, order, health or morals or the fundamental rights and freedoms of others. The limitations within Article 5(5) include the physical health, mental health and full development of the child; therefore it is covered under Article 1(3)'s reference to 'health' as well as its 'fundamental rights and freedoms' clause. However, the legitimate question posed by Sullivan emerges of what should be the fate of the child whose preferences regarding the practice of religion or belief differ from that of his parents or guardians and are not injurious to his physical and mental health or full development?[42]

Overall, the weaknesses encapsulated in Article 5 can be summarised in the following: the lack of delineation of who should be considered a 'child' (something that had also not been defined in the 1959 Declaration of the Rights of the Child[43] but was dealt with later in Article 1 of the CRC); that its overall emphasis is on parental control rather than the rights of the child; the lack of definition for 'best interests', 'mental health' and 'full development' of the child; the lack of acknowledgement of the right of children to choose their own religion or belief and the possibility of allowing discrimination against children by limiting their freedom of religion or belief.[44]

Whilst this Article is replete with remaining questions of definition and tensions between the values upheld, its inclusion in this Declaration is to be very much welcomed. It is somewhat ironic that children are included in this Declaration, and women[45] and religious minorities are not.

---

42. Sullivan, supra note 2 p. 513.
43. 1959 UN Declaration of the Rights of the Child.
44. Tahzib, *supra* note 13 pp. 175-179.
45. For a discussion of areas where major conflicts may emerge between women's rights and religious law, see: Sullivan, *supra* note 2 pp. 515-517.

Article 6

Article 6 is the key article of the Declaration and it goes some way towards tracing the scope of the right to freedom of thought, conscience, religion or belief—subject to the limitations on manifestation already outlined in Article 1(3). The Article should not be taken as a definitive guide to all such freedoms, but as an indication of the extent of these freedoms. Lerner refers to the freedoms outlined as, 'a catalog of rights that seem to be the universally agreed minimum standard in the area of religious human rights'.[46]

These rights can be categorised under the delineation of manifestation of religion or belief as outlined already in Article 1(1): 'worship, observance, practice and teaching'. However, the Article facilitates an extrapolation of what may be subsumed under these four categories. Only two of these paragraphs seem to go beyond the obvious elaboration of 'worship, observance, practice and teaching': (b) to establish and maintain appropriate charitable or humanitarian institutions and (i) to establish and maintain communications with individuals and communities in matters of religion and belief at the national and international levels.

The Article seems to shift from the more material aspects required for such freedoms to the more community dimensions of religion or belief. Worship and assembly, as well as establishing and maintaining places for such purposes, is covered in Article 6(a). Article 6(b) covers the establishment and maintenance of 'appropriate' charitable or humanitarian institutions (the implication of the word 'appropriate' not being clear here). The next section addresses necessary articles and materials that may be required by particular rites and customs of a religion or belief. The writing, issuing and dissemination of relevant publications is addressed in Article 6(d), and the teaching of a religion or belief in suitable places in 6(e). 6(f) covers the solicitation and receipt of 'voluntary financial and other contributions from individuals and institutions', and the next section allows for the training, appointment, election or designation of 'appropriate leaders called for by the requirements and standards of any religion or belief' (the implication of the word 'appropriate' not being clear here either). Finally, sub-paragraphs (h) and (i) cover days of rest and holidays or ceremonies and the possibility of establishing and maintaining communications at national and international levels with other individuals and communities in matters of religion and belief.

The scope of Article 6 is broader and more specific than the UDHR's Article 18 and the ICCPR's Article 18, which just refer to the categories of teaching, practice, worship and observance. Tahzib comments that this provision of 'specific illustrations' of the manifestation of religion constitutes

46. Lerner, *supra* note 1 pp. 117-118.

'a particularly important contribution'[47] of the Declaration to the protection of human rights. Whereas previous UN studies, especially the 1960 Krishnaswami Study,[48] had gone further than this Article in outlining what freedom of religion or belief encapsulated, this is the widest scope given to this freedom in a UN *instrument*. Article 6 also includes many rights that can prove contentious to realise in practice. Religious minorities are often accused of misappropriating financial contributions, States may try to politicise and interfere with the process of the designation of religious leadership and communications between religious communities can be considered threatening, especially where religious persecution may be occurring. If one contrasts Article 6 with the 1960 Krishnaswami Study, however, one is guided to a notable number of freedoms that were excluded from Article 6. These include the right to undertake pilgrimages, to be married/divorced/buried in accordance with one's religious laws or traditions and the right to conscientious objection in accordance with one's beliefs.

Despite its omissions, this Article can be seen as the most crucial Article of the Declaration, as it goes some way to expanding and elaborating manifestation of religion or belief in an international instrument, and specifying which spheres of life are to be protected as central to religion or belief.

Article 7

Article 7 calls for the freedoms put forward in the Declaration to be made effective through national legislation 'in such manner that everyone shall be able to avail himself of such rights and freedoms in practice'. The emphasis is on access to, and realisation of, such freedoms in practice. This echoes the need to look beyond legislation to 'all appropriate measures' to combating intolerance, as outlined in Article 4(2). This focus on access and realisation of rights is similar to provisions in other International Conventions, such as Article 24 of CEDAW: 'States Parties undertake to adopt all necessary measures at the national level aimed at achieving the full realization of the rights recognized in the present Convention.'

However, since this is not a binding instrument with a monitoring body, it is not clear how the compliance of national legislation is actually to be overseen.

47. Tahzib, *supra* note 13 p. 180.

48. A. Krishnaswami, *Study of Discrimination in the Matter of Religious Rights and Practices*, UN Doc.E/CN.4/Sub.2/200/Rev.1, 1960. Reprinted in the *NYU Journal of International Law and Politics* Vol. 11, p. 227 (1978).

Article 8

Article 8 emphasises that none of the provisions of this Declaration should be interpreted in a manner that would diminish its reach below that of the UDHR and the International Covenants on Human Rights (the ICCPR and ICESCR), or lead to any derogation from those standards. This is highly significant in relation to the apparent weakening of the freedom to change one's religion or belief as discussed under Article 1. It means that no such derogation has occurred in legal terms, though in political terms there has undoubtedly been some slippage. The protection granted by this Article is discussed in 'Omissions in the Declaration, Coercion and Inducements' below.

According to Sullivan, this Article also, 'appears to regulate conflicts between religious rights and other rights',[49] for example in relation to proselytism where the human rights of both the promoter and listener need consideration.

Overview

Omissions in the Declaration

Amongst the most glaring omissions of the Declaration, in this author's view, are the following four areas:

1) Non-theistic & atheistic beliefs

Surprisingly, nowhere in the Declaration is there an explicit acknowledgement that this Declaration is set out to protect 'theistic, non-theistic, and atheistic beliefs'. Whereas this language is not explicitly used in Article 18 of the ICCPR either, the Human Rights Committee asserted in General Comment 22 of 1993 that Article 18 of the ICCPR protects theistic, non-theistic, and atheistic beliefs, as well as the right not to profess any religion or belief.[50] This language is also found in the 2001 Madrid Declaration.[51] This lack of overt language regarding the protection of atheistic beliefs was, in fact, the cause of some US-Soviet disagreements at the time of the drafting of the Declaration. However, the inclusion in the third paragraph of the Preamble of the word

49. Sullivan, *supra* note 2 p. 498.

50. UN Doc.CCPR/C/21/Rev.1/Add.4, Human Rights Committee, 48th session, 27 September 1993, General Comment 22 adopted by the Human Rights Committee under Article 40, para. 4, of the International Covenant on Civil and Political Rights, Addendum, Adopted by the Committee at its 1247th meeting on 20 July 1993.

51. See: *supra* note 36 footnote 1 to preambular paragraph (b).

'whatever' in the context of 'the right to freedom of thought, conscience, religion or whatever belief' brought about the necessary understanding of the inclusion of non-religious beliefs. It is therefore clear that this Declaration protects non-theistic and atheistic beliefs equally to theistic beliefs and, indeed, the reference in the fourth paragraph of the Preamble to 'fundamental elements in his conception of life' would be consistent with this finding. However, this inclusion remains tacit rather than explicit.

2) Coercion and Inducements

Whereas Article 18(2) of the ICCPR states that 'no one shall be subject to coercion which would impair his freedom to have or to adopt a religion or belief of his choice', Article 1(2) of the Declaration merely forbids coercion towards a person 'having' rather than both 'having' *and* 'adopting' a religion or belief of his choice. The Declaration further omits the word 'change' of religion or belief. This marks a step back from existing international standards in this regard.[52] Indeed, General Comment 22 of the Human Rights Committee defines coercion as

> the use of threat of physical force or penal sanctions to compel believers or non-believers to adhere to their religious beliefs and congregations, to recant their religion or belief or to convert. Policies or practices having the same intention or effect, such as, for example, those restricting access to education, medical care, employment or the rights guaranteed by article 25 and other provisions of the Covenant, are similarly inconsistent with article 18.2.[53]

It is therefore clear from this General Comment that coercion either to bring about change of religion or belief or to coerce continued association with a religion or belief are equally unacceptable under international standards. It is therefore unfortunate that the Declaration remains silent on the unacceptability of coercion towards the latter, and also does not expand on actions which constitute coercion.

The Human Rights Committee also emphasises that the reference to restrictions that may be imposed on the manifestation of religion or belief in Article 18(3) of the ICCPR does not mean that 'the freedom from coercion to have or adopt a religion or belief' can be restricted.[54] One can similarly assert,

52. Exclusion of 'change' of religion in the Declaration is particularly ominous regarding those who may be accused of apostasy and heresy, and the human rights violations that may be imposed upon them. See: Sullivan, *supra* note 2 pp. 495-496.

53. *Supra* note 50 para. 5.

54. Natan Lerner's understanding of UN Doc.A/48/40, Annex VI, paragraph 2. Lerner, *supra* note 1 p. 97.

in the context of this Declaration, that the limitations outlined in Article 1(3) do *not* provide grounds for restricting freedom from coercion as protected in Article 1(2) regarding having 'a religion or belief of his choice'.

3) Religious Minorities

Though the focus of this Declaration is on eliminating intolerance and discrimination, and though religious minorities suffer most from such religious discrimination, it is startling that no reference is made to religious minorities in this Declaration. References to non-discrimination and equality underlie the protection of minorities in a very weak manner, but mention of freedom of religion or belief 'either individually or in community with others'[55] does not go so far as to recognise religious minorities as such.

Article 27 of the ICCPR recognises the rights of religious minorities to 'profess and practise their own religion'. Dinstein holds that Article 27 of the ICCPR grants 'collective human rights to members of a religious minority qua a group'.[56] The Human Rights Committee's General Comment on Article 27 confirms that Article 27 provides that ethnic, religious and linguistic minorities not be denied the right '*in community with the other members of their group*, to enjoy their own culture, to profess and practise their own religion, or to use their own language'.[57] The purely individualistic reading of Article 27 is therefore challenged by this statement, as well as in the emphasis that 'The terms used in Article 27 indicate that the persons designed to be protected are those who belong to a group and who share in common a culture, a religion and/or a language'.[58] It is the collective dimensions recognised by Article 27, in association with Article 18 of the ICCPR, that together offer a promising overlap for religious minorities discriminated on the grounds of religion or belief. This overlap, however, has not been explicitly recognised in this Declaration.

Since the 1981 Declaration, the Human Rights Committee General Comment has rejected 'any tendency to discriminate against any religion or belief for any reasons, including the fact that they are newly established or represent religious minorities that may be the subject of hostility by a predominant religious community'.[59]

55. Declaration on the Elimination of All Forms of Intolerance and of Discrimination Based on Religion or Belief, Article 1(1).

56. Y. Dinstein, 'Freedom of Religion and the Protection of Religious Minorities' in Y. Dinstein and M. Tabory (eds.), *The Protection of Minorities and Human Rights* p. 157, quoted in Lerner, *supra* note 1 p. 94.

57. Emphasis added. General Comment 23, Human Rights Committee, on Article 27 of the ICCPR, the rights of minorities, 15th session, 8/4/94, para. 1.

58. *Ibid.* para. 5.1.

59. *Supra* note 17 para. 2.

Furthermore, the 1992 Declaration on the Rights of Persons Belonging to National or Ethnic, Religious or Linguistic Minorities registers the need for States to 'protect the existence' and religious identity of minorities, 'encourage conditions for the promotion of that identity', allow them to 'profess and practice' their own religion, 'participate effectively' in decision-making, and 'establish and maintain' their own associations as well as free and peaceful contacts with co-members across frontiers.[60] It furthermore upholds the full equality before the law of religious minorities,[61] and the need for States to take measures to create 'favourable conditions'[62] allowing persons belonging to minorities to express their religion.

Whereas the description of the freedoms encompassed within the right to freedom of thought, conscience, religion or belief, as outlined in Article 6 of this Declaration, strongly suggest the inclusion of its collective dimensions, there is no language that explicitly caters for this. Since this collective dimension is *precisely* where most of the intolerance and discrimination is suffered, its exclusion from this Declaration is indeed a very serious absence. However, Article 8 of the Declaration emphasises that nothing in this Declaration should be construed as 'restricting or derogating from' any of the rights established in the UDHR or the International Covenants. Article 27's inclusion (along with, or without, Article 18) therefore, can be read into this Declaration, particularly within Article 6. Indeed, Lerner has expounded the collective dimensions encapsulated within Article 6: 'It is important to stress that Article 6 of the Declaration deals with individual rights, collective rights of the persons, and rights that can only be exercised by the group as such. In this regard, it involves progress as compared to previous instruments. Only groups can establish and maintain places of worship and institutions, or appoint religious leaders, or establish federations. The Declaration thus contemplates the needs of religious communities or congregations'[63]—but it still does not recognise religious minorities as such.

4) Incitement to Religious Hatred

Considering the pivotal role of incitement of religious hatred in the mobilisation of intolerance and discrimination against religious or belief communities worldwide, it is very surprising that no mention is found of the harmful

60. All references are from Articles 1 and 2 of the 1992 UN Declaration on the Rights of Persons Belonging to National or Ethnic, Religious and Linguistic Minorities.

61. *Ibid.* Article 4(1).

62. *Ibid.* Article 4(2).

63. Lerner, *supra* note 1 p. 120.

impact of religious incitement in this Declaration. However, Article 2(1)'s assertion that no discrimination should stem from 'any State, institution, group of persons or person on the grounds of religion or other belief' would seem to include incitement, as would Article 2(2)'s definition of intolerance and discrimination as including any distinction which effectively impairs the 'enjoyment and exercise' of human rights and freedoms on an equal basis.

Furthermore, Article 20(2) of the ICCPR should also be read in conjunction with the Declaration, as this Declaration is not to be construed as derogating from the standards established in the Covenants.[64] Article 20(2) states that 'Any advocacy of national, racial or religious hatred that constitutes incitement to discrimination, hostility or violence shall be prohibited by law' (it should be noted that, contrary to the definition of genocide, such incitement 'does not require intent')[65]. In the *travaux préparatoires* it is evident that this, and the fact that preventative action in the form of anti-incitement legislation[66] is implied, caused much controversy. However, in its General Comment 11 on Article 20 of the ICCPR (Prohibition of Propaganda for war and inciting national, racial or religious hatred) the Human Rights Committee states that, 'In view of the nature of Article 20, States parties are obliged to adopt the necessary legislative measures prohibiting the actions referred to therein.'[67] Obviously this is an issue that the Human Rights Committee is able to take up on a case-by-case basis with relevant States through the State reporting procedure. This echoes Article 7 of the UDHR regarding protection against any incitement towards such discrimination. ICERD also makes 'all dissemination of ideas based on racial superiority or hatred, incitement to racial discrimination, as well as all acts of violence or incitement to such acts against any race or group of persons' illegal. In the ICERD 'Any group of persons' obviously includes religious groups as well, and it can therefore be seen also to infer the illegality of incitement towards religious hatred. The absence of a more explicit reference to incitement in the Declaration is unfortunate.

Overall then, this Declaration omits very central aspects of religion or belief which, it is hoped, would be elaborated before any attempt is made towards a binding instrument.[68]

64. UN Declaration on the Elimination of All Forms of Intolerance and of Discrimination Based on Religion or Belief (1981), Article 8.

65. Lerner, *supra* note 1 p. 93.

66. Article 4 of the Convention on Racial Discrimination (*supra* note 3) also imposes on governments the obligation to enact anti-incitement legislation.

67. General Comment 11, Human Rights Committee, on Article 20 of the ICCPR, 19th session, 29/7/83, para. 1.

68. This proposal still stands, even though the inclusion of incitement was discussed and rejected during negotiations leading to this Declaration.

Prospects and Implementation

Since it is not known when, or *if*, the Declaration will be crystallised in the form of a binding Covenant, numerous attempts have been made to ensure that its provisions are nevertheless rendered effective. These have included measures such as the two UN-convened Geneva seminars on the Encouragement of Understanding, Tolerance, and Respect in Matters Relating to Freedom of Religion or Belief.[69] In 1985, Elizabeth Odio-Benito was appointed as Special Rapporteur by the Sub-Commission to explore the problem of intolerance based on religion or belief and propose measures to counteract the phenomenon. In 1986, the Commission on Human Rights also appointed a Special Rapporteur who has since been monitoring incidents and governmental actions in all parts of the world that were inconsistent with the provision of the 1981 Declaration.[70] The Special Rapporteur's mandate extends to recommending remedial measures including dialogue between governments and religious communities.[71]

Many have noted that the political environment for the support of this right has deteriorated over recent decades. They therefore argue against the drawing up of a Convention at present. This is because lack of consensus and support may significantly reduce the current legal status for the freedom of religion or belief and reduce the margin for interpretation that currently exists. Tahzib, for example, argues that, 'however desirable a legally binding instrument may be for the protection of freedom of religion or belief, there seems to be little inclination on the part of at least the majority of states to incur further legally binding obligations in this domain'.[72] This position has also been echoed by the Special Rapporteur himself. This opinion was given in the context of a discussion on the possibility of re-opening discussions on a new international Convention on the freedom of religion and belief. He is reported to have stated: 'I'm afraid that opening a new discussion on conventions would lead us a step backward on religious freedom.'[73] For Malcolm Evans, however, the delay is not just due to States, but to the international community as a whole. 'Clearly, the time is not yet ripe for a convention: not because of the unwill-

69. UN Doc.ST/HR/SER.A/16, 1984, quoted in M. Roan, 'The Role of Secular Non-Governmental Organisations in the Cultivation and Understanding of Religious Human Rights' in J.D. van der Vyver and J. Witte Jr (eds.), *Religious Human Rights in Global Perspective, Legal Perspectives* p. 138 (The Hague: Martinus Nijhoff Publishers, 1996).

70. UN Doc.E/CN.4/1986/65, Commission on Human Rights, Res. 1986/20.

71. See chapter 2 in this book by Carolyn Evans for a detailed analysis of the effectiveness of the role of the Special Rapporteur.

72. Tahzib, *supra* note 13 p. 441.

73. Reported from a panel discussion which took place on 5 November 1998. Bahá'í International Community, *One Country* Vol. 10, Issue 3, p. 3 (October-December 1998).

ingness of States to adopt such an instrument, but because of the reluctance of the international community to accept that in the religious beliefs of others the dogmas of human rights are met with an equally powerful force which must be respected, not overcome'.[74] For different reasons, therefore, Tahzib, Amor and Evans all suggest awaiting a more favourable milieu before the codification of the 1981 Declaration is attempted.

What, therefore, can be done with the present Declaration? Lerner comments that, 'Of course, a Declaration is not a treaty and is not binding. However, it carries with it the weight of a UN solemn statement, giving expression to the trends prevailing in the international community at a given moment. It does have a certain legal effect, and it implies an expectation of obedience by members of the international community to the extent that it may be seen as stating rules of customary international law ... the Declaration unquestionably shows progress in a sensitive area of human rights that, in comparison with other rights, had been neglected.'[75] Elizabeth Odio-Benito holds that 'It cannot be denied that the adoption of the Declaration represents an advance of enormous importance along the difficult road toward abolishing discriminatory practices and intolerant attitudes in regard to the human right of religious liberty in all its aspects. With this Declaration, the General Assembly has reminded the nations of the world that it is among the superior interests of humanity to put an immediate end to the persecutions and manifestations of religious prejudice'.[76] She also believes that it would take a very long time to adopt a Convention on the issue. In the meantime, however, and as van Boven argues, the Declaration sets out 'a valuable set of norms which lends itself both as a yardstick to measure compliance by governments and as a tool to promote respect and tolerance'.[77]

This Declaration is currently the best platform we have. We need to work on it as the basis (albeit an *incomplete* basis) of activism in an arena where few international platforms and standards actually exist. The Declaration makes a tenuous but welcome start in a field where *much* progress remains necessary—in elaborating legal standards, focusing on *implementation* of protected rights, and acknowledging the need to respond effectively to violations. It is highly necessary to bring the considerable normative force of the Declaration

74. M.D. Evans, *Religious Liberty and International Law in Europe* p. 261 (Cambridge: Cambridge University Press, 1997).

75. Lerner, *supra* note 1 p. 123.

76. E. Odio-Benito, 'Keynote Address' in L. Swidler (ed.), *Religious Liberty and Human Rights in Nations and in Religions* p. 3 (Philadelphia: Ecumenical Press and New York: Hippocrene Books, 1986).

77. T. van Boven, 'Advances and Obstacles in Building Understanding and Respect Between People of Diverse Religions and Beliefs', *Human Rights Quarterly* Vol. 13, p. 439 (1991).

to the attention of activists worldwide, to disseminate knowledge of it through educational activities and to use it alongside other initiatives[78] to gradually change the political impediments standing in the way of the effective implementation of its provisions. Despite its many weaknesses, it 'stands as a major advance in the development of international norms governing the subjects that it addresses'.[79]

78. One such initiative stems from de Jong's very interesting proposal to establish a Council representing major religions or beliefs with the task of examining tensions between religions or beliefs, developing educational methods for the teaching of tolerance, cataloguing rights of religions or belief and submitting regular reports and proposals to relevant UN bodies. de Jong, *supra* note 19 pp. 736-737.

79. Sullivan, *supra* note 2 p. 518.

Chapter 2

The Special Rapporteur on Freedom of Religion or Belief

Carolyn Evans

Senior Fellow, Faculty of Law, University of Melbourne

The reports of the Special Rapporteur on Religious Freedom are a record of the violence, brutality and discrimination visited upon people who attempt to exercise their freedom of religion or belief in many parts of the world.[1] The reports paint a grim picture of the tools of oppression used to control those who are considered to deviate from the publicly accepted religious norm. These tools vary from the discriminatory use of planning permits and visas to the horrors of widespread torture, rape and imprisonment. In light of such widespread abuses, the under-resourced office of the Special Rapporteur seems an inadequate response by the international community. Yet as this office is the most tangible sign of commitment by the members of the United Nations to the principles set out in the *Declaration on the Elimination of All Forms*

1. For a general overview of the types of complaints investigated by the Special Rapporteur see M.D. Evans, *Religious Liberty and International Law in Europe* pp. 245-250 (Cambridge: Cambridge University Press, 1997).

of Intolerance and Discrimination Based on Religion or Belief,[2] it is worth considering the way in which the Special Rapporteur has carried out his mandate.

In 1986, the Commission on Human Rights decided to appoint a Special Rapporteur to investigate governmental actions that were inconsistent with the rights set out in the *Declaration on the Elimination of All Forms of Intolerance and Discrimination Based on Religion or Belief* (henceforth Declaration on Religion or Belief or 'the Declaration') and to recommend measures to remedy any such breaches.[3] Mr d'Almeida Ribeiro was appointed as Rapporteur and he presented his first report to the Commission in 1987.[4] The Commission decided to extend his appointment and he continued to act in the role until 1993.[5] He was succeeded by Mr Abdelfattah Amor who has remained in the role ever since.[6] The Commission has continued to extend the mandate of the Rapporteur. In 2001, at the request of the Rapporteur, his title was changed from the Special Rapporteur on Religious Intolerance to the Special Rapporteur on Freedom of Religion or Belief[7] and the United Nations Commission on Human Rights requested that he continue to 'examine incidents and Governmental actions in all parts of the world that were incompatible with the provisions of the Declaration' and called on all governments to 'cooperate fully' with him.[8]

The first part of this chapter outlines the methodology adopted by the Rapporteur in order to fulfil his mandate. The second part examines three areas—extremism, women and religion, and religious defamation—that have been the focus of particular attention by the Rapporteur in recent years. The third section considers the positive strategies that the Rapporteur has used to try to help societies move away from religious intolerance and discrimina-

2. United Nations General Assembly, *The Declaration on the Elimination of All Forms of Intolerance and Discrimination Based on Religion or Belief*, UN Doc. A/36/684 (1981).

3. For a discussion of the establishment of the role of Rapporteur and of the first nine reports see B. Tahzib, *Freedom of Religion or Belief: Ensuring Effective International Protection* pp. 198-212 (The Hague: Martinus Nijhoff, 1996).

4. Commission on Human Rights, UN Doc. E/CN.4/1987/35.

5. His final report was A. Vidal d'Almeida Ribeiro, *Implementation of the Declaration on the Elimination of All Forms of Intolerance and of Discrimination Based on Religion or Belief*, U.N. Doc. E/CN.4/1993/62 (1993). A brief overview of the relevant resolutions extending the Rapporteur's Mandate can be found in this report at paras. 1-3.

6. His first report was A. Amor, *Implementation of the Declaration on the Elimination of All Forms of Intolerance and of Discrimination Based on Religion or Belief*, U.N. Doc. E/CN.4/1995/91 (1994). At the time of writing (August 2002) his most recent report is A. Amor, *Elimination of All Forms of Religious Intolerance*, U.N. Doc. A/56/253 (2001).

7. Commission on Human Rights, UN Doc. E/CN.4/RES/2001/42 para. 11 (2001). Because of the name change, the term 'Rapporteur' will be used for the rest of this chapter.

8. *Ibid*. para. 9.

tion. The final part of the chapter explores the effectiveness of the Rapporteur and concludes that, given the limitations placed on him by his position and resources, the current Rapporteur has done an impressive, if not perfect, job of carrying out his mandate.

Methodology of the Rapporteur

Complaints

The methodology of the Rapporteur has changed over time. In his first commissioned report, the Rapporteur was asked only to report on the general situation regarding religious discrimination and intolerance worldwide.[9] He kept his report to generalities and did not raise particular allegations against States.[10] Initially, Mr d'Almeida Ribeiro emphasised the non-specific nature of his role, but by his second report he had already moved to discussing the situation in particular States.[11] By his final report he stressed the 'dynamic nature' of his mandate and the increased importance of identifying 'more precisely particular situations where inconsistencies with the Declaration might have been reported.'[12]

Under the current Rapporteur, this trend has continued and one of the primary functions of the Rapporteur's annual reports is to record complaints made to him by those who claim that their right to freedom of religion or belief is being infringed or who make the claim on behalf of others. The sources of information used by the Rapporteur include 'Governments, non-governmental organizations and other sources, religious and lay' to ascertain whether States have complied with the Declaration.[13] Typically, his reports outline the allegation and also record the response (if any) from the State against which the allegation has been made. On the whole the Rapporteur

9. A. Vidal d'Almeida Ribeiro, *Implementation of the Declaration on the Elimination of All Forms of Intolerance and of Discrimination Based on Religion or Belief*, U.N. Doc. E/CN.4/1987/35 (1986).

10. *Ibid*.

11. A. Vidal d'Almeida Ribeiro, *Implementation of the Declaration on the Elimination of All Forms of Intolerance and of Discrimination Based on Religion or Belief*, U.N. Doc. E/CN.4/1988/45 para. 9 (1986).

12. A. Vidal d'Almeida Ribeiro, *Implementation of the Declaration on the Elimination of All Forms of Intolerance and of Discrimination Based on Religion or Belief*, U.N. Doc. E/CN.4/1993/62 para. 10 (1993). The Rapporteur sets out the way in which the Human Rights Commission extended his mandate to make this increased role possible at para. 11.

13. A. Amor, *Implementation of the Declaration on the Elimination of All Forms of Intolerance and of Discrimination Based on Religion or Belief*, U.N. Doc. A/50/440 para. 19 (1995).

avoids any comment on whether the allegation, even if true, would constitute a breach of religious freedom[14] and he almost never makes a factual finding that the allegation is true, except implicitly when recording a response from a State that admits to the breach. Given the lack of independent investigation of complaints and the need to keep governments engaged in dialogue, the Rapporteur has made clear that the transmission of an allegation does not amount to an accusation.[15]

Such lack of comment is understandable given the limited resources with which the Rapporteur works, but can leave the disturbing impression of nothing being done in the face of allegations of horrific breaches of religious freedom. In 1986, for example, the Rapporteur wrote ten pages outlining claims made against Myanmar/Burma and the government's response.[16] Those making the allegations spoke of forced labour, rape, murder and expulsion on the basis of religion. Detailed claims were made of both the general practice and specific examples of men from religious/ethnic minorities being forced to act as porters for the army (sometimes literally being worked to death in the process) and women being forced to provide sex. The government gave very general denials of most of this behaviour and assurances of the importance of religious freedom in Myanmar. Despite the appalling and widespread nature of the alleged practice, the Special Rapporteur felt that he could only criticise the government for failing to give an adequately detailed reply and to suggest that further investigation *by the government* (which could hardly be presumed to be acting in good faith) was warranted.[17] In the conclusion to his report he says that he has been 'preoccupied by allegations of systematic violations of a wide range of the human rights of members of the Muslim community in Myanmar', but went no further than this very general statement.[18]

14. Although many of the accusations are so serious (including murder, torture, and imprisonment on the basis of religion) that the conclusion that they are in breach of religious freedom goes without saying. In some more controversial areas, such as conscientious objection, the Rapporteur has been prepared to at least implicitly find that the allegation of failing to provide an alternative to military service would, if true, amount to a breach of the principles in the Declaration. See A. Amor, *Implementation of the Declaration on the Elimination of All Forms of Intolerance and of Discrimination Based on Religion or Belief*, U.N. Doc. E/CN.4/1995/91 p. 36 (1994).

15. See, for example: A. Vidal d'Almeida Ribeiro, *Implementation of the Declaration on the Elimination of All Forms of Intolerance and Discrimination Based on Religion or Belief*, U.N. Doc. E/CN.4/1993/62 para. 14 (1993); A. Amor, *Implementation of the Declaration on the Elimination of All Forms of Intolerance and of Discrimination Based on Religion or Belief*, U.N. Doc. E/CN.4/1995/91 p. 5 (1994).

16. A. Vidal d'Almeida Ribeiro, *Implementation of the Declaration on the Elimination of All Forms of Intolerance and Discrimination Based on Religion or Belief*, U.N. Doc. E/CN.4/1993/62 para. 45 (1993).

17. *Ibid.* para. 47.

18. *Ibid.* para. 80.

There are, however, some limited instances in which the Rapporteur has been critical of the response of States, albeit in a rather muted way. For example, in regard to four people who were allegedly imprisoned for their religion or belief in Iran (Iran claimed that they were held on charges of spying), Iran noted that the people involved would hopefully be released under an amnesty at some point in the near future. Without directly challenging Iran's claim that the men were held for spying, the Rapporteur welcomed the information and 'expressed the wish to see the accused persons released as soon as possible.'[19] This wish implicitly preferred the explanation of imprisonment given by supporters of the men, as the Rapporteur has no mandate to plead for those imprisoned for ordinary criminal offences. On another occasion, possibly provoked by the claim by Saudi Arabia that he was engaged in a 'crusade' against Muslims, the Rapporteur questioned the claim by Saudi Arabia that '100% of all the citizens of Saudi Arabia are adherents of the Muslim religion.'[20] In response to this claim the Rapporteur took the rare step of contesting the factual position by saying that 'such uniformity does not exist in either political or religious matters. Mankind has a right to diversity...'[21]

The first Rapporteur also sometimes made brief comments that were critical of particular actions (such as the fatwa issued against Salman Rushdie or the destruction of the Babri mosque in Ayodya, India) in the final section of his report.[22] The current Rapporteur originally did not seem to have been so prepared to make categorical criticisms of States, but has developed an 'urgent appeals' process of communicating for States in cases where the allegations made against it are particularly serious and require immediate action.[23] He is sometimes prepared to make critical comments about particular States or State actions or to note his concern in regard to the most serious situations of alleged religious oppression.[24]

---

19. A. Amor, *Elimination of All Forms of Religious Intolerance*, U.N. Doc. A/56/253 pp. 63-64 (2001). This referred to 4 members of the Jewish community.

20. A. Vidal d'Almeida Ribeiro, *Implementation of the Declaration on the Elimination of All Forms of Intolerance and of Discrimination Based on Religion or Belief*, U.N. Doc. E/CN.4/1993/62 para. 53 (1993).

21. *Ibid.*

22. *Ibid.* para. 80.

23. A. Amor, *Implementation of the Declaration on the Elimination of All Forms of Intolerance and of Discrimination Based on Religion or Belief*, U.N. Doc. A/50/440 para. 54 (1995). He also does make some specific criticism, e.g. of the Marxist States that control religion in A. Amor, *Elimination of All Forms of Religious Intolerance*, U.N. Doc. A/56/253 para. 158(a) (2001).

24. For a pronounced example of cases where the Rapporteur was prepared to at least briefly attribute breaches to particular States see A. Amor, *Interim Report on the Elimination of All Forms of Intolerance and Discrimination Based on Religion or Belief*, U.N. Doc. A/54/386 paras. 129-137. (1999).

The Rapporteur appears to be less concerned with the propriety of making criticisms of States that fail to respond to requests or that give responses that are inadequate.[25] To cite one of many examples, when Laos replied to a series of specific allegations with a brief, political statement condemning such allegations as 'false and groundless' and reiterating the importance of religious freedom in Laos, the Rapporteur thanked it for its reply, but noted tartly that he had been hoping 'to receive specific information on allegations that were submitted.'[26] He regularly notes States who have failed to respond to requests for information and calls on them to assist him in carrying out his mandate by replying promptly to his questions.[27]

In Situ Visits

A different philosophy, however, appears to prevail in regard to the reports on specific States to which the Rapporteur has made *in situ* visits. These visits have become an increasingly important part of the Rapporteur's role with the current Rapporteur visiting, by 2001, China, Pakistan, Iran, Greece, Sudan, India, Australia, Germany, the United States, Vietnam, Turkey, Bangladesh, and Argentina.[28] Unlike his predecessor, the current Rapporteur clearly considers these visits to be essential to his function and has emphasized a number of times the importance that he attaches to these visits in order to increase dialogue with States and to 'better appreciate the full complexity of the situations of religious intolerance' which he encounters during his mandate.[29]

Such visits also allow the Rapporteur to better assess problem areas of religious intolerance and persecution than is possible in relation to all the allegations that are put into the annual report. Because of the scope of the annual report and the severely restricted financial backing that has been given to the Rapporteur, it is impossible for him to reach any considered conclusion about the truth or otherwise of complaints that are made. Thus he must be cautious

25. See, for example: A. Amor, *Elimination of All Forms of Religious Intolerance*, U.N. Doc. A/55/280 para. 20 (2000), 'The Special Rapporteur regrets the lack of effort and care taken over this reply [from Egypt], which is no reply at all'.

26. A. Amor, *Elimination of All Forms of Religious Intolerance*, U.N. Doc. A/56/253 p. 65 (2001).

27. A table outlining the 'evolution of communications' to the Rapporteur can be found at A. Amor, *Elimination of All Forms of Religious Intolerance*, U.N. Doc. A/56/253 paras. 81-88 (2001).

28. A. Amor, *Elimination of All Forms of Religious Intolerance*, U.N. Doc. A/56/253 table 1 (2001).

29. See, for example: A. Amor, *Implementation of the Declaration on the Elimination of All Forms of Intolerance and of Discrimination Based on Religion or Belief*, U.N. Doc. E/CN.4/1995/91 p. 5 (1994).

with his criticisms of governments, especially when those governments deny the allegations outright. The *in situ* visits, however, offer greater scope for the Rapporteur to come to independent and informed assessments of the state of religious freedom in the country being visited. These reports, therefore, tend to be far more willing to evaluate problems and reach general conclusions about the protection given to religious freedom.[30]

The example of the way in which the Rapporteur has dealt with issues of religious freedom in China in general reports, as compared to his report on his *in situ* visit, illustrates this point. In his report of 1994, for example, the Rapporteur outlined a series of serious allegations about the treatment of people on the basis of their religion or belief in China. He listed numerous people, particularly monks and nuns in Tibet, who had reportedly been imprisoned (and, in some cases, tortured) for practicing their religion.[31] The report also contained the response of China to a list of similarly serious allegations made the year before.[32] The Rapporteur made no comment as to the truth of these allegations, nor did he make any recommendations as to action that was required, reforms that were needed, or investigations that should be held. In comparison, his *in situ* report on China was more detailed and reflected personal contact with both governmental and non-governmental people with an interest in religious issues.[33] In his subsequent report he made thirteen recommendations for changes in legislation and policy, including the inclusion of a right to manifest a religion or belief in the Chinese constitution, more precision in the definition of the criteria for establishing places of worship, and the release of people held on the basis of their religion or belief.[34] The degree to which the Rapporteur felt able to draw factual conclusions and express (albeit in very diplomatic language) criticisms of the Chinese government in this type of detailed report, illustrates the importance of *in situ* visits.

---

30. See, for example, recommendations regarding Greece, India and Sudan in A. Amor, *Elimination of All Forms of Religious Intolerance*, U.N. Doc. A/52/477/Add. 1 (1997).

31. A. Amor, *Implementation of the Declaration on the Elimination of All Forms of Intolerance and of Discrimination Based on Religion or Belief*, U.N. Doc. E/CN.4/1995/91/Add. 1 para. 8 (1994).

32. *Ibid.*

33. A. Amor, *Implementation of the Declaration on the Elimination of All Forms of Intolerance and of Discrimination Based on Religion or Belief*, U.N. Doc. E/CN.4/1995/91 chp. 3 (1994).

34. A. Amor, *Implementation of the Declaration on the Elimination of All Forms of Intolerance and of Discrimination Based on Religion or Belief*, U.N. Doc. A/51/542 para. 22, annex 1 (1996). The Chinese response is in annex 2 of the same report.

Conferences

Another important method by which the Rapporteur carries out his role is through contributions to international conferences and the work of other United Nations bodies. Most notable in this regard is his contribution to the World Conference on Racism held in Durban in 2001. The Rapporteur presented a detailed and thoughtful preparatory report for that conference on the overlap between multiple forms of discrimination, in particular the problems caused when people are targeted for both racial/ethnic and religious reasons (a phenomenon that he calls aggravated discrimination).[35]

As well as contributing to the debates occurring in other parts of the United Nations, the Rapporteur has also initiated a number of studies in relation to specific issues of religious freedom that he considers to be of importance or complexity. A particular focus for the current Rapporteur has been the role of education in promoting religious freedom, which is discussed in more detail below. He has also proposed a conference on the issue of new religious movements or so-called 'cults'.[36]

Key Issues in Religious Freedom

In the general sections of his annual reports, the Rapporteur has tended to return to a couple of key themes. In a longer annual report in 2001 that looked at the achievements of the twenty years since the 1981 Declaration was adopted, he summarised some of his conclusions about the trends in religious freedom. He observed that over the first twenty years of the existence of the Declaration there had been a decline in the total control of religion in the name of hard-line Marxist ideology, but the maintenance of discriminatory or intolerant policies by States with an official religion and a marked increase in activities against groups described as sects.[37] There had been an increase in extremism, which often involved the 'active or tacit complicity of national and foreign States'.[38] He noted a gradual increase in militant non-belief that entered into competition with religion, but also an increase in inter-reli-

35. General Assembly, *Racial Discrimination and Religious Discrimination: Identification and Measures*, UN Doc. A/CONF.189/PC.1/7 (2000).

36. A. Amor, *Implementation of the Declaration on the Elimination of All Forms of Intolerance and of Discrimination Based on Religion or Belief*, U.N. Doc. E/CN.4/1997/91 para. 103 (1996).

37. A. Amor, *Elimination of All Forms of Religious Intolerance*, U.N. Doc. A/56/253 para. 158 (2001).

38. *Ibid.*

gious dialogue.[39] He believed that religions themselves could be oppressive to women and that, while those who suffered religious persecution came from a diverse range of backgrounds, women and minorities are particularly vulnerable to discrimination and intolerance based on religion or belief.[40]

These changes are all mentioned in his annual reports, but there are a number of areas that stand out as ones to which the Rapporteur regularly returns. One theme that has emerged is that of actively promoting religious freedom and creating a 'culture of tolerance'. This will be discussed in the next section. Three other themes also emerge as areas that the Rapporteur believes need special attention. They are religious extremism, the negative impact of religion on women, and religious defamation.

Religious Extremism

Religious extremism has been one of the key areas of focus in the Rapporteur's reports.[41] The Rapporteur is vigorous in his condemnation of the phenomenon, describing it as an 'ever-growing and all-pervasive menace to peace that breaks up society and poses a particular threat to vulnerable groups (women and minorities)'.[42] He includes within his definition both extremism that is violent in nature and that which 'takes on less spectacular forms of intolerance', and calls on the international community to react firmly to the threat through the elaboration of rules and principles of conduct towards religious extremism.[43]

The term 'extremism' is used frequently[44] and as though its meaning is self-evident and rather broad. In the context of a discussion about extremism, for example, he states that:

39. *Ibid.*

40. *Ibid.*

41. In his 1994 report, for example, the Rapporteur lists the fall of the Soviet bloc, the Gulf War and 'the emergence and development of religious extremism' as three of the most fundamental political changes that have occurred since the first appointment of a Rapporteur in 1986. A. Amor, *Implementation of the Declaration on the Elimination of All Forms of Intolerance and of Discrimination Based on Religion or Belief*, U.N. Doc. A/50/440 para. 16 (1995). See also A. Amor, *Elimination of All Forms of Religious Intolerance*, U.N. Doc. A/55/280 paras. 77-86 (2000).

42. A. Amor, *Elimination of All Forms of Religious Intolerance*, U.N. Doc. A/56/253 para. 165(a) (2001).

43. *Ibid.*

44. In his most recent report, A. Amor, *Elimination of All Forms of Religious Intolerance*, U.N. Doc. A/56/253 para. 165(a) (2001) for example, the Rapporteur describes religious groups as extremist in Georgia (p. 11), India (p. 11), Indonesia (p. 12), Pakistan (p. 16), and Sri Lanka (p. 18). In A. Amor, *Implementation of the Declaration on the Elimination of All Forms of Intolerance and of Discrimination Based on Religion or Belief*, U.N. Doc. A/51/542 para. 33 (1996) he described extremism as a 'cancer in any religious group'.

> It is a fact that freedom of religion does not seem to have won over the minds of all men and women. Each religion tends to believe that it is the sole guardian of the truth and that it has a duty to make everyone bear witness to that truth. That does not always contribute to tolerance among religions. Moreover, each religion may be tempted to fight what it may consider to be deviance within its own ranks or around it. That does not always contribute to tolerance within religions, especially tolerance of religious minorities.[45]

In another report he argues that the repression of the Jehovah's Witnesses in Greece 'is certainly not unconnected to their religious militancy as expressed through their proselytising activities, their conscientious objection to military service and the various public demonstrations they stage which challenge the Orthodox Church and aspects of State legislative and political activity'.[46] He also stated in his 1999 report that extremism can 'result from sheer religious fanaticism, where a given individual or group believes that he or it possess the absolute truth and wishes to impose it on others'.[47] He then goes on to make the claim that extremism is aberrant as all religions are based 'fundamentally on the values of human rights, tolerance and non-discrimination'.[48] The previous Rapporteur was also concerned with the growth of religious extremism and he too adopted a broad approach to defining it, seeming to include 'sectarian or dogmatic intransigence' within its scope.[49] As his discussions of extremism deal primarily with the issue of extremist religious groups rather than extremist governments, this raises concerns that religious individuals and groups can be criticised for believing in the truth of their own religious teachings even if they do not take any violent action in an attempt to force these beliefs on anyone else. The precise borderline between an extremist and a person who has a deep commitment to their religious beliefs is not easily drawn. Some see unhealthy fanaticism in door to door proselytising, where others see an exercise of religious freedom.[50]

Of course, there are many religious groups that potentially do pose a serious threat to religious tolerance and discrimination. Even so, the issue of the

---

45. A. Amor, *Implementation of the Declaration on the Elimination of All Forms of Intolerance and of Discrimination Based on Religion or Belief*, U.N. Doc. A/51/542 para. 48 (1996).
46. A. Amor, *Implementation of the Declaration on the Elimination of All Forms of Intolerance and of Discrimination Based on Religion or Belief*, U.N. Doc. E/CN.4/1997/91 para. 49 (1997).
47. A. Amor, *Elimination of All Forms of Religious Intolerance*, U.N. Doc. A/55/280 para. 80 (2000).
48. *Ibid*.
49. A. Vidal d'Almeida Ribeiro, *Implementation of the Declaration on the Elimination of All Forms of Intolerance and of Discrimination Based on Religion or Belief*, U.N. Doc. E/CN.4/1993/62 para. 78 (1993).
50. N. Lerner, 'Proselytism, Change of Religion and Adherence to International Human Rights', *Emory International Law Review* Vol. 12, p. 477 (1998).

best way to deal with such groups is a complex one. The Rapporteur sometimes argues to governments that they should respect religious freedom because religious persecution tends to lead to fanaticism and religiously-inspired violence.[51] Once such violence has begun, however, a simple policy of tolerance may not be sufficient, especially if the religious leadership is actively involved in promoting violence. Yet crackdowns on religious communities because of the militant actions of a few (or even a large number) of co-religionists can lead to religious persecution. The fight against extremism can also be used as a façade by governments for taking action against a politically troublesome religious group. China, for example, has used the excuse of clamping down on religious extremism in Xinjiang to justify highly repressive actions.[52] Yet the call of the Rapporteur for States to 'curb religious extremism of any kind by acting on both its cause and effects, without selectivity or ambivalence' could be used by States as a justification for repressive actions.[53]

The rather blunt approach taken to this issue by the Rapporteur can be contrasted with the more nuanced view put forward by the former United Nations High Commissioner for Human Rights, Mary Robinson, in a speech to the Oslo Conference on Freedom of Religion or Belief. In it she spoke of the *gift* and threat of fundamental belief. She notes that 'faith is understood at its best as progressively liberating into aspects of the truth and only the truth sets free... That is the gift of fundamental belief—liberation in truth. The threat is that of a belief or unbelief which the agent believes that he possess in its fullness and therefore must impose on others.'[54] It is worrying that, despite this more moderate approach, she includes proselytising as one of the fundamentalist forces that 'have so often disfigured our world'.[55]

The reports of the Rapporteur are not, and should not become, lengthy academic works on definitional matters or detailed explorations of the complexities of particular issues. Given the emphasis that has been put on extremism, however, it might be useful for the Rapporteur to consider whether this issue would be suitable for an issue based conference and/or report. While

51. In his recommendations to China, for example, he recommends compromise on religious freedom to 'avoid the deeply religious being tempted by religious extremism'. A. Amor, *Implementation of the Declaration on the Elimination of All Forms of Intolerance and of Discrimination Based on Religion or Belief*, U.N. Doc. E/CN.4/1995/91 (1994).

52. Human Rights Watch, *World Report 2002: China and Tibet*, http://www.hrw.org/wr2k2/asia4.html

53. A. Amor, *Implementation of the Declaration on the Elimination of All Forms of Intolerance and of Discrimination Based on Religion or Belief*, U.N. Doc. A/50/440 para. 77 (1995).

54. High Commissioner for Human Rights, The Universal Declaration of Human Rights: Hope and History, Address to the Oslo Conference on Freedom of Religion or Belief, University of Oslo, 14 August 1998.

55. *Ibid*.

few would contest his reminder to States that it is their duty to 'calm rather than exacerbate religious problems',[56] his conclusion that the relationship between the political and religious realm cannot 'encompass extreme positions and that wisdom lies in moderation'[57] is insufficient. Calling on governments to take unspecified actions to deal with ill-defined extremist behaviour has the potential to encourage or legitimate government action that infringes on religious freedom.[58]

The Impact of Religion on Women

In response to directions from the Commission on Human Rights,[59] the impact of religious doctrine and practice on women has become one of the focal points of the Rapporteur's attention.[60] He has been prepared to be critical to a remarkable degree of the role that religion can play in the oppression of women. Unlike many commentators on religious freedom, who tend to marginalise the role that religion can play in encouraging discrimination against women, he has repeatedly raised these issues making them a separate section of his report, despite Saudi Arabia challenging his mandate to investigate these issues.[61] His reports have given full recognition to the immensity of the problem and his language in condemning expressions of religiosity that result in women's oppression have been unequivocal. In 2001, for example, he stated bluntly that,

> Not all traditions are equally valid, and those which run counter to human rights must be combated. It is essential to distinguish between tolerance, which is necessary, and blind acceptance of customs which may involve degrading treatment or blatant violations of human rights. In order to ensure that freedom of religion does not under-

56. A. Amor, *Elimination of All Forms of Religious Intolerance*, U.N. Doc. A/52/477/Add. 1 para. 4(2) (1997).

57. A. Amor, *Implementation of the Declaration on the Elimination of All Forms of Intolerance and of Discrimination Based on Religion or Belief*, U.N. Doc. E/CN.4/1997/91 para. 88 (1996).

58. M.D. Evans, 'Religion, Law and Human Rights: Locating the Debate' in P. Edge and G. Harvey (eds.), *Law and religion in Contemporary Society: Communities, Individualism and the State* p. 186 (Aldershot: Ashgate, 2000).

59 See, for example, Commission on Human Rights, UN Doc. E/CN.4/RES/2001/42 para. 7 (2001) which stresses the 'need for the Special Rapporteur to continue to apply a gender perspective, *inter alia* through the identification of gender-specific abuses, in the reporting process, including information collection and in recommendations'.

60. A. Amor, *Interim Report on the Elimination of All Forms of Intolerance and Discrimination Based on Religion or Belief*, U.N. Doc. A/54/386 paras. 133-145 (1999); A. Amor, *Elimination of All Forms of Religious Intolerance*, U.N. Doc. A/55/280 para. 88 (2000).

61. *Ibid*. para. 42.

> mine women's rights, it is vital that the right to difference which that freedom implies should not be interpreted as a right to indifference to the status of women.[62]

Combined with this bluntness is a preparedness to make criticisms of specific States for using religion as a justification for restricting women's rights. It is interesting that the Rapporteur tends to take a vigorously feminist perspective on these issues. He seems to assume in cases of a conflict between women's rights and religious practices that the religious practices must be changed or abandoned. No sense is given in these reports that he is arguing for a balancing of competing rights or some compromise position to be reached, as do most authors in this field.[63] It may be that this is because the situations that he has in mind are the most egregious violations of women's rights in the name of religion. Examples of complaints received include the murder by militants of a 17 year old Algerian school-girl for failing to wear a hijab (head-scarf)[64] and the oppressive regime for women created by the Taliban in Afghanistan.[65] There are, however, more complex areas of conflict, such as discrimination on the basis of religion in regards to the selection of religious leadership, and it is not clear if the Rapporteur would include these types of situations in his call for the abandonment of sexist religious practices. If so, such a call would further enlarge the scope of the State to interfere with the internal organisation of religions with potentially negative effects for religious freedom.

Religious Defamation

The Human Rights Commission has called on the Rapporteur to pay particular attention to the issue of religious defamation.[66] Over the last couple of years

62. A. Amor, *Elimination of All Forms of Religious Intolerance*, U.N. Doc. A/56/253 para. 146 (2001).
63. D. Sullivan, 'Gender Equality and Religious Freedom: Toward a Framework for Conflict Resolution', *New York University Journal of International Law and Politics*, Vol. 24, p. 795 (1992); *cf.* S. Moller Okin, 'Is Multiculturalism Bad for Women?', http://bostonreview.mit.edu/BR22.5/okin.html
64. A. Amor, *Implementation of the Declaration on the Elimination of All Forms of Intolerance and of Discrimination Based on Religion or Belief*, U.N. Doc. E/CN.4/1995/91 p. 8 (1994).
65. A. Amor, *Elimination of All Forms of Religious Intolerance*, U.N. Doc. A/54/386 para. 41 p. 6 (1999), which notes that 'women are subjected to total segregation within society'. See also A. Amor, *Implementation of the Declaration on the Elimination of All Forms of Intolerance and of Discrimination Based on Religion or Belief*, U.N. Doc. A/52/477 paras. 31 and 87 (1997); A. Amor, *Elimination of All Forms of Religious Intolerance*, U.N. Doc. A/54/386 para. 41 (1999); A. Amor, *Elimination of All Forms of Religious Intolerance*, U.N. Doc. A/55/280 para. 77 (2000).
66. A. Amor, *Elimination of All Forms of Religious Intolerance*, U.N. Doc. A/56/253 para. 135 (2001).

this issue has been brought to the forefront by 'Islamophobia', engaged in by some media organisations and governments. While Islamophobia has been of particular concern to the Rapporteur, he has also noted cases against other religions such as the propagation of anti-Semitism or campaigns conducted against new religious movements (sometimes referred to as 'cults' or 'sects').[67]

Once again the definition of 'defamation' seems broad and unclear. In criticising the plans of the Taliban to require non-Muslims to wear a distinctive emblem, the Rapporteur used some of his most critical language and argued that the action would use religion for political purposes and was obscurantist. He concluded that 'the negative image of Islam that has been conveyed by the Taliban not only misrepresents the religion, but constitutes a betrayal and a downright defamation of religion'.[68] This seems to lead to the bizarre position that a religious group that behaves in a manner that is abusive of human rights can be condemned not only for rights violations, but also for bringing that religion into disrepute—even when the aim of the group was to promote their religion and belief.

The problems with a simplistic approach to this problem are illustrated by the allegations that were made to the Rapporteur of negative portrayals of Muslims and Islam in the British media. The United Kingdom responded to these allegations (with information that the Rapporteur described as of 'admirable quality and relevance') by stating that the media in the United Kingdom was free, but that there were detailed guidelines to try to ensure that portrayals of religious people or groups in the media did not encourage intolerance nor give undue offence.[69] The Rapporteur agreed that press freedom was important but made one of his rare determinations of fact by saying that negative stereotypes of minorities, including Muslims, still featured in some media outlets. He concluded that the 'State must remain vigilant in that connection and take action in the event of any lapses by the organs concerned'.[70] This is an unhelpful analysis. The United Kingdom's response illustrated its awareness of the tension between religious intolerance and press freedom, and it claimed that its position appropriately balanced the two interests. Simply saying that it does not—and even implying that *any* negative portrayal of religious minorities implicated the State—does not give States much idea of the appropriate

67. A. Amor, *Implementation of the Declaration on the Elimination of All Forms of Intolerance and of Discrimination Based on Religion or Belief*, U.N. Doc. E/CN.4/1997/91 para. 94 (1996); A. Amor, *Elimination of All Forms of Religious Intolerance*, U.N. Doc. A/54/386 para. 106 (1999).

68. A. Amor, *Elimination of All Forms of Religious Intolerance*, U.N. Doc. A/56/253 para. 30 (2001).

69. *Ibid*. para. 25 (annex).

70. *Ibid*. para. 26.

manner in which to regulate this area. The Rapporteur's reference to 'organs' presumably referred to independent media organisations, but gave the unfortunate impression of implying that that such organisations were organs of the State and could be subjected unproblematically to 'action' by the government for any 'lapses.'

His suggestions as to concrete ways in which States could reduce defamation are rare and sometimes do not appear to be very well thought out. The suggestion that media organisations should be the target of campaigns to develop awareness of their importance in shaping a culture of tolerance seems reasonable.[71] Less unobjectionable is his approval in early reports of (carefully defined) laws against blasphemy to protect religions from defamation.[72] Such laws are controversial because of their openness to abuse and selective prosecutions.[73] In later reports, the Rapporteur treats the use of blasphemy laws with more circumspection.[74]

Once again this issue is a complex one. In a society that respects human rights, people have a right to be critical, even strongly critical, of the doctrine and practices of religious groups. The Rapporteur himself, as discussed above, has been critical of religious practices that encourage extremism or are degrading to women. In one report where he comments that the hostility towards sects can be 'largely explained by the excesses, the breaches of public order and, on occasion, the crimes and despicable conduct' engaged in by these groups, he is arguably engaging in the stereotyping and generalisation that he condemns as defamatory.[75] It would be most inappropriate for States to take action to protect religions from fair criticism.[76] By the same token, there have been examples of vitriolic hate campaigns that have intimidated their victims and led to violence. While the potential problems that can result from religious defamation can be easily identified, the solutions are not as clear. The Rapporteur certainly highlights the issue but he provides little assistance to States that are struggling to find an appropriate way of dealing with it.

71. A. Amor, *Elimination of All Forms of Religious Intolerance*, U.N. Doc. A/54/386 para. 106 (1999).

72. *Ibid.* para. 111.

73. *Ibid.* para. 118 where the Rapporteur gives examples of this practice.

74. A. Amor, *Elimination of All Forms of Religious Intolerance*, U.N. Doc. A/55/280 para. 97 (2000).

75. A. Amor, *Implementation of the Declaration on the Elimination of All Forms of Intolerance and of Discrimination Based on Religion or Belief*, U.N. Doc. E/CN.4/1997/91 para. 99 (1996).

76. A. Amor, *Elimination of All Forms of Religious Intolerance*, U.N. Doc. A/54/386 para. 113 (1999).

Developing a Culture of Tolerance

The Rapporteur clearly conceives his role as going beyond criticism of current practices and extending into assisting States towards constructive methods for combating intolerance and discrimination. The change of his title from Rapporteur on Discrimination and Intolerance on the Basis of Religion or Belief to the Rapporteur on Freedom of Religion or Belief in part reflects this increased recognition of this positive role. According to the Rapporteur, the change of title helps to ensure 'full recognition of the role of [his] mandate in management and prevention, which are complementary and indispensable activities'[77] to the campaign to eliminate discrimination and intolerance. There are two particular methods that the Rapporteur has focussed on in his campaign to attempt to create what he calls a 'culture of tolerance'. These methods are education and inter-religious dialogue.

Education

Education has the potential to play a significant role in developing a culture of tolerance and non-discrimination.[78] Schools can be places in which children are taught to respect basic human rights and the freedoms of others. They can also be places that inculcate religious bigotry or ignorance. Yet the appropriate way in which education can be used to promote religious tolerance is far from clear. Even some very basic questions are contentious. Whether religious education should be permitted in government funded schools, the nature of that education, and who should be required to attend are deeply controversial questions.[79]

The Rapporteur has taken a number of steps in an attempt to reach a consensus on using education to promote tolerance and non-discrimination. He devised a questionnaire for States about their current policies that asked them

77. A. Amor, *Elimination of All Forms of Religious Intolerance*, U.N. Doc. A/56/253 para. 161 (2001).

78. The Rapporteur argues that education 'could be the prime means of combating discrimination and intolerance'. A. Amor, *Implementation of the Declaration on the Elimination of All Forms of Intolerance and of Discrimination Based on Religion or Belief*, U.N. Doc. E/CN.4/1996/95 para. 66 (1995). See also A. Amor, *Implementation of the Declaration on the Elimination of All Forms of Intolerance and of Discrimination Based on Religion or Belief*, U.N. Doc. A/51/542 para. 22 (1996).

79. For a general discussion of the problems that these issues have given rise to in Europe, see C. Evans, *Freedom of Religion under the European Convention on Human Rights* pp. 88-97 (Oxford: Oxford University Press, 2001). For a United States' perspective see M.E. Marty and J. Moore, *Education, Religion and the Common Good: Advancing a Distinctly American Conversation about Religion's Role in our Shared Life* (New York: Jossey-Bass, 2000).

19 questions on the law and practices of religious instruction and education in principles of religious tolerance in their States.[80] The results of this survey and the Rapporteur's response to them were issued as a report that formed the basis for discussion at a conference in November 2001 attended by representatives of States, inter-governmental organizations, the main religions and other religious and spiritual communities, non-governmental organizations and experts.'[81]

This conference produced a Final Document in which participants recognised the importance of human rights education in eliminating religious hatred and intolerance.[82] The Final Document of the Conference consists of a lengthy preamble and 19 operative clauses. The operative clauses focus in on the issue of using education to promote tolerance and tend to be overlapping and repetitive in some areas. They make a number of useful, concrete recommendations, such as encouraging students and teachers to meet with counter-parts of different beliefs[83] and developing units to assist students in critically analysing information about religions in the mass media.[84] The contentious issues surrounding religious education itself are not dealt with in the document, except to note that a student has a right 'not to receive religious instruction inconsistent with his or her conviction'.[85]

Strangely, right at the end of the document, with no article number attached, there is a statement that 'With understanding that freedom of religion or belief includes theistic, non-theistic and atheistic beliefs, as well as the right not to profess any religion'. While such professions have become common from international human rights bodies, it is unusual to see such a declaration in a document to which States have agreed, where any attempt to define religion is usually avoided.[86]

While the Final Document itself is a rather bland and general commitment to using education for the purposes of increasing tolerance, it is a positive step. The process that was used to reach agreement on the wording was perhaps more useful than the wording itself. The Rapporteur brought together rel-

80. A. Amor, *Implementation of the Declaration on the Elimination of All Forms of Intolerance and of Discrimination Based on Religion or Belief*, U.N. Doc. A/50/440 p. 16 (1995), annex 1.

81. A. Amor, *Elimination of All Forms of Religious Intolerance*, U.N. Doc. A/55/280 para. 130 (2000).

82. International Consultative Conference on School Education in Relation with Freedom of Religion and Belief, Tolerance and Non-Discrimination, Final Document, preamble at para. f, Madrid 23-25 November 2001.

83. *Ibid*. para. 10(d).

84. *Ibid*. para. 11(c).

85. *Ibid*. para. 4.

86. Evans, *supra* note 79 chp. 4.

evant experts and government representatives and wrote a detailed and useful report on ways forward in this area.[87] As education is one of the key strategies pursued by the Rapporteur in fulfilling the positive side of his mandate, it is likely that he will use the Final Document as a basis for further activity in this area, rather than seeing it as the end of the process.

Inter-religious Dialogue

Another important element of the Rapporteur's proactive approach to religious freedom is his commitment to inter-religious dialogue. In his summary of the past twenty years, he noted with satisfaction the increased role of direct dialogue and cooperation between religious groups, including those who have been hostile towards one another at some points in history. The Rapporteur has tried to ensure that this issue stays on the international agenda by participating, for example, in the UNESCO International Congress on Inter-religious Dialogue and a Culture of Peace and working with non-governmental organizations and religious groups that are involved in managing and preventing inter-religious conflict.[88]

The Rapporteur also intends to extend the traditional *in situ* programme and make what he describes as 'visits to the major communities of religion or belief'.[89] This programme began with a visit to the Holy See in September 1999.[90] While direct dealing with religious groups is a useful way to ensure that the mandate of the Rapporteur is not captured by State interests (especially given the essential role of inter-faith dialogue), it will be interesting to see how he carries out his plan to visit 'other religions, including, Islam, Judaism, non-Catholic Christianity, Buddhism, Hinduism, and the belief system of indigenous populations'.[91] While Catholicism has a clearly identifiable central religious leader, the selection of those who will be considered the representatives of other religious groups may prove more controversial.

87. A. Amor, *Elimination of All Forms of Religious Intolerance*, U.N. Doc. A/55/280 paras. 121-131 (2000).

88. A. Amor, *Elimination of All Forms of Religious Intolerance*, U.N. Doc. A/56/253 para. 164 (2001).

89. *Ibid*. para. 15.

90. *Ibid*.

91. *Ibid*.

Effectiveness

The current methodologies adopted by the Rapporteur to carry out his mandate have allowed religious freedom to gain a greater prominence within the United Nations and among some States than might have been the case if he had restricted himself to making the very general annual reports that were at first considered the only proper role for the Rapporteur.

There are, however, real limitations on his ability to fulfil his role. The Rapporteur's reports are reliant on recording allegations made by individuals or groups about abuses of religious freedom and noting the response (if any) that the State makes to these allegations. As the Rapporteur himself has argued, this methodology can have a distorting effect, making one State appear to be involved in widespread religious persecution simply because a large number of unsubstantiated claims have been made against it, while failing to consider religious freedom in another, possibly more abusive State because no allegations have been made. In order to combat this problem, the Rapporteur would prefer to present Reports that gave an overview of the state of religious freedom in all States in a form that makes comparison and the drawing of proper conclusions far easier than in currently the case.[92]

At present, however, the funding available to the Rapporteur barely covers the expenses generated by his current practices.[93] At a conference in the United States in 1998, the Rapporteur expressed his irritation at the limitations placed on his role by a lack of funding. He noted that he, like most people working in human rights bodies in the United Nations, was unable to deal with the wealth of information that he was sent by governmental and non-governmental bodies. He continued,

> Why is this not possible? It is because the human and material resources needed to deal with this material are simply lacking particularly in the area of human rights. In fact, you could almost say that the Human Rights section of the United Nations is the Third World of it. United Nations resources are simply not adequate for what has to be done.[94]

---

92. *Ibid*. para. 168(b).

93. The Rapporteur was unable to publish communications and replies in his 1996 report because of severe budgetary restraints. He described these constraints as 'detrimental' and a 'form of information censorship that seriously undermines the Special Rapporteur's mandate'. A. Amor, *Implementation of the Declaration on the Elimination of All Forms of Intolerance and of Discrimination Based on Religion or Belief*, U.N. Doc. A/51/542 para. 26 (1996).

94. A. Amor, 'The Mandate of the Special Rapporteur on Religious Freedom', *Emory International Law Review*, Vol. 12, p. 945 (1998).

In his reports, the Rapporteur makes the thoroughly reasonable point that various United Nations bodies have asked ever more of those with responsibilities in human rights, but have not provided the resources to match that increase in responsibilities.[95] Recently, the support of some non-governmental organisations and the government of Norway, Spain and the Holy See have alleviated the financial strain to some degree,[96] but it is clear that some desirable reforms to the way in which the Rapporteur carries out his mandate (such as the development of a more comprehensive, global reporting system) are unlikely to be feasible in the near future. In this regard he has warned that any 'savings made at the expense of human rights at the present time is a lost opportunity for human rights which will translate into less freedom, less tolerance and less humanity'.[97]

The Rapporteur has also suggested that steps should be taken at both the international and national level to establish legal mechanisms through which individuals could seek protection from violations of their rights to religious freedom and in which States could be penalised for such violations.[98] One assumes that an international body set up for these purposes would be a committee established under a Convention along the lines of such bodies as the Human Rights Committee.[99] Such a committee would have the advantage of being able to deal with individual complaints in a more consistent and fair manner by taking evidence and hearing both sides in a structured manner. Of course, such committees have not been an unmixed success in other contexts and while, if the committee system worked in practice as it should in theory, it would have real advantages over the current system, it is unrealistic to expect that it will not be plagued by the same kind of problems that beset the system elsewhere.[100] It is also extremely unlikely that the political consensus required

95. A. Amor, *Elimination of All Forms of Religious Intolerance*, U.N. Doc. A/54/386 para. 153 (1999).

96. A. Amor, *Elimination of All Forms of Religious Intolerance*, U.N. Doc. A/56/253 para. 168(a) (2001).

97. A. Amor, *Implementation of the Declaration on the Elimination of All Forms of Intolerance and of Discrimination Based on Religion or Belief*, U.N. Doc. A/51/542 para. 60 (1996).

98. A. Amor, *Implementation of the Declaration on the Elimination of All Forms of Intolerance and of Discrimination Based on Religion or Belief*, U.N. Doc. A/50/440 para. 22 (1995). See also the early recommendation by Ribeiro that a convention that required States to make regular reports might 'encourage greater respect for religious rights and freedoms'. A. Vidal d'Almeida Ribeiro, *Implementation of the Declaration on the Elimination of All Forms of Intolerance and of Discrimination Based on Religion or Belief*, U.N. Doc. E/CN.4/1988/45 para. 66 (1986).

99. General Assembly, *International Covenant on Civil and Political Rights*, UN Doc. A/6316 (1966), 999 UNTS 171, Part IV.

100. J. Crawford, 'The UN Human Rights Treaty System: A System in Crisis?' in P. Alston and J. Crawford (eds.), *The Future of UN Human Rights Treaty Monitoring* (Cambridge: Cambridge University Press, 2000); P.R. Ghandhi, *The Human Rights Committee and the Right of Individual Communication: Law and Practice* chp. 15 (Aldershot: Ashgate, 1998).

to create both a treaty and a protocol allowing for individual complaints will be found in the near future. The current Rapporteur acknowledges that an international convention on religious intolerance and discrimination is 'a necessary but premature step'[101] at this point in time. Patrick Flood, a critical commentator on the way in which Ribeiro carried out his role, argued that the Rapporteur should move away from the abstract debate over the desirability of a convention and recognise instead the useful, flexible nature of the current arrangements.[102]

The lack of resources and 'hard' treaty obligations are compounded by the essentially voluntary nature of State participation with the Rapporteur. In particular, the Rapporteur has no power to require States to comply with his recommendations or to respond to his requests. Recognising these limitations, the Rapporteur has taken a pragmatic and flexible approach to encourage the voluntary cooperation of States. The first Rapporteur, for example, said that his role was 'not to make accusations or value judgments, but to help arrive at a better understanding of the circumstances surrounding (religious) intolerance and discrimination ... to mobilize international public opinion and to establish a dialogue with the Governments and all other parties concerned'.[103] The current Rapporteur has claimed that, in order to promote religious freedom, it is necessary to avoid 'categorical, inflexible attitudes, impulsive and ineffectual initiatives, ill-considered behaviours, blind obstinacy, gratuitous accusations, inconsistent judgments and grandiose but futile gestures'.[104] He reiterates that his role is to work with States progressively over time to develop a culture of religious tolerance and to work to 'dynamic compromises based on events [which] should be reached pragmatically'.[105]

This pragmatic approach may have assisted in promoting religious free dom in States that might have balked at more heavy-handed treatment. There have, however, been some situations in which it is clear that attempts by the Rapporteur to intervene have been entirely ineffective. In February 2001, for example, the Rapporteur sent an urgent appeal to the Taliban representa-

101. A. Amor, *Implementation of the Declaration on the Elimination of All Forms of Intolerance and of Discrimination Based on Religion or Belief*, U.N. Doc. A/50/440 para. 85 (1995).

102. P.J. Flood, *The Effectiveness of UN Human Rights Instruments* pp. 74-75 (Westport: Praeger, 1998); R. Brody and D. Weissbrodt, 'Major Developments in the 1989 Session on the United Nations Commission on Human Rights', *Human Rights Quarterly*, Vol. 11, p. 602 (1989).

103. A. Vidal d'Almeida Ribeiro, *Implementation of the Declaration on the Elimination of All Forms of Intolerance and of Discrimination Based on Religion or Belief*, U.N. Doc. E/CN.4/1993/62 para. 73 (1993).

104. A. Amor, *Implementation of the Declaration on the Elimination of All Forms of Intolerance and of Discrimination Based on Religion or Belief*, U.N. Doc. A/50/440 para. 86 (1995).

105. *Ibid.*

tive asking for a halt to the plan to destroy the Buddhist statutes of Bamayan in Afghanistan. There was no response from the Taliban and the destruction went ahead as planned.[106] A particularly worrying example of the ineffectiveness of the Rapporteur in cases where the State is opposed to his mandate is that of the venerable Yulo Dawa Tsering, a Tibetan monk to whom the Rapporteur spoke during his visit to China. The Chinese government promised that no negative consequences would arise from the meeting, but the Rapporteur later issued an urgent appeal in regard to the monk who had been placed under house arrest.[107]

Requests for *in situ* visits have also met with mixed success. While a number of States have agreed to requests for visits, and others have even extended an invitation to the Rapporteur, a number of other States have not cooperated with his requests. In his 2001 report, for example, the Rapporteur notes that he requested permission to visit Indonesia, Mauritius, the Russian Federation, and Democratic People's Republic of Korea without receiving any response, in some cases over a period of several years.[108] Similarly, a request to the government of Israel to be allowed to inspect the occupied Palestinian territories as part of a mission with other Rapporteurs met with Israeli refusal.[109]

Conclusion

In most ways, the current Rapporteur has done an extraordinary job, particularly given his limited financial and human resources. He has certainly brought more energy to the role than his predecessor, whose record was more mixed.[110] There are, however, some areas in which improvement could still be

106. A. Amor, *Elimination of All Forms of Religious Intolerance*, U.N. Doc. A/56/253 para. 27 (2001).

107. A. Amor, *Implementation of the Declaration on the Elimination of All Forms of Intolerance and of Discrimination Based on Religion or Belief*, U.N. Doc. E/CN.4/1997/91 para. 10 (1996). The Chinese government later claimed that he was at liberty and that the allegations that he had been arrested were false. A. Amor, *Implementation of the Declaration on the Elimination of All Forms of Intolerance and of Discrimination Based on Religion or Belief*, U.N. Doc. A/52/477 para. 26 (1997).

108. A. Amor, *Elimination of All Forms of Religious Intolerance*, U.N. Doc. A/56/253 table 2 (2001).

109. *Ibid*. paras. 13-14.

110. Flood, *supra* note 102 pp. 75-77. For a less critical overview see T. van Boven, 'Advances and Obstacles in Building Understanding and Respect between People of Diverse Religions and Belief' *Human Rights Quarterly*, Vol. 13, pp. 445-447 (1991).

made. Most notable among these is giving greater acknowledgement to the complexities inherent in some of the areas that the Rapporteur has focussed upon. As is too often the case in United Nations human rights organisations, banal generalities are used to paper over areas of controversy, giving little guidance to States or individuals about their respective duties and rights.[111] Now that schooling and the intersection of racial/religious discrimination have been given in-depth exploration in specific reports, it might be time to consider issues such as extremism and the position of what the Rapporteur describes as 'sects' in more depth.[112] It is of concern that some comments of the Rapporteur seem to downplay the importance of religious freedom as compared to other laudable social goals.

Whatever the limitations there are inherent in his mandate or criticisms one might make of the way in which the Rapporteur carries out his role, his overall performance has been extraordinary. The current Rapporteur averages two *in situ* visits a year,[113] as well as preparing his annual report and responding to initiatives by United Nations and non-governmental bodies. He brings an extraordinary commitment and energy to a largely thankless role. His own description of the modest, complex and limited role that he plays perhaps best summarises the strengths and weaknesses of the role:

> [C]ompromises make it possible to go beyond what is hateful and move forward in the search for the best that can be achieved without ever failing—even when there is very little latitude or room to manoeuvre—to take a stand against tyranny, totalitarianism and everything else which is likely to impose a uniformity of attitudes and behaviour, to deny freedom of conscience or to mortgage intelligence.[114]

111. Evans, *supra* note 1 p. 365.

112. The Rapporteur has called for a high-level intergovernmental meeting on sects. A. Amor, *Implementation of the Declaration on the Elimination of All Forms of Intolerance and of Discrimination Based on Religion or Belief*, U.N. Doc. E/CN.4/1997/91 para. 103 (1996).

113. A. Amor, *Elimination of All Forms of Religious Intolerance*, U.N. Doc. A/56/253 para. 7 (2001).

114. A. Amor, *Implementation of the Declaration on the Elimination of All Forms of Intolerance and of Discrimination Based on Religion or Belief*, U.N. Doc. A/50/440 para. 87 (1995).

Chapter 3

The Dimensions and Dynamics of Religious Discrimination: Findings and Analysis from the UK

Paul Weller[1]

Professor of Inter-Religious Relations, University of Derby

Discrimination and unfair treatment on the grounds of religion takes a variety of forms in a range of different contexts throughout the world[2]. How it is experienced, analysed and understood has a significant bearing upon how it is addressed in terms of policy initiatives and legal instruments. This chapter therefore aims to explore the various dimensions and dynamics of what, in

---

1. Paul Weller is Professor of Inter-Religious Relations and Subject Group Manager, Humanities and Social Sciences at the University of Derby. He is editor of *Religions in the UK: Directory 2001-3* (Derby: Multi Faith Centre at the University of Derby, 2001) and was project Director of the British Government Home Office commissioned Religious Discrimination in England and Wales Research Project. He is co-author (P. Weller, K. Purdam *et al*) of *Religious Discrimination in England and Wales: Interim Report* (Derby: University of Derby, 2000) and of the project's final report, P. Weller, A. Feldman and K. Purdam *et al*, *Religious Discrimination in England and Wales*, Home Office Research Study 220 (London: Research, Development and Statistics Directorate, Home Office, 2001).
2. K. Boyle and J. Sheen (eds.), *Freedom of Religion and Belief: A World Report* (London: Routledge, 1997).

popular debate, is often described in an undifferentiated way simply as 'religious discrimination'.

This chapter proceeds by exploring these themes with reference to the work of the Religious Discrimination in England and Wales Research Project (1999-2001) which was the first major research study[3] of religious discrimination to be commissioned from within the United Kingdom Government. The empirical results of the project were published in Home Office Research Study 220, *Religious Discrimination in England and Wales*, by Weller, Feldman and Purdam.[4]

Prior to that, the project had published its own *Interim Report*,[5] which was based upon a literature review of published and other relevant materials that were available and/or submitted to the project. The main body of this chapter draws upon[6] the results of the empirical study in order to illustrate some

3. The project was commissioned by the Home Office and conducted by a research team from the University of Derby of which the present author was Project Director. It was carried out by means of quantitative and qualitative research methods, with a postal questionnaire being sent to 1,830 religious organisations, of which 628 were returned (including 154 from national, 16 from regional, and 458 from local organisations). Fieldwork was conducted in Leicester (November-December 1999), Newham (January-February 2000), Blackburn (March-April 2000) and Cardiff (May-June 2000), including meetings and interviews with religious organisations, public, private and voluntary sector bodies, and also biographical interviews with individuals. The aims of the project, as commissioned by the Home Office, were to:
   - assess the evidence of religious discrimination, both actual and perceived.
   - describe the patterns shown by this evidence including: its overall scale; the main victims; the main perpetrators; and the main ways in which it manifests.
   - indicate the extent to which religious discrimination overlaps with racial discrimination.
   - identify the broad range of policy options available for dealing with religious discrimination.
4. P. Weller, A. Feldman, K. Purdam *et al*, Home Office Research Study 220, *Religious Discrimination in England and Wales* (2001). The report can be viewed electronically through the Research Development and Statistics Directorate's section of the Home Office web site at http://www.homeoffice.gov.uk/rds/pdfs/hors220.pdf.
5. The interim report was published in January 2000: P. Weller, K. Purdam *et al*, *Religious Discrimination in England and Wales, Interim Report, January 2000* (2000). It reviewed the historical background, described the current religious diversity of Britain, and provided information on anti-discrimination legislation in the UK and a number of other countries. Printed copies are no longer available, but it can be accessed on the internet through the University of Derby's *MultiFaithNet* website at http://www.multifaithnet.org/projects/religdiscrim/reports.htm.
6. The following sections of the chapter draw on text in Weller, Feldman, Purdam *et al*, *supra* note 4, which is © Crown Copyright, 2001, as well as on the project's *Interim Report* (Weller, Purdam *et al*, *supra* note 5) and other research materials gathered in the course of the Religious Discrimination in England and Wales Research Project. Contributions to the empirical report were also made by Ahmed Andrews, Anna Doswell, John Hinnells, Marie Parker-Jenkins, Sima Parmar and Michele Wolfe. The authors and contributors also express their acknowledgements to the fieldwork informants and questionnaire respon-

aspects of the varied dimensions and dynamics of unfair treatment on the basis of religion. It does so within an overall analytical framework for delineating these dimensions and dynamics that was outlined by the project's *Interim Report*. It also includes some personal and professional reflections by the author, especially in the section following which sets out the contemporary and historical context of religious discrimination, as well as in the chapter's concluding reflections on evidence, analysis, policy and community development.

Reflections on Religious Discrimination in Contemporary and Historical Context

Even taking account of the religious discrimination that has been a feature of the long-running sore of national and religious conflict in Northern Ireland,[7] the position with regard to religious discrimination and conflict in the United Kingdom as a whole has been one that has been comparatively positive in comparison with such contexts as the religious and ethnic cleansing in Bosnia-Herzogovina and the outbreaks of communalism in the Indian subcontinent. In addition, in recent years within the public, private and voluntary sectors, there have been significant developments with regard to recognition of the place of religious identity and the role of religious communities in the aspiration to build an inclusive society.

Within the Office of the Deputy Prime Minister, the Inner Cities' Religious Council[8] (originally created under the former Conservative Government within the then Department of the Environment) acts as a channel of communication and engagement for five of the largest religious communities in relation to agendas of urban regeneration. In the National Health Service, the Patient's Charter explicitly requires 'respect for privacy, dignity and religious

---

dents, whose experiences and views form the basis of the research findings. The views expressed in both this part of the chapter and in the chapter as a whole are those of the author of the chapter, and not necessarily those of the authors of the project report, or of the Home Office, nor do they reflect Government policy.

7. P. Badham, 'The contribution of religion to the conflict in Northern Ireland' in D. Cohn-Sherbok (ed.), *The Canterbury Papers: Essays on Religion and Society* pp. 119-128 (London: Bellew, 1990); R. Comerford, M. Cullen and J. Hill, *Religion, Conflict and Coexistence in Ireland* (London: Gill and Macmillan, 1990); J. Hickey, *Religion and the Northern Ireland Problem* (Dublin: Gill and Macmillan, 1984); B. McSweeney, 'The Religious Dimension of the 'troubles' in Northern Ireland' in P. Badham (ed.), *Religion, State and Society in Modern Britain* pp. 68-83 (Lampeter: Edwin Mellen Press, 1989).

8. C. Beales, 'Partnerships for a Change: The Inner Cities Religious Council' in *World Faiths Encounter* No. 8, July 1994, pp. 41-47.

and cultural beliefs'. In the private sector, a number of employers, such as the B&Q home improvement chain, have sought to take account of religion within the evolution of their diversity policies and practices. In the voluntary sector, various inter-faith and multi-faith initiatives and structures have also been developed at local, national, and United Kingdom-wide levels. These include the important evolution of the Inter Faith Network for the United Kingdom[9] that has acted as a partner with both the Commission for Racial Equality and the Government in relation to a number of concerns and events.

At the same time, these positive developments are no reason for complacency. The summer 2001 disturbances in the northern towns and subsequent reports[10] on these have underlined the potentially dangerous cocktail that can explode when the ingredients of social and economic deprivation, and religious and ethnic identity become unstable. In addition, it is important to remember that the United Kingdom has an historical inheritance that differs significantly from the liberal contemporary self-image in respect of religious diversity. Historically, religious and political belonging were often seen as being co-terminal. When and where this has been the case, religious diversity has often been seen as being at least potentially dangerous to the fabric of the state and of society. In this context, being a Nonconformist or Roman Catholic Christian was perceived as being a potential 'fifth columnist'. The former would not worship according to the legally required forms of worship, while the latter were associated with the extra-territorial institution of the Papacy. Throughout their history in these islands Jews have also suffered from such perceptions and have often been charged with 'dual loyalties'.

As a result, British history has seen attempts to impose varying degrees of uniformity in the public profession of belief and in religious worship, in which the law itself has also been an instrument of discrimination. In England and Wales, such discriminatory legal provisions included a number of *Acts of Uniformity*, the *Test and Corporation Acts*, the *Conventicle Acts*, and the *Five Mile Act*. Arising from this inheritance, issues related to religion as an axis of discrimination undergirding the civic and political disabilities of Nonconformist[11]

9. P. Weller, 'The Inter Faith Network for the United Kingdom' in *The Anglo-Indian Historical Review: A Journal of History* Vol. XX, No. 1, pp. 20-26 (1994).

10. T. Cantle and The Community Cohesion Team, *Community Cohesion: A Report of the Independent Review Team Chaired by Ted Cantle* (London: The Home Office, 2001); and J. Denham and the Ministerial Group on Public Order and Community Cohesion, *Building Cohesive Communities: A Report of the Ministerial Group on Public Order and Building Cohesive Communities* (London: The Home Office, 2001).

11. D. Bebbington, *The Nonconformist Conscience: Chapel and Politics, 1870-1914* (London: George Allen and Unwin, 1982); T. Larsen, *Friends of Religious Equality: Nonconformist Politics in Mid-Victorian England* (Woodbridge: The Boydell Press, 1999).

and Roman Catholic Christians, Jews,[12] Atheists,[13] Humanists, Freethinkers and other groups outside the Established religious tradition, were at the forefront of social, religious and political debate.

When examining the dynamics and dimensions of religious discrimination, although the historical context and the groups involved were different, there are perhaps important things that can be learned from the past and some of these potential lessons will be reflected upon in the concluding section of this chapter. The contemporary context of the United Kingdom and of other European societies is, after all, not much more than a century away from a time in which the main (including Christian) religious minorities still had to contend with religious discrimination that was enshrined in law as well as in social attitudes and behaviour. In fact, in the United Kingdom there are still some religious privileges and constraints enshrined in the law. For example, on taking the Throne, under the terms of the *Act of Settlement* the monarch must pledge to uphold Protestant Christianity and the *Act of Succession* prevents anyone with a claim to the Throne from embracing the Roman Catholic tradition of Christianity. However, although these matters are arguably still important in their own right, and also of wider symbolic and constitutional significance for a society which aspires to be multi-cultural and multi-faith, they do not explain how the issue of religious discrimination has re-emerged as a broader contemporary concern.

By the mid-twentieth century, much of the 19th century debate around religious discrimination had subsided. From the 1960s onwards, it had become increasingly assumed that, as part of a process of 'secularisation'[14] religion would come to be viewed as a matter for the private, as distinguished from the public, sphere. By the 1970s and early 1980s the politics of identity and diversity had become primarily concerned with issues related to race and ethnicity. But although there have undoubtedly been shifts in adherence to religious belief and practice, the nature of secularisation has itself been fiercely contested,[15] and in more recent times religion has begun to re-emerge as a marker of individual and community identity for a significant number of people. That this was likely to happen was presciently identified by Bishop John Taylor who, as early as a 1977 Church of England General Synod debate on the British

12. M. Salbstein, *The Emancipation of the Jews in Britain: The Question of the Admission of the Jews to Parliament, 1828-1860* (London & Toronto: Associated University Press, 1982).

13. D. Berman, *A History of Atheism in Britain: From Hobbes to Russell* (London: Croon Helm, 1988).

14. A. Gilbert, *The Making of Post-Christian Britain: a History of the Secularisation of Modern Society* (London: Longman, 1980).

15. S. Bruce, *Religion and Modernisation: Sociologists and Historians Debate the Secularisation Thesis* (Oxford: Oxford University Press, 1992).

Council of Churches' Community and Race Relations Unit's hard-hitting 1976 report *The New Black Presence in Britain*,[16] argued that:

> The existence of religious minorities presents us with both problems and opportunities which are distinct from those that arise in the presence of racial and cultural minorities, and should not be lost sight of or evaded.[17]

Setting this within a context of global change Vincent Cable, in his Demos booklet *The World's New Fissures: Identities in Crisis*,[18] linked the rise in importance of cultural and the religious factors of self-identification and organisation with the phenomenon of globalisation. In a world that is rapidly shrinking and becoming the 'global village' of Marshall McLuhan's 1960s prophecy, the old political polarities of left and right, and of identities based on nation-state formations, have weakened and individuals and groups are looking for ways of connecting the local and the global.

Religions are prime exemplars of this possibility with their participative communities centred on localised groups in villages, towns and cities but which, at the same time, are connected with wider transnational networks in which primary allegiance is owed to value systems which claim to transcend the national, ethnic and legal systems of all human societies. Therefore, in the closing decades of the 20th century, a shift began to take place in which, in the context of a developing identity politics, religion once again emerged as a major factor in the public sphere.

Once again, the tensions between particular (national) and global (religious) forms of belonging formed the backcloth to these debates, and especially in relation to the Muslim population of the United Kingdom and the global Ummah. During the 1991 Gulf War,[19] in the long running Rushdie controversy,[20] and in the climate of fear[21] and suspicion about 'Islamic terrorism'

16. British Council of Churches, *The New Black Presence in Britain: A Christian Scrutiny* (London: British Council of Churches, 1978).
17. Quoted in J. Wolffe (ed.), *The Growth of Religious Diversity: Britain From 1945. A Reader* p. 193 (Sevenoaks: Hodder and Stoughton, 1993).
18. V. Cable, *The World's New Fissures: Identities in Crisis* (London: Demos, 1994).
19. T. Benn, 'Religion, War and the Gulf' in D. Cohn-Sherbok and D. McClellan (eds.), *Religion in Public Life* pp. 29-37 (London: Macmillan, 1992).
20. L. Appignanesi and S. Maitland (eds.), *The Rushdie File* (London: Fourth Estate, 1989); M.M. Ahsan and A.R. Kidwai (eds.), *Sacrilege Versus Civility: Muslim Perspectives on the Salman Rushdie Affair* (Leicester: Islamic Foundation, 1991). The Muslim writer Rana Kabbani (in *Letter to Christendom* p. 8 (London: Virago, 1989)) argued that: *'Rushdie's book brought into the open the frustrations of a Muslim minority for whom the much-vaunted multicultural society was a sham....Faced by the majority community, still overwhelmingly Christian in law and institutions if not in belief, Muslims felt powerless and unprotected'*.
21. C. Allen and J. Nielsen, *Summary Report on Islamophobia in the EU after 11 September 2001* (Vienna: European Monitoring Centre on Racism and Xenophobia, May 2002).

following the Al-Qaida Network's September 11th attacks on the World Trade Centre and the Pentagon, Muslims frequently found themselves inheriting the historic mantle of Roman Catholics and Jews in being perceived, at least potentially, as 'fifth columnists'.

For other religious groups, too, events such as the storming of the Golden Temple in Amritsar[22] and the discrimination against Hindus in Fiji have heightened awareness of the significance of religion as a key marker of self-identification and as a basis for self-organisation. In the UK, the struggles over legislation affecting the wearing of turbans by Sikhs[23] and the planning battle over the use of Bhaktivendanta Manor[24] for Hindu worship and festivals have also played a part.

Whether or not these developments are seen as welcome, an observable shift has been taking place in social and political realities. Through these symbolically charged major social and political events and their associated debates, underlying and day-to-day experiences of unfair treatment in employment, education, the media and a whole range of other aspects of life in an increasingly plural society have been brought into sharper focus. It was these dimensions of religious discrimination that were the main focus of the findings of the Religious Discrimination in England and Wales Research Project.

Clearing the Terminological Ground

As noted in the project's Interim Report, the terminology of 'religious discrimination' is not unproblematic. There is, first of all, the problem of what constitutes religion. This is not simply an abstract and theoretical question. Rather, how it is answered has concrete and practical consequences. The notion of a religion has often simply been assumed according to one or more of its popular senses or, as in charitable law, its appropriateness to describe a particular form of corporate life has been evaluated in relation to the particular kinds of activities of an organisation claiming to be religious.

22. D. Singh Tatla, 'The Punjab Crisis and Sikh Mobilisation in Britain' in R. Barot (ed.), *Religion and Ethnicity: Minorities and Social Change in the Metropolis* pp. 96-109 (Kampen: Kok Pharos, 1993).

23. A.W. Helweg, *Sikhs in England: The Development of a Migrant Community (2nd edition)* (Delhi: Oxford University Press, 1986).

24. M. Nye, 'Hare Krishna and Sanatan Dharm in Britain: The Campaign for Bhaktivedanta Manor' *Journal of Contemporary Religion* Vol. XXI, No. 1, pp. 37-56 (1996).

As with 'ethnicity',[25] there is no straightforward or uncontested definition of 'religion'. In both popular usage, and some legal usage in connection with charity law, religion has often been considered to be something to do with belief in a God or divine being. Such an understanding is, however, problematic, since it does not take account of the world religions of Buddhism or Jainism that are 'a-theistic', let alone the beliefs of newer movements such as Scientology. In addition, such definitions locate the significance of belief more centrally than would be the case in some traditions. As the sociologist of religion, Grace Davie[26] has argued, there is also a phenomenon of 'believing without belonging' which means that identification with a religion is likely to be considerably wider than active involvement in a religious tradition or community.

In the academic study of religion, the best that exists are various 'working definitions' of religion which tend to reflect the various disciplinary traditions within which the definitions are made. Etymologically, the English word 'religion' derives from the Latin word *religio* which has a root meaning related to the idea of a 'binding' together and which contains the sense of an organised culture. The sociologist Emile Durkheim's[27] definition of religion is that of 'a unified system of beliefs and practices relative to sacred things'. The anthropologist Clifford Geertz's[28] definition sees religion as,

> (1) a system of symbols which acts to (2) establish powerful, pervasive and long-lasting moods and motivations in men [sic] by (3) formulating conceptions of a general order of existence and (4) clothing these conceptions with such an aura of factuality that (5) the moods and motivations seem uniquely realistic.

By contrast, the theologian and historian of religion Wilfred Cantwell Smith[29] has critiqued the usefulness of the very idea of a 'religion' itself. Instead, he argued that what are today described as distinct 'religions' are, in fact, historical constructions superimposed upon what are actually the very diverse experiences of people of 'personal faith' who live within what Cantwell Smith prefers to call 'cumulative traditions.'

An appreciation of the complexity of the issues involved is important for avoiding simplistic pitfalls in the potential responses to unfair treatment on the

25. A. Bacal, *Ethnicity in the Social Sciences: A View and Review of the Literature on Ethnicity* Reprint Paper on Ethnic Relations, No. 3 (Coventry: Centre for Research in Ethnic Relations, University of Warwick, 1991).

26. G. Davie, *Religion in Britain Since 1945: Believing Without Belonging* (London: Blackwell, 1994).

27. E. Durkheim, *The Elementary Forms of Religious Life* (New York: The Free Press, 1947).

28. C. Geertz, 'Religion as a Cultural System' (1966) in M. Bainton (ed.), *Anthropological Approaches to the Study of Religion* p. 4 (London: Tavistock, 1990).

29. W. Cantwell Smith, *The Meaning and End of Religion* (London: SPCK, 1978).

basis of religion, whether such responses might be of a legislative or a non-legislative kind. The problem of defining religion has often been adduced as a reason for not bringing in new legislation to respond to religious discrimination, or to develop law to take account of the extended religious plurality of contemporary society. For example, The Law Commission[30] argued on these grounds that it would not be possible to legislate for a more inclusive law protecting religious sensitivities to replace the current common law offences of blasphemy and blasphemous libel.

In practical and legal terms, some countries try to deal with this difficulty by having a list of religions that are recognised by the state, together with a process and criteria for such recognition. But this approach has often caused significant difficulties for newer communities seeking recognition, and in Britain the tradition has been much more pragmatic, based neither on a list of recognised religions, nor a single working definition of what constitutes a religion. However, to acknowledge the complexity of an issue and the imperfection of any working definition does not, of itself, provide a necessary reason for discarding the policy response of legislation. If uncontested definitions were a prior requirement of law-making, then race relations legislation would never have been contemplated since the concepts of 'race' and 'ethnicity' were not originally defined by Parliament. As with the concept of religion, the meanings of 'race' and 'ethnicity' have also been highly contested in both social science theory and in community politics.

But if the basic concepts of 'religion', 'ethnicity' and 'culture' are themselves contested ones when considered separately, then the question of the relationship between them is even more highly complex, with debates centred on the degree of overlap and distinction between what the concepts signify.[31] In actual populations, religion, ethnicity and culture are often closely linked[32] as a consequence of the history of when and where religious traditions developed. However, the patterns of overlap between religion and ethnicity are not always straightforward and most religious communities are ethnically diverse. Moreover, just as one religious tradition may embrace many ethnicities, so one national or regional origin can be shared by people from within several religions. 'Culture' and 'religion' are clearly often connected in interdepen-

30. The Law Commission, *Offences Against Religion and Public Worship*, Law Commission Report No. 145 (London: HMSO, 1985).

31. See K. Clements, 'The Religious Variable: Dependent, Independent or Interdependent' in M. Hill, *A Sociological Yearbook of Religion* No. 4, pp. 36-45 (London: SCM Press, 1971); K. Knott, *Religion and Identity in the Study of Ethnic Minority Religions in Britain*, Community Religions Project Research Papers, ns. 2, (Leeds: University of Leeds, 1986); 'Ethnicity and religion' (editorial), *Runnymede Bulletin* No. 253, p. 1 (March, 1992).

32. R. Barot (ed.), *Religion and Ethnicity: Minorities and Social Change in the Metropolis*.

dent ways even if they are, in principle, distinguishable, but the nature of their relationship is evaluated differently both among and between the different religious traditions and within varied approaches to the study of religions.

Within the social sciences, the dominant tradition has understood religion to be a dependent variable of ethnicity and/or culture. In this tradition, to varying degrees, religion has been seen as certainly a functional, and sometimes an almost instrumental reinforcement of the primary category of ethnicity. Others have argued that religion and ethnicity are to be seen as much more clearly distinct, or in a reciprocal relationship. By contrast, some[33] have argued for the importance of religion itself as a 'social determinate'.

In the Religious Discrimination Project's field research, a group of Bahá'ís observed in relation to their experience of unfair treatment on the basis of religion that: '…it's not out and out discrimination; not as bad as what ethnic minorities experience, but there's a whole part of your life people don't care about.' A white, male, police inspector noted that: '…an incident may start as a road rage incident and then move to racial insults, even if it wasn't initially motivated by race. There's the same problem with religion: it might begin as racial harassment but then elements of religion are brought into it'. A Muslim woman stated that: 'If someone throws two stones through someone's window, that's racism. If they throw two pigs heads [as did happen in this person's experience], it's about religion'. However, an African-Caribbean race equality worker observed about this: 'I don't care what they threw, but why they threw anything at all—the whole gambit of 'ifs'. You're usually dealing with a multiplicity of issues'.

In this highly problematic and controversial area, the development of policy and practice in relation to self-definition perhaps represents the most practical way forward. It is one that, for all its problems, at least allows policy and practice to connect with 'where people are at'. In this, religion is perhaps best understood as a way of living in which some form of identification (either in a weaker and more general sense, or in a stronger and more specific sense of alignment with particular movements, communities and/or organisational forms) is often (though not always or necessarily) to be found in conjunction with different forms of 'believing' (in various combinations of certain values, ideals and doctrines) and can be expressed through 'practice' (that is related to shared symbols, rituals, observances and ethical orientations).

A strong theme that emerged from the Religious Discrimination in England and Wales Research Project was that individuals, organisations and communities who see their primary identity in terms of religion have frequently experienced a sense of their 'invisibility'. This was highlighted in the image used by a

33. R. Gill, *Social Context of Theology: A Methodological Enquiry* (London: Mowbrays, 1975).

youth interviewed in the course of the project's fieldwork who spoke of those who discriminate on the grounds of religion as having 'a brick in front of their eyes'. This 'invisibility' has been manifested in the frequent failure of individuals, organisations and the society as whole to take account of the distinctive needs, experience, and legitimate expectations of religious individuals, communities and organisations. But it also relates to the relative invisibility of the positive contributions that such individuals, communities and organisations can make to the wider societies of which they are a part.

The 'invisibility' of religion, highlighted by the image of the 'brick in front of their eyes', underlines the nature and scope of the problem of unfair treatment on the basis of religion. But the image also suggests the possibility that once the presence of this blockage is identified, it is possible to remove it. With a clearer perception of the role and significance of religion in the lives of individuals, communities and organisations, actions can be taken that will result in both challenge to, and remedy for, unfair treatment on the basis of religion. Positive measures can then be taken at all levels of society to promote greater inclusivity, in which the distinctive contributions represented by all of its religious traditions and communities will be welcomed and valued for the contributions that they can make to the common good.

Overall the terminology 'religious discrimination' is perhaps best understood as 'shorthand' terminology for 'discrimination on the basis of religion'. In other words, the term is used to describe those attitudes, actions, circumstances and dynamics in which, in relation to factors concerned with religion, an individual or group is treated less favourably than another individual or group either of a different religion, or of no religion. Such treatment, perhaps may, as in the Religious Discrimination project's empirical report, most inclusively be characterised as 'unfair treatment on the basis of religion'. In this understanding, the notion of 'fairness' is important, in the sense that what is deficient is not an impossible to achieve abstract position of mathematical equality, but a sense of basic and achievable 'equity'. The lack of such equity, or 'religious discrimination' can, as with 'racial discrimination', be understood in a variety of ways.

As with the category of race, so also with religion, it is important to distinguish between dimensions of unfair treatment as well as to consider how these dimensions might relate to one another in order that possible responses are appropriate to the nature of the issues involved. As suggested in the Religious Discrimination Project's *Interim Report*,[34] when examining the reported experiences and perceptions that are often colloquially grouped together under the term 'religious discrimination' it can be illuminating to consider the parallel

34. Weller, Purdam *et al*, *supra* note 5.

terminological, definitional and policy debates that have taken place in respect of 'race' and 'ethnicity'. In respect of the agendas set by 'race' and 'ethnicity', it has proved important to distinguish between 'racial prejudice', 'racial hatred', 'racial disadvantage', 'racial discrimination' (including 'direct' and 'indirect' racial discrimination), and 'institutional racism', and it is to parallel analytical categories used in relation to unfair treatment on the basis of religion, that this chapter now turns.

Religious Prejudice

'Religious prejudice' involves the stereotyping of particular religious groups through attitudes that can wound individuals and form a basis for exclusion and unfair treatment. Stereotyping is, for example, deeply entrenched in relation to the perceptions of Muslims[35] in western societies. 'Religious prejudice' is often, but not only, rooted in the historical inheritance of a conflictual relationship that has developed over many centuries involving the overlap of religion, politics and warfare.

Religious prejudice is often manifested in an ignorance that, in the project's[36] field interviews, was one of the most frequently cited reasons for unfair or discriminatory treatment on the basis of religion.

Despite living side by side, sometimes for decades, a large number of interviewees from minority religions and communities felt that members of the majority society knew very little about them. For example, one individual explained that a neighbour was 'shocked' to find out that Jews don't celebrate Christmas/Jesus. A Zoroastrian youth reported that when other young people ask about her religion, they often ask if she attends church. When she tells them her temple is in London they reply that 'it can't be a real religion if you only have one temple'. A Sikh noted that people think because someone is wearing a kirpan then he is aggressive or dangerous. A Jehovah's Witness observed that people believe that they are 'uneducated and brainwashed' and spoke of a public perception of Jehovah's Witnesses being involved in a 'controlling American organisation' despite the fact that a central part of their beliefs centre upon actively developing and following their own conscience.

35. N. Daniels, *Islam and the West: The Making of an Image, 1000-1300 AD, Volume I* (Edinburgh: Edinburgh University Press, 1960); N. Daniels, *Islam and the West: Islam, Europe and Empire, Volume II* (Edinburgh: Edinburgh University Press, 1967); F. Hussain, *The Anti-Islamic Tradition in the West* (Leicester: Muslim Community Studies Institute, 1990).

36. Weller, Feldman, Purdam *et al*, *supra* note 4.

Interviewees reported that those who are not religious often seem to exhibit considerable levels of fear and suspicion towards people who have a strong religious identity and commitment. It was noted that, especially if others have had a bad experience of religion or of religious people, they can tend to generalise this to all other members of that particular religious group, or even towards all religious groups. One person felt that there is a section of the general public which believes that people who maintain strong religious beliefs and distinctive practices are: '...dangerous, clinging to old, outmoded ways, clinging to their identity—people don't understand and are suspicious of those who don't want to conform, who want to keep their distinct identity and not completely integrate'.

Ignorance leading into prejudice may take the form of comments like, 'what's wrong with your head', as a Sikh man reported that he used to be asked, whilst taunts relating to the traditional clothing of Muslim women such as, 'where's the fancy dress?', are not uncommon. Often, those who were the recipients of what they experienced as offensive comments found it hard to know whether the ignorance and/or lack of common sense derives from a lack of interest, or whether it is related to a deep-seated hostility. Such hostility relates to another dimension and dynamic of 'religious discrimination' in which 'religious prejudice' shades over into what can, perhaps, best be identified as 'religious hatred'.

Religious Hatred

Attitudes of religious prejudice may result in no specific discriminatory outcomes. At the same time, when both intensified and developed in a settled attitude of mind, emotion and will, 'religious prejudice' can spill over into, and fan, manifestations of 'religious hatred'. When such 'religious hatred' becomes intense, in certain circumstances it can result in intimidatory and/or violent behaviour towards the religiously 'other'. 'Religious hatred' can also be stimulated and nurtured by organised cadres such as those of extreme racist and fascist groups. In Europe, this 'religious hatred', which has traditionally been directed towards the Jews, has in more recent times also become directed towards Muslims as representatives of what is often perceived as an alien civilisation that is fundamentally at odds with the European heritage. The reports of the enquiry teams[37] into the 2001 summer disturbances in the northern English towns of Burnley and Oldham also underline the role of

37. Cantle, *supra* note 10; Denham, *supra* note 10.

organised fascist activity in this regard, and especially with regard to its particular targeting of 'Muslims' as a specific category of 'undesirable other'.

Such specific prejudicial hatred has been characterised by some as having its roots in what has been described as the phenomenon of 'Islamophobia', identified in the Runnymede Trust report[38] of the same name. But 'religious hatred' is not only experienced and reported by Muslims. In the responses to the Religious Discrimination project questionnaire, hostility and violence were also very real concerns for organisations representing Sikhs and Hindus. In the project fieldwork, Hindu interviewees explained that at one temple there had been damage to the cars of devotees and that, despite security arrangements, some worshippers had been physically attacked when seeking to attend the temple at festival times.

Jews,[39] of course, also continue to be targets of such 'religious hatred', with attacks on synagogues and cemeteries not being uncommon. Pagans and people from 'New Religious Movements' complained of open hostility and discrimination, and of being labelled as 'child abusers' and 'cults', particularly by the media. In the field research, Pagans reported that they feel that they have to take measures to keep their religious lives secret while at work. One said that, if confronted about his Pagan identity, he would need to lie. As a consequence, therefore, they feared they may be perceived as being suspect and dishonest and they were worried that negative stereotypes would be perpetuated if anyone found out.

The findings of the research project highlight the attitudes and behaviour of individuals, whether manifested as 'religious prejudice' or in its more extreme form of 'religious hatred', as being generally the most frequent and widespread form of unfair treatment on the basis of religion. 'Religious hatred', especially, can be very serious, threatening and destabilising in its consequences for individuals and groups, leading to violence against both person and property.

However, even in the absence of 'religious prejudice' and 'religious hatred', the findings of the Religious Discrimination research project underline that more day-to-day and structural dimensions of unfair treatment on the basis of religion can play as significant a role in the lives of many who report unfair treatment on the basis of religion. Because of this, it is also important to take account of how the practices and policies of organisations work and how they result in either 'direct' or 'indirect' religious discrimination. But, in addition, there are also dimensions and dynamics of religious discrimination that arise

38. Runnymede Trust, *Islamophobia: A Challenge for Us All* (London: Runnymede Trust, 1997).

39. Runnymede Trust, *A Very Light Sleeper: The Persistence and Dangers of Antisemitism* (London: Runnymede Trust, 1994).

from the underlying social position of religious minorities which can perhaps best be described by the concept of 'religious disadvantage'.

Religious Disadvantage

'Religious disadvantage' is a structural expression of unfair treatment on the basis of religion that can, in at least some measure, be experienced by all non-Established religious groups. Established religions have traditions of historical presence and rights of access to a range of social institutions that are not available to non-Established religions or, if they are to some extent available, are not available on the same terms as to Established religions. Such factors can impact significantly upon the possibilities of social inclusion that are open to religious minorities. In the United Kingdom, the Church of England is numerically the strongest religious body. As an Established Church, it has a special relationship with English history. However, in addition to being a national Church within England, the particular history and contemporary form of its Establishment means that the Church of England has a distinctive and privileged position, both in relation to the Monarchy and in respect of the institutions of the State and Parliament.[40]

In contrast with the national Churches of some other European countries, the Church of England is not funded by the state in any direct way. But, as Stewart Lamont, a Scottish writer on Church and State relationships points out, although 'The British Constitution has never been formulated as a single written document', nevertheless, 'the bond of the Church of England with the Crown and the parliament of England is clearly spelt out.'[41] In the Religious Discrimination research project, some Christian interviewees raised aspects of constitutional law that embody unfair treatment on the basis of religion. A Roman Catholic drew attention to the fact that, under the law, Roman Catholic Christians are still the only religious group to which a direct successor to the Throne is not allowed to belong. This interviewee believed that these legal constraints remained in force because of persistent perceptions and myths about Catholic disloyalty. He felt that such things would be considered an outrage if they were in force in respect, say, of black people, and argued that a failure to alter this legal position helped to perpetuate the myths. He noted that the Government had challenged the hereditary principle in relation

40. A. Hastings, *Church and State: The English Experience* (Exeter: Exeter University Press, 1991).

41. S. Lamont, *Church and State: Uneasy Alliances* p. 183 (London: Bodley Head, 1989).

to the composition of the House of Lords and he could not therefore see why the *Act of Settlement* should not be repealed.

Christian clergy of various denominations noted that Church of England cathedrals received money for improvements from the local authority, whereas other Christian churches and the places of worship of other religious groups do not seem to have the same possibilities. It was accepted that Anglican cathedrals are often located in the town centre and may be seen as buildings of wider 'public interest', or even as tourist sites. However, a representative of the Roman Catholic Church reported that even though their own cathedral was one of the major sites in the city centre, it was not treated equitably in comparison with a Church of England cathedral.

Some of the implications of the inheritance of the Establishment of the Church of England might seem to be only rather quaint historical quirks. But in the context of a religiously plural society, those 'entails'[42] of the Establishment that are to do with education, the law and the constitution have substantial consequences for people of other than the Established religious traditions. Such examples of 'religious disadvantage' can be found in respect of the provisions made for religious chaplaincy services in public institutions such as prisons,[43] the health service, and the armed forces, as well as also in institutions of higher education.[44]

Christianity, especially in its Established forms, has a privileged presence, sometimes as of right, and sometimes as a consequence of tradition, which is not available to other non-Established traditions. In each of these areas there are now often advisers of other faith traditions playing a role, and the research by Beckford and Gilliat and by Gilliat alluded to above has shown that the privileges of Establishment can sometimes be used creatively to involve minority groups. However, this relies upon the approaches taken by individual personnel and is thus highly dependent upon these individuals rather than being structurally supported and embedded. At best, such a state of affairs might be seen by minority religions as one of enlightened paternalism, and at worst as a structural expression of unfair treatment on the basis of religion.

Interviewees from secular agencies as well as from Christian religious groups pointed out that there was a Christian 'default position' built into

42. P. Weller, 'Equity, Inclusivity and Participation in a Plural Society: Challenging the Establishment of the Church of England' in P. Edge and G. Harvey (eds.), *Law and Religion in Contemporary Society: Communities, Individualism and the State* pp. 53-67 (Aldershot: Ashgate, 2000).

43. J. Beckford and S. Gilliat, *Religion in Prison: Equal Rites in a Multi-Faith Society* (Cambridge: Cambridge University Press, 1998).

44. S. Gilliat, *Higher Education and Student Religious Identity* (Department of Sociology, University of Exeter, Exeter, in association with the Inter Faith Network for the United Kingdom, London, 1999).

some existing laws. Many felt that this amounted to unfair treatment of other religions and should be reviewed, although what might take the place of the default position was the subject of much more diverse comment.

Direct Religious Discrimination

'Direct religious discrimination' occurs where there is deliberate exclusion of people from opportunities or services on grounds related to their religious belief, identity or practice. 'Direct discrimination' would, for example, include decisions made by potential employers to exclude Muslims from employment because of their religious belief, identity or practice.

In the draft Equality Bill [45] prepared by the Independent Review of the Enforcement of U.K. Anti-Discrimination Legislation, a definition of 'direct discrimination' which is intended also to embrace such discrimination on the ground of religion, is offered as: 'A person ("A") directly discriminates against another person ("B") if, for a reason related to any of the prohibited grounds.' This is then illustrated by 'A treats B less favourably than another person ("C") is, has been or would be treated in a comparable situation' or 'A subjects B to a detriment'. A further illustration is, 'A comparison of the situations of B and C must be such that the relevant circumstances in the one case are the same, or not materially different, in the other.'

'Religious prejudice', 'religious hatred' and 'religious disadvantage' do not necessarily lead to 'direct religious discrimination'. But, as with racial prejudice, it is possible for these dimensions and dynamics to translate into directly discriminatory behaviour when they inform decisions taken by individuals holding positions of power within the public, private and voluntary sectors. For example, a Hindu educationalist recalled Sikh children being embarrassed by teachers who derided them and their hair by saying things like 'why can't they chop off that bun'?

It was noted that because of the status and power of teachers, such negative and prejudicial attitudes on their part can have an adverse influence on the behaviour of other students. As a Jehovah's Witness explained it: 'If a teacher gives a student a hard time in the class, then you can guarantee that the other students will do so at lunchtime. The reality is that a six-year-old is not intellectually able to articulate his or her views when challenged by teachers'.

---

45. Independent Review of the Enforcement of U.K. Anti-Discrimination Legislation, *Equality Bill* p. 9 (University of Cambridge Faculty of Law, 10 July 2002).

However, as in the lessons learned from tackling discrimination on the basis of ethnicity, gender and disability, conscious and deliberate 'direct religious discrimination' is not the only, or perhaps in its effects even the most widespread, form of unfair treatment on the basis of religion. 'Indirect religious discrimination', although not intended, can be at least, and perhaps even more significant as 'direct religious discrimination' in its effects, because 'indirect discrimination' usually extends beyond individual instances affecting single persons to impact upon the experience and opportunities of whole groups.

Indirect Religious Discrimination

'Indirect religious discrimination' is rooted in the policies and practices of organisations which can result in patterns of exclusive recruitment policies, employment practice and service provision. Such discrimination is therefore to be understood in terms of the exclusionary effects of historical decisions, contemporary structures or patterns of behaviour and organisation that may not at all be informed by attitudes of 'religious prejudice' or 'religious hatred', although they may be related to aspects of 'religious disadvantage'. But where such historic patterns have not been explicitly reconsidered in the light of the implications of religious plurality, then they can unintentionally result in discrimination against people of various religious traditions. Examples of this can include culturally exclusive requirements and provisions in terms of diet, clothing, religious festivals and a range of other matters.

In the draft Equality Bill, 'indirect discrimination' is defined (again as intending to encompass religion as a ground of such discrimination) as:

> A person indirectly discriminates against another person where he applies an apparently neutral provision, criterion or practice which, in its application to persons who are members of a relevant group (a) is, or would be, to the detriment of a considerably larger proportion of persons in the group compared with other persons; or (b) has, or would have, the effect that members of the group are put at a particular disadvantage when compared with other persons.

But 'A person (P) does not indirectly discriminate against another person if P shows (a) that the application by him of any provision, criterion or practice is objectively justified by a legitimate aim; and (b) that the means of achieving that aim are appropriate and necessary' and that a person may not rely on the foregoing 'unless he also shows that he has taken such steps as it is reasonable in the circumstances of the case for him to have to take to change the provision, criterion or practice in question so as to prevent it having the effect described in paragraph (b).' In determining whether something is 'reasonable', then 'regard is to be paid to whether taking the step would place a disproportionate burden on P',[46] including the practicability, financial cost, and disruption to activities involved.

In the Religious Discrimination Project fieldwork a Sikh woman, who worked in a medium-sized bakery, related the following story through her son:

> For 8 years, it was never a problem. Then, for one and a half years they picked on this (Sikh) woman for wearing her bangle. Finally, they moved her to a different part of the [organisation]. They said she must take it off, but she said no. Representatives from the Sikh temple had a meeting with Personnel to explain, but they said no because it was classed as jewellery.

Other interviewees mentioned that tests were done to see if there were any bacteria in the bangle, and that these came out negative. They also made the point that her apron sleeves covered the bangle. This controversy had important knock-on effects for other Sikh women who came forward in support of this woman to state that they themselves also wore bangles, and who then also became subject to harassment by other employees as well as by the management. The woman lost her case at a tribunal, but after years of fighting a special sleeve was developed, and the management and staff were required to attend diversity training.

Others who commented on this case believed that it represented an instance of discrimination, especially as a very persuasive and clear argument was made by religious community representatives, and other employees were wearing wedding rings. However, a white, male, employment tribunal representative (and who was not associated with the case) commented:

> ...knowing how diverse society is, sometimes situations are just unfair. People will have to be aware of say, hygiene regulations, and if they have to wear a bangle, they may have to do something else either within the organisation or as a job. You have to find a balance...the average employer couldn't really care less about religion unless it affects the running of her or his business which usually can be covered by race protections.

Institutional Religionism

The admittedly somewhat inelegant neologism 'institutional religionism', as used in the Religious Discrimination project's *Interim Report*, attempts to

46. *Supra* note 45.

describe the endemic and structurally embedded forms of discrimination that can occur within organisations. As the recent *Macpherson Report*[47] following the murder of Stephen Lawrence has shown with regard to racism, the prejudicial attitudes of individuals can combine with several factors into a mutually reinforcing environment and ethos.

By analogy with the Lawrence Inquiry report's analysis of 'institutional racism', what the project's *Interim Report* identifies by the neologism of 'institutional religionism' can be understood as the product of a combination of several factors into a mutually reinforcing environment and ethos. Such 'institutional religionism' or 'institutional religious discrimination' can occur in a context in which 'religious prejudice', 'direct' and 'indirect' religious discrimination and sometimes, also, 'religious disadvantage', combine in the collective failure of an organisation to provide an adequate and professional environment and/or service.

Tackling Religious Discrimination

As well as gathering reported evidence in respect of the nature and extent of unfair treatment on the basis of religion, the Religious Discrimination Research Project postal questionnaire and fieldwork also asked about the most appropriate ways of responding to such religious discrimination.[48] As well as giving respondents a free opportunity to respond, the project itself also identified[49] a

47. *Sir William Macpherson's Inquiry into the Matters Arising from the Death of Stephen Lawrence on 22nd April 1993 to date, in order Particularly to Identify the Lessons to be Learned for the Investigation and Prosecution of Racially Motivated Crimes*, 24 February 1999, Cm 4262-I, (London: The Stationery Office, 1999).

48. The people completing questionnaires on behalf of religious organisations were asked for their personal views about the measures that should be considered in order to combat unfair treatment. Each respondent was asked to tick up to three items from a list of six (to which they could also add their own suggestions) or to indicate that they did not think any new measures were necessary. In practice, some people ticked up to six measures from the list and the average number varied between religious groups. This means that comparisons between traditions need to be treated with caution. Therefore the comparative summary of the results of this question concentrates on the two or three options most likely to be chosen by respondents.

49. It should be noted that the remit of the project, as commissioned by the Home Office, did not include the making of any recommendations, but only the identification of a range of possible options. This section of the chapter includes, in a descriptive way, some reporting of how the various religious groups that participated in the research relatively evaluated these options. Where it goes beyond this, the section reflects the individual views of the author of the chapter rather those of either the research participants, the research project team, or the Home Office.

range of possible responses to such discrimination, which included:[50]

No new action

Monitoring and evaluation of policy and practice in the light of the Human Rights Act

Curricular initiatives within the formal education system at school and University levels

Partnership initiatives of public education with religious and inter-faith groups

Staff development and personnel initiatives

The drawing up and implementation of codes of practice

The evolution of equity policies and programmes on religion and equal opportunities

The use of legal instruments by amendment to existing law or introduction of new law such as:

i. introducing law on religious discrimination to Britain
ii. amending the Race Relations Act to include religion
iii. extending, amending or abolishing current blasphemy laws
iv. extending existing criminal law in the Public Order Act and the Crime and Disorder Act to include measures against religious hatred and religiously motivated offences
v. introducing a new right of Manifestation of Belief
vi. consolidating anti-discrimination legislation into a single statute including explicit consideration of religion in all constitutional reviews

In the responses to the postal questionnaire, more teaching of comparative religion in schools was the first or second most favoured option for all the non-Christian traditions, and for representatives of organisations in the Christian (other)[51] category of the research. Public education programmes and better training of staff/employees were the two most popular options for Christian respondents whilst both of these measures (especially public education) were also well favoured by respondents from the other religions.

The remaining three measures (changes in the law, policy reviews to promote equal treatment and voluntary codes of practice) were generally less popular among respondents of all religions. However, for Muslims change in the law was the single most popular option (chosen by slightly more respondents than comparative religion). It was the least favoured measure for

50. These options, together with a range of the issues that they raise, are explored in Weller, Feldman, Purdam *et al*, *supra* note 4 pp. 59-89.

51. In the project categories, this included groups such as Christian Scientists, Jehovah's Witnesses and Mormons.

Christian respondents, although within this tradition it had more support from representatives of black-led Christian organisations.

Sikh respondents were more likely than respondents from other religions to favour policy reviews, although they gave higher priority to comparative religion overall. Voluntary codes of practice were one of the least favoured options for all religions, whilst only a tiny minority favoured no new action (six per cent of Christian respondents and smaller percentages for the other religions).

Reflections on Evidence, Analysis, Policy and Community Development

Thus far, the chapter has highlighted some evidence from the Religious Discrimination in England and Wales Research Project findings and has undertaken some exploration of this within the analytical framework that was developed by the project's *Interim Report*. The final section of this chapter now goes on to offer some personal and professional reflections on the relationship between this evidence and analysis, and a range of contemporary issues for policy and community development in a religiously plural society.

The question of which response or responses to religious discrimination might be the most effective is, perhaps, most appropriately decided when the question and the possible answers are differentiated according to which particular dimension or dynamic of unfair treatment on the basis of religion is being considered. In relation to 'religious prejudice', it may be that the law can achieve little directly, but school-based education and wider public education programmes may be more appropriate and, if properly planned and resourced, could be capable of achieving much. At the same time, the dynamic inter-relationship between law and what is viewed as being socially 'acceptable' and 'unacceptable' should not be underestimated.

In the field of employment, though, whilst there may be an important role for staff development programmes, it may be that (as in the case of Northern Ireland) legislation is required, both to provide individuals with a means of redress and to act as a lever for change. This has been recognised by the European Union in its Directive 2000/78/EC that established a general framework for equal treatment in employment and occupation without discrimination 'on grounds of religion or belief, disability, age or sexual orientation'.

In respect of religious disadvantage, the promotion of debate on constitutional review and reform—such as the recent debates on reform of the

Second Chamber of Parliament, and debates about the disestablishment of the Church of England—may offer the most appropriate way forward.

As can be seen then, the analytical differentiation of the various dynamics and dimensions of religious discrimination is not a matter of purely theoretical import. Quite to the contrary, the attainment of such a differentiated understanding is critically important in the development of effective policy and, if judged appropriate, of workable legislation. At the same time, in relation to the issues of religious discrimination it is important not to see those who report experiencing such discrimination simply as passive recipients of policy and/or legal processes coming from 'outside' and from 'above'. Rather, they are also themselves empowering themselves by addressing these issues from 'inside' and 'below'.

The chapter began with a reminder that the dynamics and dimensions of religious discrimination are not new, and that perhaps significant things can be learned from the history of the 19th century struggle for the ending of civil disabilities and the development of wider social and political participation. An understanding of the past demonstrates that these historic disabilities were not removed simply as the product of an automatic evolutionary process based on social and economic developments, nor only due to the enlightened good will of those who did not themselves experience such disabilities but recognised the inequity of the position and sought to change it.

Although both economic development and changes of position on the part of the relatively powerful played their part, the removal of civil disabilities related to religious identity and belonging primarily came about in response to organised struggle and campaigning on the part of those who were negatively affected by them. Numerous bodies were formed which engaged in campaigning against religious privilege and civil disabilities. Reflecting on the developments towards religious equality in the 19th century, the legal academic St John Robilliard commented that: 'The early story of the struggle for religious liberty' is one that was concerned with groups who experienced prejudice, discrimination, disability and disadvantage 'establishing an identity of their own' ...and then 'From the struggle for existence we pass to the struggle for equality'.[52]

The element of struggle within civil society is often necessary to bring about social, political and legal change. It is only recently that religion has once again become recognised in the UK as a potentially significant axis of discrimination in its own right. In finding ways to address such discrimination, policies and laws from 'outside' and from 'above' are seen by those who

52. St. J. Robilliard, *Religion and The Law: Religious Liberty in Modern English Law* p. ix (Manchester: Manchester University Press, 1984).

experience such discrimination fundamentally as instruments that can either impede or facilitate positive change. They can be imposed upon those primarily affected by the problems concerned, or they can be developed in partnership with them. They can create more divisions and difficulties, or help to move things along in a more positive and inclusive direction.

The way in which policy developments and possible laws are considered and decided upon is critical to the effects that they might have. Therefore ways need to be identified and nurtured, at all levels—locally, nationally and internationally—of working on these issues in a complementary but distinctive way from 'inside' and from 'outside', from 'below' and from 'above'. In this way, the processes involved will themselves already have begun to contribute to the development of a more inclusive society in which, at all levels, the religious diversity of its citizens and communities is more clearly recognised and valued.

The increasing religious diversity of European societies and the intersection of this diversity with many issues of social and public life is posing many new questions and possibilities. Among the recommendations of a report by the Council of Europe's Group of Consultants on Religious and Cultural Aspects of Equality of Opportunities for Immigrants is one that states:

> The increasing religious diversity of Europe constitutes a major challenge to both the governments of the member states and to their societies. The governments and the historical religious communities must adopt a policy which aims to establish an effective equality of rights and treatments for the new religious minorities in Europe. Failure to establish such a policy would amount to a violation by Europe of its declared principles and those of the Council of Europe.[53]

Finally, in considering religious discrimination, it is important to recall that the followers of various religions have themselves also been perpetrators as well as victims of religious discrimination, both in relation to other religious groups and also in relation to those who do not understand themselves in terms of religion. The rights to question and believe did not come about without historic struggles and represent important social gains. They can also be seen as religious gains, too, since they helped to establish the principle of religious identity as something that is freely chosen and/or affirmed rather than being something that is merely the product of history or convention.

Therefore, in giving consideration to the contours of religious discrimination and also the possible measures for tackling it, it is important to maintain an approach that includes an equal concern for the rights of Atheists,

53. Group of Consultants on Cultural Aspects of Equality of Opportunities for Immigrants, *Study* para. 4.2.1 (Strasbourg: Council of Europe, 1996).

Humanists and Agnostics as well as for those of religious believers and practitioners of various kinds. Indeed, such an approach is itself required under the terms of the European Convention on Human Rights defence of the freedom of 'thought, conscience and religion'. Pragmatically, too, if religious believers wish to have their concerns taken seriously as part of an agenda to create a fully inclusive plural society, those of all backgrounds will need to affirm the importance of tackling discrimination on the grounds of religion wherever it appears and by whomever it is committed, including majority Christians, minority Muslims, Hindus, Sikhs and others, as well as Atheists, Agnostics and Humanists.

Chapter 4

A Human Rights Framework for Defining and Understanding Intra-Religious Persecution in Muslim Countries[1]

Mohamed S.M. Eltayeb

Lawyer, activist and author of 'A Human Rights Approach to Combating Religious Persecution'

Religious persecution is a worldwide phenomenon. Practices of intolerance and discrimination based on religion or beliefs are reported almost every day. In his report to the United Nations Commission on Human Rights, the Special

1. The term 'Muslim countries' is used here in a broader sense. It refers to both Islamic countries, where the laws are derived from Islamic law (Shari'a), and to those countries where the majority of the population are Muslims, but Islam is neither the state religion nor the formal source of law. Some scholars, like Donna E. Arzt, have used the term 'Islamic states' to refer to the countries which have officially proclaimed Islam to be the state religion or for which Islamic law is a formal source of legislation. It is the contention of this author that a distinction has to be drawn between countries that have only proclaimed Islam as state religion or the primary source of legislation within the framework of a secularized legal system, and those countries where the legal system has been Islamized and the laws are derived from Islamic law (Shari'a). The term 'Islamic states' has

Rapporteur on Religious Intolerance concluded from the information he had collected:

> It is apparent that intolerance and discrimination based on religion or belief is a common phenomenon throughout the world.[2]

Religious persecution, in general, is a form of persecution based on difference of belief. Such belief may take the form of religious or ideological belief. Within the genre of religious persecution, particularly state-sponsored persecution, we may distinguish the following forms: inter-religious persecution; intra-religious persecution; secular v. religious; and religious v. secular. While inter-religious persecution is directed against other religions and beliefs, intra-religious persecution is directed against communities belonging to the same religion. The persecution of religions in the former communist countries serves as an example of the third form. The persecution of communists in Saudi Arabia exemplified the fourth form.[3] It is to be observed that these forms of persecution are not mutually exclusive, hence two or more of them may very well co-exist with each other. The case of Saudi Arabia is a clear example. Both the *Shi'is* and communists are persecuted in this country. Bearing in mind that religious persecution should be treated in the broader context of all human rights abuses, with an emphasis on avoiding a hierarchy of human suffering or abuse of rights, all these forms should be treated with equal seriousness.

This chapter focuses on the definition and understanding of the phenomenon of internal persecution among Muslims. It is premised on two claims: first, since religious persecution arises in the broader context of freedom of religion and belief, this study will use a human rights approach in examining religious persecution; and second, that the phenomenon of intra-religious persecution can only be analysed through special consideration of the contextual factors surrounding the phenomenon. Intra-religious persecution should be understood in a context encompassing political, historical, and social fac-

---

to refer to the latter rather than the former. See D.E. Arzt, 'The Treatment of Religious Dissidents under Classical and Contemporary Islamic Law' in J. Witte and J.D. van der Vyver (eds.), *Religious Human Rights in Global Perspective: Religious Perspectives* pp. 392-393 (The Hague: Martinus Nijhoff Publishers, 1996).

2. Report of the Special Rapporteur on Religious Intolerance, Mr. Angelo Vidal d'Almeida, UN Doc. E/CN.4/1987/35, p. 26. This has been reaffirmed by the present Special Rapporteur in his recent reports. See, for example, A. Amor, *Implementation of the Declaration on the Elimination of All Forms of Intolerance and Discrimination Based on Religion or Belief*, UN Doc. E/CN.4/1999/58, para. 115 (January 1999).

3. See M.S.M. Eltayeb, *A Human Rights Approach to Combating Religious Persecution: Cases from Pakistan, Saudi Arabia and Sudan* p. 2 (Antwerpen, Groningen, Oxford: Hart Intersentia, 2001).

tors as well as in terms of the purported religious rationale or justification on which intra-religious persecution is always grounded.

Religion is an inherent and integral part of culture in Muslim countries. Islam is conceived not only as a belief, but also as an organic component of culture. Today, the phenomenon of religious intolerance is to varying degrees a characteristic of most Muslim countries. Persecution of religious groups is one of the dominant forms of such religious intolerance. Internal persecution within the Islamic tradition exposes the political and sociological nature of religious persecution, since the persecuted group is of the same religion as the persecuting majority. This focus also helps in challenging the alleged religious rationale of the persecution, in that every religious majority was in the past, and may become in future, a minority. Thus, protection of freedom of belief is essential for the validity and authenticity of all religious beliefs and practices, whether of a majority or a minority.[4]

The distinction between intra- and inter-religious persecution does not pertain to state obligations deriving from international norms applicable to the protection of the right to freedom of thought, conscience, and religion or belief. International standards concerning these norms, as embodied in international human rights law, apply equally to violations resulting from both types of persecution. The normative content of the right to freedom of thought, conscience, and religion or belief guarantees freedom of religion; right to pluralism within the religion, including the right to change one's religion or belief, and equality and tolerance for non-members of the religion. Furthermore, this normative content does not permit any limitations whatsoever on freedom of thought and conscience or the freedom to have or adopt a religion or belief of one's choice. These freedoms are protected unconditionally. Limitations are only permitted on the freedom to manifest a religion or belief. The importance of the distinction between intra- and inter-religious persecution lies not in the international obligations but rather in the nature of the persecution and the strategies for combating each type. International standards on the right to freedom of thought, conscience, religion or belief apply equally to violations resulting from both types of persecution. Legal and political actions required for combating, preventing, protecting or remedying violations are dependent on whether these violations are related to intra- or inter-religious persecution.

---

4. See, generally, T. van Boven, 'Religious Freedom in International Perspectives: Existing and Future Standards' in K.J. Partsch (ed.), *Des Menschen Recht Zwischen Freiheit Und Verantworting* pp. 101-113 (Berlin: Duncker & Humblot, 1989); B. Tahzib, *Freedom of Religion or Belief: Ensuring Effective International Legal Protection* (The Hague: Martinus Nijhoff, 1996); C.D. de Jong, *The Freedom of Thought, Conscience and Religion or Belief in the United Nations (1946-1992)* (Antwerp, Groningen, Oxford: Intersentia-Hart, 2000).

The tendency of believers in each religion or belief system to consider themselves the sole guardian of the boundaries of their faith, fighting against whatever are considered as deviant views, as well as claims of exclusivity of interpretation of their faith, are issues that particularly pertain to the phenomenon of intra-religious persecution. In fact, it is more difficult to deal with intra-religious persecution than inter-religious persecution, since these issues are linked to the question of the integrity of the tradition. The phenomenon of intra-religious persecution is not peculiar to the Islamic tradition. Intra-religious persecution has been a common phenomenon for major religions, including, for example, Christianity and Hinduism. Major religions have witnessed incidents of persecution of individuals and groups who deviated from the mainstream orthodoxy. In the Muslim context, the phenomenon of intra-religious persecution started from early Islam and continues to the present day. However, neither historically nor at the present time can any one group be seen as solely the oppressed and the other group as the oppressor. Intra-religious persecution is not inherent to being *Sunni* or *Shi'i*, but rather a product of context and power-relationships. In this regard, it has to be noted that by definition, each religion or belief system has a degree of exclusion. It is the nature of all beliefs to claim an exclusive truth for themselves and to discard others as lacking the truth. The question is how to uphold the integrity of a religion without persecution. It can be seen from the history of every major religious tradition that dissident religious views have always been repressed. However, dissident persons have not always been *persecuted* in the name of protecting the integrity of the faith, the community, and/or the moral wellbeing of others.

Defining religious persecution

The difficulty in defining religious persecution arises from a lack of any formal definition of the term in international human rights instruments.[5] Human

5. It is worth mentioning that the recent developments in international criminal law have included references to the notion of persecution. Art. 5(h) of the Statute of the International Tribunal for the Former Yugoslavia (adopted May 1993 and amended May 1998) lists persecution on political, racial and religious grounds among the crimes against humanity over which the Tribunal would have jurisdiction. Art. 7 [1(h)] of the Rome Statute of the International Criminal Court, which was adopted on 17 July 1998, includes persecution among crimes against humanity. This Article reads:

> For the purpose of this Statute, "Crimes against humanity" means any of the following acts when committed as part of a wide-spread or systematic attack directed against any civilian population, with knowledge of the attack:

rights instruments have instead used the terms 'religious discrimination' and 'religious intolerance'. Analysing international standards protecting the right to freedom of thought, conscience, and religion or belief reveals the following points, which are of the utmost importance for the purpose of defining religious persecution.[6] First, the existing international standards have neither included nor addressed the specific or particular nature of the phenomenon of intra-religious persecution. It appears that the drafters of the existing international standards were more concerned with issues of inter-religious persecution. Furthermore, the existing standards do not take into account the broader social, economic and political context for all forms of religious persecution, whether intra- or inter-religious. For example, a sub-article in one of the relevant instruments could have included the obligation of states to address those social, economic and political factors in order to reduce reasons for religious persecution. Consequently, either new standards should be adopted to address these deficiencies in the existing texts, or the existing standards should be interpreted broadly to include freedom from intra-religious persecution. What is particularly necessary is to secure and guarantee the right of dissent within a religious community. This requires attention to the broader social, economic and political context for *all* types of persecution, whether intra- or inter-religious.

(h) Persecution against any identifiable group or collectivity on political, racial, national, ethnic, cultural, religious, gender or other grounds that are universally recognised as impermissible under international law, in connection with any act referred to in this paragraph or any crime within the jurisdiction of the Court.

Furthermore, art. 7 [2(g)] defines persecution as meaning 'the intentional and severe deprivation of fundamental rights contrary to international law by reason of the identity of the group or collectivity'.

The jurisprudence of the International Criminal Tribunal for the Former Yugoslavia has dealt with the crime of persecution in the case of the *Prosecutor* v. *Tihomir Blaskic*. Blaskic was accused and convicted of a crime against humanity for persecution of the Muslim civilian population of Bosnia throughout the municipalities of Vitez, Busovaca, Kiseljak and Zenica on political, racial or religious grounds during the period of May 1992 to January 1994. The persecution allegedly took the form of widespread, large-scale and systematic attacks upon towns, villages and hamlets inhabited by Bosnian Muslims. During and after the attack, Bosnian Muslim civilians were allegedly murdered and subjected to serious bodily harm whilst dwellings, buildings, private property, livestock and businesses belonging to Bosnian Muslims as well as their institutions dedicated to religion or education were all allegedly plundered and wilfully destroyed. Furthermore, the Prosecutor alleged that hundreds of Bosnian Muslim civilians were systematically arrested, interned, treated inhumanely, intimidated and coerced to leave their homes or forcibly transferred by the HVO (the Croatian Defence Council) to zones outside the municipalities of Vitez, Busovaca and Kiseljak (for the text of the judgement, see the home page of ICTY: www.un.org/icty/).

6. For the analysis of the international standards protecting the right to freedom of thought, conscience, and religion or belief, see Eltayeb, *supra* note 3 pp. 10-25.

Second, during the drafting history of the three major international instruments protecting the right to freedom of thought, conscience, and religion or belief,[7] the debate, as mentioned earlier, revolved around three issues: the nature and concept of freedom of religion or belief, the right to change one's religion or belief, and the scope of legitimate limitations on the right to manifest one's religion or belief. There was no debate on the right to dissent within a religious community. However, the concept of the right to dissent is broader than the right to change one's religion or belief. The concept of the right to dissent includes both the rights to change views within one's religion or belief as well as the right to change one's religion or belief. Basically, intra-religious persecution entails a violation of the right to dissent within a religious tradition. The right to pluralism within one's religion or belief is a perquisite for securing and guaranteeing the right to dissent within a religion or belief. Thus, freedom from intra-religious persecution necessitates protecting and securing the right to dissent within a religion or belief.

Third, since all forms of religious persecution, whether intra- or inter-religious, arise in the broader context of the right to freedom of thought, conscience, and religion or belief, a human rights approach for defining religious persecution is indispensable. However, such a human rights approach must be seen against the background of both the constraints and possibilities of the application of human rights in general. The implementation of human rights presupposes the existence of many factors, including legal enforcement, quality of political commitment, availability of resources, civil society activism, and the implementation of administrative, educational, and other policies. Legal protection, which is often considered as the primary mechanism for implementing human rights, should be seen as a part of wider strategies of implementation. Successful legal protection requires a certain degree of political stability, economic resources, institutional capacity, and the willingness of the public at large to resort to court for the enforcement of their rights. Legal protection also assumes the prevalence of the conception of the rule of law, the independence of the judiciary, and executive compliance with judicial pronouncements.[8]

The permeation of human rights norms in domestic systems is often dependent upon whether there is political repression or, in other words, whether the political situation is conducive for the observance of human rights. A related issue is the question of cultural resistance to human rights norms. Needless to say that international relations also affects the credibility of the

7. These three international instruments are the UDHR, ICCPR, and the 1981 Declaration.

8. A.A. An-Na'im, 'The Legal Protection of Human Rights in Africa: Doing More with Less' (Unpublished. Forthcoming).

human rights discourse, and especially poses the problem of double standards with regard to human rights violations. In this regard, it has to be noted that all governments are likely to engage in double standards because of conflicting objectives in their foreign policies. However, double standards by powerful states (such as the USA and Western governments) are generally more visible because of the extent of their international activities. Double standards by such governments can lead to human rights advocates in the South being hampered in their activities by charges of being agents of western powers. The problem is even more serious in that context, because of the history of colonialization and post-colonial hegemony. In other words, governments of Muslim countries are just as likely to engage in double standards as Western governments,[9] but history and context make double standards by the latter lead to difficulties for human rights advocates in Muslim countries, in having to deal with the problem of legitimacy and credibility. Notwithstanding these limitations and constraints, the human rights approach has its possibilities too. The human rights approach has universal moral power; human rights are no longer a matter exclusively within the domestic jurisdiction of states but have become a matter of international concern.

Fourth, the experience of the drafting history of the three major international human rights instruments protecting the right to freedom of thought, conscience, and religion or belief, supports the view that a broad interpretation of existing standards is better than adopting new standards, in order to include the right to dissent within a religion or belief. The adoption of new standards would be time-consuming, and whether a consensus would exist is rather questionable. There is also a fear that the new standards might even erode the existing ones. However, it is possible for the UN Human Rights Committee to use its innovative techniques of adopting 'General Comments' and 'Concluding Observations' to broadly interpret the right to freedom of thought, conscience, and religion or belief to explicitly embrace the right to dissent in a religious community, as a complement to freedom from intra-religious persecution.[10] The Special Rapporteur on Freedom of Religion or Belief can also use his (or her) mandate and propose a broad interpretation that includes the right to dissent within a religion or belief. Since the Special Rapporteur usually receives communications and reports testifying to inci-

9. For example, governments of Muslim countries would condemn Israeli human rights violations against Palestinians while not condemning other Muslim countries for even more serious human rights violations.

10. For a thorough discussion of these innovative techniques, see I. Boerefijn, *The Reporting Procedure under the Covenant on Civil and Political Rights: Practice and Procedure of the Human Rights Committee* Chapters 14 and 15, pp. 285-343 (Antwerp, Groningen, Oxford: Intersentia-Hart Publishers, 1999).

dents of intra-religious persecution, 'Conclusions and Recommendations' can be used to advocate a broader definition for the right to freedom of thought, conscience, and religion or belief which encompasses the right to dissent as a prerequisite for freedom from intra-religious persecution. In fact, such approaches would be preferable to awaiting the development of a binding international Convention on the Elimination of All Forms of Intolerance and Discrimination Based on Religion or Belief before this issue is tackled. In this regard, Bahiyyih Tahzib has observed:

> A special legally binding international instrument with its own supervisory mechanism is not feasible and desirable for ensuring effective international legal protection of freedom of religion or belief. Rather, other ways and means of enhancing international legal protection should be pursued, most notably the adoption of general comments, general recommendations or suggestions by supervisory human rights treaty bodies. In the long term, a legally binding instrument specifically pertaining to freedom of religion or belief should be adopted. Although an optional protocol to an existing multilateral human rights treaty has preference over a separate convention, the option of a convention should not be categorically ruled out.[11]

Returning now to the broader issue of 'religious persecution', three considerations must be taken into account in formulating a working definition for this term. First, religious persecution has to be defined not only along the lines of international standards of freedom of thought, conscience and religion, but also by adding the element of severity of persecution which might result in attacks and assaults on personal liberty and integrity. Second, one should consider the active nature of religious persecution, i.e. persecution signifies active state policy and action to harass, intimidate, and punish religious groups. And third, one should consider what distinguishes religious persecution from other types of persecution. Accordingly, the formulation of a working definition needs to begin by first defining and clarifying the relationship between religious persecution and closely related terms, such as 'gross and systematic violations of human rights' and 'intolerance and discrimination based on religion or belief'. The types of human rights violations encompassed by the term should also be identified.

Religious persecution and gross violations of human rights

In its common usage, the term 'religious persecution' is used to describe a particularly serious situation of discrimination where a campaign or program

11. Tahzib, *supra* note 4 pp. 493-494.

is initiated to harass, intimidate, and punish a group because of its religious or moral beliefs. This definition comprises the elements of both a systematic plan and policy and an element of severity and repression to force a change in the religious beliefs of the group in question. In this way religious persecution can be seen as an extreme example of religious discrimination in the same way as torture has been viewed by international human rights law as an aggravated form of cruel, inhuman or degrading treatment or punishment. However, this definition is confronted by the difficulty of drawing a distinctive line between those discriminatory acts tantamount to persecution and those that are not.

The definition that has been given for the term 'gross, systematic violations of human rights' may be deemed useful in identifying criteria for such a distinction. The term 'gross, systematic violations of human rights' has been defined as follows:

> Gross, systemic violations of human rights are those violations, instrumental to the achievement of government policies, perpetrated in such a quantity and in such a manner as to create a situation in which rights to life, to personal integrity or to personal liberty of the population as a whole or of one or more sectors of the population of a country are continuously infringed or threatened.[12]

Thus, a situation of gross human rights violations exists when the rights to life, personal integrity or personal liberty are violated. This criterion, which is based on violations of certain *types* of rights, could be used in distinguishing those discriminatory acts tantamount to religious persecution from those that are not. Acts tantamount to religious persecution would be those acts that basically entail violations of the right to freedom of thought, conscience, and religion or belief in a manner that continuously infringes or threatens the right to life, personal integrity or personal liberty. Thus, the distinctive criteria will be whether or not the discriminatory acts that violate the right to freedom of thought, conscience, and religion or belief would amount to a violation of the right to life, personal integrity or personal liberty. By using such criteria, religious persecution can be viewed as constituting a situation of gross human rights violations. Or in other words, religious persecution constitutes a situation of gross violations of the right to freedom of thought, conscience, and religion or belief where there is a consistent pattern of gross violations of the right to freedom of religion that includes violations of the right to life, to personal integrity or personal liberty.

12. C. Medina, *The Battle of Human Rights: Gross, Systematic Violations and the Inter-American System* p. 16 (Dordrecht: Martinus Nijhoff Publishers, 1988).

Distinguishing religious persecution from intolerance and discrimination based on religion or belief

The term 'intolerance and discrimination based on religion or belief' has been defined under Article 2(2) of the 1981 Declaration on the Elimination of All Forms of Intolerance and Discrimination Based on Religion or Belief as

> Any distinction, exclusion, restriction, or preference based on religion or belief and having as its purpose or as its effect nullification or impairment of the recognition, enjoyment or exercise of human rights and fundamental freedoms on an equal basis.

Whereas religious persecution and discrimination based on religion or belief signify active state policy and action, religious intolerance in most cases emanates from sections of the population, though it might be tolerated or even encouraged by the state concerned. It can be said that, while religious persecution results in denying freedom of religion *ab initio*, religious intolerance leads to distinction, exclusion, restriction, or preference on account of adhering to a particular religion or belief. However, the group subject to discrimination might still have a right to religious freedom, i.e. to profess and practice its religion or belief. In other words, religious persecution means denying both aspects of freedom of religion (*forum internum* and *forum externum*), whereas religious discrimination relates only to denying the aspect of freedom from discrimination in the enjoyment of human rights and fundamental freedoms in general.

Since religious persecution can be viewed as an extreme situation of religious discrimination, combating religious persecution may only be accomplished through combating all forms of intolerance and discrimination based on religion or belief. Intolerance and discrimination based on religion or belief can shift into religious persecution during times of societal stress, when discriminatory laws and practices provide a legal justification for government-sponsored persecution policies and action to harass, intimidate and punish individuals and religious groups.

Types of human rights violations encompassed by religious persecution

It has been established above that acts tantamount to religious persecution basically entail violations of the right to freedom of thought, conscience, and religion or belief in a manner that continuously infringes or threatens the right to life, personal integrity or personal liberty. Since not *all* acts that are deemed not to conform with the normative content of the right to freedom of thought, conscience, and religion or belief can amount to religious persecution, a distinction has to be made between those acts whose violations would be tantamount to religious persecution and those that are not. It is suggested that any breach of the right to have or to adopt a religion or belief of one's choice—*forum internum*—or any discriminatory or non-emergency abrogation of the right to manifest one's religion or belief—*forum externum*—is tantamount to persecution. Infringements and violations of the right to life, to personal integrity or to personal security cover a wide range of violations. However, it has to be noted that it is not exclusively the nature of these rights that renders the violation of the right to freedom of thought, conscience and religion or belief tantamount to religious persecution. The character of the violation itself has to be taken into account. Thus, for example, the gross violation of the right to personal security is limited only to torture.[13] In this regard, it is important to note that the violation-based approach does not necessarily require a quantitative element. Smaller number of victims, or even a single victim, may amount to religious persecution when the violations of human rights are directed against certain individuals who are important and highly influential to the religious group in question. Thus, for determining whether the violations of the right to freedom of thought, conscience, and religion or belief that continuously infringe or threaten the right to life, personal integrity or personal liberty amount to religious persecution, we have to consider the three combined factors: (i) types of right violated; (ii) the character of the violation; and (iii) the status of the victims of the violation.[14]

A working definition of 'religious persecution'

In light of the previous discussion, religious persecution can be defined as including a situation of gross violation of the right to freedom of thought, conscience, and religion or belief emanating from systematic and active state policy and action to harass, intimidate and punish individuals and religious groups in a manner that continuously infringes or threatens the right to life, personal integrity or personal security. The question of how many victims are treated in this way, or how many rights or which set of rights must be violated, may vary from one case to other, and cannot be answered in terms of a general rule. It has to be decided within the specific context of each case.

This definition applies to both intra- and inter-religious persecution. However, the focus of this chapter is confined to the phenomenon of intra-

13. *Ibid.* p.15.

14. *Ibid.* p. 13.

religious persecution within the Islamic tradition. This type of persecution, as shall be seen in, is linked to the exclusive, oppressive, and abusive nature of the theocratic state.

This chapter argues that the phenomenon of intra-religious persecution cannot be exclusively analysed and understood by reference to religious rationale, but should be seen as a product of a broader context that also incorporates economic, social and political factors. In each case study, we should understand how this multi-factor analysis operates in a particular context. The very fact that we can show the relationship between religious persecution and the broader economic, social and political context will help in overcoming the religious justification. Simultaneously, this may give people and governments the confidence to challenge religious persecution as a product of social and political dynamics rather than divine will.

Religious Exclusion in Islam

Prior to examining a framework of understanding intra-religious persecution in the Muslim context, an analysis of the doctrinal tools of religious exclusion in Islam is needed.[15] Such analysis will highlight the nature and process of the phenomenon of intra-religious persecution in this context, and help in understanding the origin, nature, and dynamics of the phenomenon of intra-religious persecution in the Muslim context.

First, the phenomenon of intra-religious persecution is not peculiar to Islam or to particular groups within Islam. In the Muslim context, the phenomenon is not new. It started from the early history of Islam and continues to the present day. However, neither historically nor at the present time can any one group be seen solely as the oppressor nor the other as the persecuted. Intra-religious persecution is thus not inherent to being *Sunni*, *Shi'i*, *Kharijite* or *Mu'tazilite*, but rather a product of power-relationships and political context.

Second, the development of schism in Islam as well as theological schools came as a result of conflicts over political power and who should have the legitimate right to rule the Muslim community. Thus, at the beginning of the schism, political questions were of utmost concern. However, the religious issue was to become a decisive element in perpetuating the schism.

Third, pre-modern Islamic culture was generally tolerant of diverging views on questions of Islamic theology and law. However, Muslim history also testifies to the fact that Muslims are simultaneously capable of both sectarian diversity and sectarian intolerance. The notion of a state-sponsored orthodoxy

15. For such analysis, see Eltayeb, *supra* note 3 chapter 2.

has been responsible for harassing, intimidating, and persecuting individuals and groups who deviated from the state creed.

Fourth, throughout Muslim history, much of the persecution of alleged apostates and heretics has been politically motivated and designed to benefit hegemonic orthodox groups. These groups resorted to religious justifications to legitimise their abusive power.

Fifth, the classical Islamic law of apostasy is not only in contradiction to the concept of freedom of religion, but it also lends itself to being manipulated to suppress and punish political dissidents. Thus, the Islamic law of apostasy can be used to punish Muslims who adhere to doctrines that do not conform to official Islam as it is imposed by a government claiming an Islamization policy. As Ann Elizabeth Mayer has observed:

> When contemporary Middle East governments have pressed forward with Islamization campaigns, they have tended to impose a uniform standard of orthodoxy on their Muslim citizens and reject the legitimacy of the positions of Muslim groups that do not accept what is being presented as the official norms of Islam. As the official orthodoxy becomes identified with the regime's own ideology and legitimacy, modern governments have shown themselves inclined to label Muslims who do not accept the official Islam as 'heretics' and 'apostates'.[16]

Apostasy, Heresy, and State-sponsored Religious Persecution

As can be seen above, the Islamic Sharia encompasses a broad spectrum of tools of religious exclusion, which includes categories of apostates and blasphemers, heretics and renegades, and non-Muslims and infidels. It is the first two categories of apostasy and heresy that are linked to intra-religious persecution. In orthodox literature, apostasy is deemed to be an act of rejection of belief, while heresy is more about content that resembles false belief or the denial of orthodox belief by a rival school of thought. In the case of Islamic scripture, which is held to be immutable and sacrosanct, non-orthodox interpretations are vulnerable to charges of apostasy as well as heresy. In contrast with apostasy, however, heresy has developed from Muslim history rather than having been ordained in religious texts.[17] The concept of heresy in

16. A.E. Mayer, *Islam and Human Rights: Tradition and Politics* p. 165 (Boulder, Colorado: Westview Press, 1991).

17. *Ibid.*

Islam can be traced back to early conflicts between *Sunnis*, *Shi'is* and subsequently *Kharijites* over the question of the legitimate successor to the Prophet Muhammad.

Regardless of its historical antecedents, it has been the notion of a state-sponsored orthodoxy that has been responsible for harassing, intimidating, and persecuting individuals and groups who deviated from the state creed. The purported religious rationale or justification of a policy of religious persecution, whether allegedly being justified due to apostasy or heresy, must be seen as a product of power relationships and the political context. Theological differences are only tolerated to the extent that they are not seen as undermining or threatening the legitimacy of the state. In the case of a theocratic state in which state authority is fused with, and embraces, a particular religious creed; it has been the claims of superiority, exclusivity, and monopoly of interpreting religious texts that has lead to harassment, intimidation, and punishment of those individuals and groups who, though they belong to the majority faith, dissent from the official position claimed by the state.

Although the alleged religious rationale offers *a* basis for religious persecution, it can not be singled out as *the* sole factor for the phenomenon of intra-religious persecution. Carrying out and executing a policy of persecution requires the backing and support of state entities. Religious persecution, therefore, signifies an active state policy and action to harass, intimidate, and punish religious groups. Such state policy may take the form of direct involvement with, condoning, or tolerating acts which are tantamount to religious persecution, as already defined above.

What makes the alleged religious rationale more visible and acute is a political variable expressing the choice of the ruling elite to conduct, condone, or tolerate a policy of harassment, intimidation, and persecution when such policy serves its political interests. Hence, there is a direct relationship between an elite's motivation to opt for a state policy and action of religious persecution and the timing where acts tantamount to religious persecution take place. However, such policies cannot serve the political interests of the elite if the society at large is not involved. In other words, what might be called 'scapegoat policies' depend on pre-existing prejudices as well as the social and political isolation of the persecuted groups within the wider society, since otherwise it will not be useful or politically possible for a government to persecute individuals and groups. Three cases—the Ahmadiyya in Pakistan, *Shi'is* in Saudi Arabia, and the Republican Brothers in Sudan—can be used to demonstrate this understanding.

Intra-religious Persecution amongst Muslims: The Ahmadiyya in Pakistan, the Shi'is in Saudi Arabia and the Republican Brothers in Sudan

In the Ahmadiyya case,[18] it was the movement's loyalty to British rule coupled with the exclusive nature of the community and its political isolation rather than its theology, which helped to seed prejudices within the wider (Muslim and non-Muslim) society against the Ahmadiyya in Pakistan. These prejudices were later reinforced by the success of the movement in its international missionary work as well as the high rate of literacy among the Ahmadiyya community, which indicated that they are likely to obtain employment and gain public office, to contribute to the antagonism and animosity between the movement and other Muslims. It was in this context that the theological differences between the Ahmadiyya and other *Sunni* Muslims should be seen.

At the heart of these theological differences lies the Ahmadiyya prophetology regarding its interpretation of the idea of the finality of the prophethood. Although the Ahmadiyya prophetology is radically different from that of other *Sunni* Muslims, it cannot be singled out as the only factor leading to the systematic and continuing persecution of the Ahmadiyya. The manipulation of this theological difference by the doctrinal forces for gaining the masses' support and vote was evident in the politics of the post-independence state of Pakistan. The transfer of the headquarters of the movement to Pakistan after the partition of India brought the case of the Ahmadiyya into the centre of the constitutional debate in Pakistan. The issue ceased to be a theological one to be decided on the Day of Judgement. The attempts of doctrinal forces to formally exclude the Ahmadiyya from the pale of Islam failed until 1974 when the Pakistani government yielded to the demands of religious groups and constitutionally declared the Ahmadiyya a non-Muslim minority. This constitutional amendment (known as the Second Amendment) marked what might be described as both state-sponsored and state-tolerated persecution. The phases of persecution of the Ahmadiyya followed a similar pattern of pressure by the *ulama*, the threat of widespread agitation, and subsequent action by the government. The adoption of its Islamization policy since 1977, and hence the government's reliance on the doctrinal forces, has further led to the adoption of anti-Ahmadiyya legislation. This Islamization policy does not only curtail the freedom of Ahmadis to practice, profess, and propagate their faith, but it has also turned the daily practices of the community into a criminal offence. The persecution of Ahmadiyya community would not have been possible

18. For a detailed discussion of the persecution of the Ahmadiyya in Pakistan, see Eltayeb, *supra* note 3 chapter 3.

without the convergence of interests of both the political elite and the doctrinal forces. The elite was looking for legitimacy and support from the masses, which are open to manipulation by the doctrinal forces. The role of *Jama'at -i Islami* and the various groups of *ulama* were instrumental in the adoption of the Second Amendment, which declared Ahmadiyya a non-Muslim minority. The doctrinal forces, on the other hand, opposed the Ahmadiyya prophetology and its reinterpretation of the idea of the finality of prophethood, which is radically different from their views. More important was the fear of the various groups of the *ulama* that the new claim of Ahmadiyya would undermine the authority vested in them by virtue of their traditional learning, and in turn, their ability to control the masses.

The persecution policy of *Shi'is* in Saudi Arabia derives its legitimacy from the Wahhabi doctrine.[19] Being the official creed of the state, the precepts of this doctrine view *Shi'is* as polytheists and apostates liable to be killed. The link of political power to the religious establishment, with its absolute Wahhabi orientation, has been further endorsed and put in practice the doctrinal views and transformed them into an institutionalised persecution policy. Tribal prejudices, regional schism, and geo-political factors have reinforced Wahhabi views on the *Shi'is*. The geographical location of the *Shi'i* minority in the Eastern Province of the Saudi Kingdom, with its proximity to Iran as the only Muslim country dominated by *Shi'is*, has further contributed to the questioning of the loyalty of the *Shi'i* population to the Saudi Kingdom. However, the existence of an institutionalised and systematic policy to harass, intimidate and persecute the *Shi'is* in Saudi Arabia emerged as a response to external factors presented in the Iranian revolution that took place in 1979 and brought the *Shi'is* to rule Iran. Thus, the persecution of *Shi'is* in Saudi Arabia demonstrates that geo-political as well as international relations factors can play a crucial role as a trigger of the phenomenon of intra-religious persecution.

The timing of an elite's adoption of state policy and action of religious persecution is also illustrated in the case of the Republican Brothers in the Sudan.[20] The political context under which the two key trials against Republican Brothers[21] took place in Sudan demonstrated that the persecution

19. For a detailed discussion of the persecution of the *Shi'is* in Saudi Arabia, see Eltayeb, *supra* note 3 chapter 4.

20. For a detailed discussion of the persecution of the Republican Brothers in Sudan, see Eltayeb, *supra* note 3 chapter 5.

21. The political context under which these two trials took place demonstrated that the persecution of the Republican movement in the Sudan was politically motivated. It was the Republican's severe criticism of the sectarian governments of the 1960s, their active campaign against the dissolution of the Sudanese Communist Party in 1965, as well as their counter-campaign against the proposal of the Muslim Brothers for an Islamic constitution, that motivated the first *ridda* trial in 1968. The second apostasy case came in response to

of the Republican movement in the Sudan was politically motivated. It was the Republicans' severe criticism of the sectarian governments of the 1960s, coupled with their active campaign against the dissolution of the Sudanese Communist Party in 1965, as well as the Republican counter-campaign against the proposal of the Muslim Brothers for an Islamic constitution, which was increasingly supported by the sectarian parties and traditional political groups, that motivated the first *ridda* trial. The second apostasy case came in response to the Republicans' mounting criticism of the religious establishment, the Muslim Brothers and further of the regime of President Nimeiri when it opted for a policy of Islamization, which resulted in the adoption of the September Laws.[22] Thus, both trials were political in the sense that they were meant to suppress, intimidate and punish political opponents. The religious arguments in both trials were used as a pretext for persecuting political opponents. The movement's social aspects that challenged the prevailing rituals, social customs, cultural values and legal practices, coupled with their outright pronouncements on politically sensitive issues, isolated the Republicans from the wider Sudanese society and made them an easy target to pick on and eliminate. However, it was the convergence of interests of President Nimeiri, the Muslim Brothers and the religious establishment that helped to facilitate the persecution of the Republicans in the Sudan.

the Republican's mounting criticism of the religious establishment, the Muslim Brothers and of the regime of President Nimeiri when it opted for an Islamization policy which resulted in the adoption of the September Laws in 1983. Thus, both trials were political in the sense that they intended to suppress, intimidate and punish political opponents. The religious arguments in both trials have been used as a pretext for persecuting political opponents. For a detailed discussion of the two cases, see Mohamed S. M. Eltayeb, supra note 3, pp. 167-179.

22. The September Laws were a series of laws based on Sharia law promulgated by President Nimeiri between 1983 and 1984. For a detailed discussion of the September Laws see: C.N. Gordon, 'Islamic Legal Revolution: The Case of Sudan', *International Lawyer* Vol. 19, p. 793 (1985) and G.R. Warberg, 'The Sharia Law in Sudan: Implementation and Repercussion, 1983-1989', *The Middle-East Journal*, Vol. 44, No. 4, (Autumn 1990); A.M. Tier, 'Islamization of the Sudan Laws and Constitution: Its Allure and Its Impracticability', *Verfassung und Recht in Uebersee* Vol 25, Issue 2, pp. 215-219 (1990); A. A. An-Na'im, *Towards an Islamic Reformation: Civil Liberties, Human Rights and International Law* pp. 127-136 (Syracuse, NY: Syracuse University Press, 1990). For an analysis of the political factors which underlined the adoption of September Laws see: John L. Esposito, 'Sudan Islamic Experiment', *Muslim World*, Vol. 76, pp. 181-202 (1986) and K. Duran, 'The Centrifugal Forces of Religion in Sudanese Politics', *Orient*, Vol. 26, No. 4, pp. 572-600 (December 1985).

The Religious Rationale and State Policy

These three cases show that the alleged religious rationale can only work in a particular socio-political setting. Pre-existing prejudices, social aloofness and the perceived exclusive nature of a group, as well as its political isolation, reinforce the religious rationale. To the extent that the purported religious rationale contributed to a state policy and its action to harass, intimidate, punish and persecute individuals and groups, this contribution is reinforced by a broader socio-economic and political context. Theological differences between religious groups adhering to the same tradition have always existed. What makes these differences amount to a purported religious rationale, that reinforces a state policy of intra-religious persecution, is the extent to which those differences are being seen as undermining or threatening the legitimacy of the state. This has been made evident in the three case studies.

The three cases have further demonstrated that the notion of a state-sponsored orthodoxy has been responsible for harassing, intimidating, and persecuting individuals and groups who deviated from the state creed. Whenever governments have pressed forward with Islamization policies, they have tended to impose a uniform standard of orthodoxy on their Muslim citizens and reject the legitimacy of the positions of Muslim groups that do not accept what is being presented as the official norms of Islam. As the official orthodoxy becomes identified with the regime's own ideology and legitimacy, modern governments have shown themselves inclined to label Muslims who do not accept the 'official Islam' as heretics and apostates. Therefore, massive violations of the rights of religious minorities often take place in countries that undergo systematic Islamization of their constitutional and legal systems. Religious persecution under the pretext of Islamization especially targets individuals and groups that are regarded as apostates from Islam and hence deviating from official Islam as interpreted and imposed by a government claiming the role of guardian of the faith. Thus, whenever and wherever a religious doctrine manifests itself as a state ideology or creed, and makes absolute claims on individuals and society, religious persecution of individuals and groups who hold different doctrines becomes inevitable.

Responding to the religious rationale

The process of challenging and undermining the religious foundation of intra-religious persecution is an internal theological issue that needs to take place within an internal religious framework. Although human rights norms target acts of discrimination based on religion or belief, it is neither appropriate nor desirable for human rights scholars to engage in internal debate or pass judgement with regard to internal religious issues that have to be decided within a religious framework. The process of combating intra-religious persecution relies largely on the legal, political, cultural, and social frameworks on which international human rights norms are to be observed, respected, and implemented.

The tendency of believers in each religion or belief system to consider themselves the sole guardians of the boundaries of their faith, fighting against whatever is considered as deviant views, as well as claims of exclusivity of interpretation of their faith, are issues that pertain in particular to the phenomenon of intra-religious persecution. It can be seen from the history of every major religious tradition that dissident religious views have always been minimized and discouraged. However, and as mentioned before, only sometimes have dissident persons been persecuted in the name of protecting the integrity of the faith, the community, and/or the moral wellbeing of others. These arguments provide the religious basis and rationale for the phenomenon of intra-religious persecution. The question that arises in this context is how to uphold the integrity of the religion without persecution.

In the three cases mentioned before, the traditional Sharia law of apostasy has been used as a pretext for harassing, intimidating, punishing and persecuting the Ahmadiyya, *Shi'is* and the Republican Brothers. Besides the criminal law consequences of apostasy—reflected in the death penalty—there are a number of civil law consequences following the conviction of apostasy. Hence, the punishment of apostasy is not only confined to the religious domain but it extends to the civil, political and social domains. This makes apostasy an extra-religious offence. Moreover, the political nature of apostasy is reflected in the commonly used argument that the punishment is inflicted in cases in which apostasy is a cause of harm to society. In this respect, a brief outlining of the modern Muslim discourse on apostasy is deemed to be useful.

Modern Muslim discourse on apostasy

Modern Islamic discourse on apostasy is based on two opposite strands of thought. One category limits the scope of freedom of religion as defined in international human rights law. In other words, it keeps the classical doctrine of apostasy intact. The second category advocates changing the legal theory of apostasy, or in other words, favouring the observance of international standard-setting for freedom of religion including, *inter alia*, the right to change one's religion or belief.

In the first category, one can identify traditionalist, fundamentalist and modernist approaches. For traditionalist scholars, Sharia needs no defence or justification while anything that is inconsistent with Sharia is necessarily wrong and bad. Therefore, the Islamic law of apostasy has to be maintained and imposed. The fundamentalists make an attempt to justify the law of apostasy on the grounds that Islam is not only a religion but also a social and political order. Abu A'la Mawdudi has argued that a person who disagrees with the basis of organised society has only two alternatives: he may either leave the boundaries of society or submit to deprivation of all his rights as a citizen. As the latter state would be worse than death, it is better to kill him.[23] Fundamentalists further emphasise the danger the apostate poses to Islamic society. To quote Muhammad al-Gazali, who can be regarded as a representative of fundamentalist thought:

> Apostasy seldom is a matter that only concerns one's inner self alone. If that would be the case, nobody would notice it. In most instances, apostasy is a psychological pretext for rebellion against worship, traditions and laws, even against the foundations of the state itself and against its stand towards external enemies. Therefore, apostasy is often synonymous with the crime of high treason.[24]

Thus, according to this argument the death penalty for apostasy is rather a protective and preventive measure for the Islamic State and society. There are even more radical fundamentalists, like Abd al-Qadir Awada, who have argued that the killing of an apostate is a duty of individual Muslims where the state fails to do so.[25]

The modernist approach distinguishes between passive apostasy and apostasy accompanied by a threat to the Islamic state. It holds that the apostate cannot be put to death on the mere ground of his apostasy. However, modernists have argued that apostasy accompanied with a danger to the state is punishable by death, not on the ground of apostasy but on the basis that the offence is treason or another serious offence against the state. This line of reasoning of modernist scholars has been soundly refuted by An-Na'im who has pointed out that if the punishment is for treason or other appropriate offence against the state such offences can be defined and enforced within the ordinary criminal law of the land without making reference to the religious

23. Quoted in S.A. Rahman, *Punishment of Apostasy in Islam* pp. 120-121 (Lahore: Institute of Islamic Culture, 1972).

24. M. al-Ghazali, *Huquq al-Insan Bayn Ta'alim al-Islam Wa- I'lan Al-Umam al-Muttahidah* (Human Rights between Islamic Principles and the United Nations' Declaration) p. 102 (Cairo: al-Maktabah al-Tidjariyyah, 1963).

25. A. al-Qadir Awada, *al-Tashri al Djina'i al-Islami* (Islamic Criminal Legislation) Vol. 1, pp. 535-538 (Beirut: al-Kitab al-Arabi House, undated).

belief of the accused. An-Na'im has further noted that this argument lacks a legal and theological foundation in Sharia law which is primarily concerned with the question of religious belief rather than with the notion of treason or offence against the state coming as a much delayed attempt at rationalisation.[26] Further, the notion of time to recant indicates religious motivations not the crime of treason.

It has been argued that the main difference between fundamentalist and modernist approaches lies in the fact that, according to the former, the apostate is automatically considered to be a dangerous enemy of the Islamic state. In the latter this is not implied in the mere condition of being an apostate, it must be proven separately.[27] In other words, while for modernists an apostate should not be killed unless he constitutes a danger to the Islamic State, for fundamentalists the act of an apostasy as such constitutes a danger to Islamic society.

The second category endorses freedom of religion as it is acknowledged in international human rights instruments and advocates rethinking the classical Islamic law of apostasy. Two groups in this category can be identified according to their terms of reference as far as rethinking the classical theory of apostasy is concerned. The first group, basing itself on the Sharia rules of construction and derivation of legal rules as earlier jurists have applied them, holds that capital punishment for apostasy is not compatible with the concept of freedom of religion. Therefore, they argue it must be abolished.[28] The scholars of this group make an attempt to refute the legal basis of the death penalty for apostasy under Islamic Sharia. Their point of departure is that, although the *Qur'an* condemns an apostate in harsh terms, it prescribes no punishment for apostasy in this world. Secondly, they contest the authenticity of the two prophetic traditions that lay down the basis for the death penalty for apostasy, as indicated earlier. Finally, they refer to pronouncements of a few earlier jurists who have stated that the apostate should forever be asked to repent, from which it can be inferred that he may not be killed.[29] The position of this group is subject to challenge from within Islamic Sharia, since according to Sharia there can be no exercise of rational legal reasoning (*Ijtihad*) in any matter covered by an explicit text of the *Qur'an* or *Sunna*. With reference to the death penalty for

26. A.A. An-Na'im, 'The Islamic Law of Apostasy and Its Modern Applicability: A Case from the Sudan', *Religion* 16, p. 214 (1986).

27. R. Peters and G.J. de Vries, 'Apostasy in Islam', *Die Welt des Islams* Vol. XVII, p. 17 (1976-1977).

28. A. al-Mota'al al-Saidi, *al-Hurriyyah al-Diniyyah Fi al-Islam* (Religious Freedom in Islam), (Cairo: al-Fikr al-Arabi House, undated); and Rahman, *supra* note 23.

29. Rhaman, *supra* note 24, pp. 72, 148 and 156; Peters and De Vries, *supra* note 27 footnote 41, p. 15.

apostasy, the above cited Prophetic traditions bar any other legal reasoning within the framework of Sharia rules of construction and derivation of legal rules. The second point of criticism against this group lies in the fact that its line of reasoning is limited to the criminal consequences of apostasy, while it is silent on the civil consequences indicated, which might be taken as endorsement of civil death for the apostate.

The second group has taken a rather radical approach, which is reflected in a historical reading of the Islamic sources with a clear emphasis on Sharia as a mere historical interpretation of the main Islamic sources. Hence, in contrast with the prevailing view, this group denies to those historical interpretations the character of divine law, and therefore opens the door to a new interpretation of the main Islamic sources (*Qur'an* and *Sunna*) outside the framework of Sharia. The late Sudanese reformer Mahmoud Mohammad Taha, who was executed in 1985,[30] can be identified as a leading scholar in this group. Taha advocated a radical and new approach for reformation of the entire Islamic law.[31] At this point a brief examination of Taha's reform technique with reference to Islamic law of apostasy may be useful.

Taha's cardinal principle was the concept of evolution of Islamic Sharia. As far as the Islamic law of apostasy is concerned, this principle indicates that Islam was originally offered in Mecca through the principle of freedom of choice and voluntary conversion. The *Qur'anic* texts of this class have been abrogated in favour of texts of compulsion revealed subsequently in Medina when the Prophet immigrated there, but they remained part of the *Qur'an*. This class of texts was manifested in the principles of Sharia providing for *jihad*, discrimination against women and non-Muslims, and penalising apostasy. Thus, Taha maintained that the legally binding principles of Sharia were not based on texts of freedom of choice, as most jurists would argue, but rather on texts of compulsion. Taha worked from the premise that the repeal of Meccan texts was actually a postponement and not a final abrogation, and he suggested that Muslims should now enact those texts and repeal again, in a legal sense only, texts of compulsion and *jihad*. An-Na'im has noted that Taha was only concerned with legal efficacy, and the repeal of texts in this sense does not tamper with the sanctity of the *Qur'an* or deny any of its texts. Taha argued that, in order to establish complete freedom of religion within Islam, Muslims must be prepared to base this aspect of Islamic law on a group of texts of *Qur'an* and *Sunna* that has hitherto been deemed to have been repealed or abrogated by operative texts that discriminate against non-Muslims and penalise apostasy.

30. See Eltayeb, *supra* note 3 chapter 5.

31. For the discussion of the reformation approach of Taha, see Eltayeb, *supra* note 3 chapter 5.

It can be said that Taha's approach not only aimed at the abolition of all civil and criminal consequences of apostasy, but rather at the abolition of the crime itself, and hence has opened the door to complete freedom of religion as envisaged in international human rights law. This indeed makes Taha's approach a unique one and distinguishes it from other approaches that have aimed only at the abolition of the death penalty for apostasy.

Conclusion

This chapter has discussed a definition, and provided a framework, for understanding the notion of religious persecution. Since religious persecution arises in the broader context of freedom of religion and belief, this chapter has used a human rights approach in examining religious persecution. As indicated in the preceding analysis, such a human rights approach should accommodate the element of severity, together with the fact that persecution in most cases involves active state policy and action. It is worth emphasising that the chapter defined religious persecution as a situation of gross violation of the right to freedom of thought, conscience, and religion or belief emanating from a systematic and active state policy; and action to harass, intimidate and punish individuals and religious groups in a manner that continuously infringes or threatens their right to life, personal integrity or personal security. The adequacy of this definition has been tested elsewhere.[32]

The central thesis of this chapter argues that the phenomenon of intra-religious persecution cannot be exclusively analysed and understood by reference to a religious rationale, but should be seen as a product of a broader context that incorporates economic, social and political factors. It follows, for the purpose of outlining a framework for understanding the phenomenon, that all these elements (social, economic and political, as well as religious) must be taken into account, and that in each case study we should understand how this multi-factor analysis operates in a particular context.

The very fact that we can show the relationship between religious persecution and the broader economic, social and political context will help in overcoming the religious justification. Simultaneously, this may give people and governments the confidence to challenge religious persecution as a product of social and political dynamics rather than divine will.

32. See Eltayeb, *supra* note 3 chapters 3, 4 and 5.

Chapter 5

Faith in Human Rights, Human Rights in Faith[1]

Nazila Ghanea

Lecturer in Human Rights and International Law and MA Convenor, University of London, Institute of Commonwealth Studies.

In recent years the lexicon of human rights[2] has gained widespread currency in international affairs. International human rights standards have been put forward as: 'the central criteria of political legitimacy',[3] a criterion with which domestic and foreign policies should be reconciled, a standard for civilisation,[4] an ethical basis for governance, 'a means of empowerment against

1. An earlier version of this chapter has been published as a book chapter by N. Ghanea-Hercock, 'Faith in Human Rights, Human Rights in Faith' in J. Thierstien and Y.R. Kamalipour (eds.), *Religion, Law and Freedom: A Global Perspective* (Westport: Praeger Publishing, 2000).
2. In this chapter the term 'human rights' is being used in its philosophical sense, rather than with its specific legal connotations, unless stated otherwise.
3. G. Luf, 'Human Rights in Christian and Islamic Thought, A Report on the Tubingen "Human Rights Project"' in L. Swidler (ed)., *Religious Liberty and Human Rights, in Nations and Religions* p. 235 (Philadelphia: Ecumenical Press and New York: Hippocrene Books, 1986).
4. The title of Jack Donnelly's article, 'Human rights, a new standard of civilization?', *International Affairs* Vol. 74, No. 1, pp. 1-23 (January 1998).

oppression by States',[5] and, 'the strongest ethical language that exists'.[6] With the parallel increase in the assertion of religion onto the international agenda,[7] the question emerges of how religion and human rights react to one another. Will both crusading normative projects collaborate in the provision of a common grounding for a new mindset, or degenerate in a cold war of words over their notional normative space in the international arena?

Effective Universalism and Human Rights

Since the end of the cold war and the 1993 Vienna World Conference on Human Rights, the call for a deepened commitment to ensuring that human rights standards are effectively implemented worldwide is becoming increasingly vocal. Such a universal respect calls for more than the enhancement of international and national human rights monitoring machinery, critical though that may be. Even with the best will in the world and consistent support across the board, it is impossible for a centralised international human rights machinery to oversee *all* international, national and local situations—especially when, as van Boven notes, this machinery contains 'within it all the limitations of a 'preponderantly inter-governmental' organisation.[8] Even if it were possible for all such abuses to be 'policed', its cost and bureaucracy would be phenomenal. Van Boven therefore concludes that the UN needs to, 'enrol also other organs of society, national and international, in order to build up a broad human rights movement with the active and vigilant participation of people at all levels, notably the grass roots level'.[9] Should such a grass roots commitment to human rights indeed be universal, it could itself act as 'guardian' to the guarantee of such standards.

However, what is assumed in such calls for the universalisation of human rights is that the human rights discourse will not face any serious challenges to becoming adopted by the masses. One serious hindrance, however, is the questionable relationship between religion and human rights. Without trying

5. R. Künnemann, 'A Coherent Approach to Human Rights', *Human Rights Quarterly, A Comparative and International Journal of the Social Sciences, Humanities, and Law* Vol. 17, No. 2, pp. 339-340 (May 1995).
6. C.E. Curran, 'Religious Freedom and Human Rights in the World and the Church, A Christian Perspective' in Swidler *supra* note 3 p. 158.
7. See, for example: J. Haynes, *Religion in Global Politics* (London: Longman, 1998).
8. T.C. van Boven, 'United Nations and Human Rights, A Critical Appraisal' in A. Cassese (ed.), *UN Law/Fundamental Rights, Two Topics in International Law* p. 130 (Alphen aan den Rijn, The Netherlands: Sijthoff & Noordhoff, 1979).
9. *Ibid.* p. 132.

to dichotomously position these two against one another, it is clear that this is an area needing further exploration. One writer has argued that, 'Religion must be seen as a vital dimension of any legal regime of human rights ... Religions will not be easy allies to engage, but the struggle for human rights cannot be won without them.'[10] Küng even argues that, 'there will be no peace among the peoples of this world without peace among the world religions'.[11] Why this claim for the indispensability of religion to human rights, when some have actually highlighted religion as a complicating factor in the human rights debate?

> If religion is so complicating, so difficult, why deal with it? Why not be content with casual recourse or wilful reversion to non- or anti-religious arguments derived from Enlightenment era understandings of secular reasoning? If religion brings as much heat as light, why not extinguish it, or at least bracket it in polite discourse?[12]

Even Küng has to agree that 'The most fanatical, the cruelest political struggles are those that have been colored, inspired, and legitimized by religion'.[13] Why, then, engage with religion whose precepts hold meaning only for those who share its perspectives and which many feel cannot participate fully in debates relating to other value structures?

The value of the engagement of religion becomes evident when the need for nurturing a 'culture of human rights'[14] is appreciated. The coming into existence of such a culture needs the creation of a new mindset. As human vision can be significantly informed through visions of faith, religion plays a significant role in deepening the vision of universal human rights. Human action is often profoundly motivated through deeply held belief. As, 'without committed individuals and groups, human rights will become a dead letter',[15] such a 'rooting' of human rights in religions will assist in the widening of both the enforcement and effectiveness of human rights.

---

10. J. Witte Jr, 'Law, Religion, and Human Rights', *Columbia Human Rights Law Review* Vol. 28, No. 1, p. 2 (Fall 1996).
11. H. Küng, *Christianity and the World Religions, Paths of Dialogue with Islam, Hinduism, and Buddhism* p. 443 (Glasgow: Collins, 1985).
12. M.E. Marty, 'Religious Dimensions of Human Rights' in J. Witte Jr and J. van der Vyver (eds.), *Religious Human Rights in Global Perspective, Religious Perspectives* p. 9 (The Hague: Martinus Nijhoff Publishers, 1996).
13. Küng, *supra* note 11 p. 442.
14. This has been proposed in many UN circles, for example by the UN Special Rapporteur on Religious Intolerance. He suggests that such a human rights culture should be 'learned and absorbed progressively through initiatives and measures over the long term', particularly through education. See: Doc. E/CN.4/1996/95, Commission on Human Rights, 52nd session, 15 December 1995, report of Mr Abdelfattah Amor, p. 15.
15. Künnemann, *supra* note 5 p. 340.

Complexity, Diversity and Human Rights

In our increasingly globalised world, varying cultures, races and beliefs have had to adjust to living in much closer proximity. One aspect of this contraction in world affairs has been the need for the emergence of a new ethic that will regulate relations between the multiplicity of groups. International human rights law has been codified in parallel with these forces, as a response to the social need for regulation in our increasingly complex societies. Janis has delegated this task of regulation to international law in claiming that, 'the greatest task, weighing on modern international lawyers is to craft a universal and legal process capable of ordering relations among diverse people with differing religions, histories, cultures, laws and languages'.[16] This legal process cannot be imposed on a void. It needs pillars to uphold it, genuine links that associate it with particular groups and a congruous platform which connects it to specific peoples. Universality does not imply blandness, shallowness or rootlessness. In fact, it cannot exist within a vacuum of pretence of universality. As An-Na'im has stated,

> If human rights are to be truly universal ... they must be based on the broadest and deepest possible consensus among all cultural traditions. This can be done through an intelligent and purposeful employment of the processes of internal discourse and cross-cultural dialogue.[17]

This ambitious role for the human rights discourse spills over into the need for a multicultural, multiethnic and multifaith approach that is able to capture the imagination of the public. At the moment, in Mitra's words,

> The question of human rights is asked and pursued in the Western context. What the rights of human beings as humans are is often described in terms of Western categories. This runs the danger of ideological neo-colonialism ... There is a need to investigate the meaning of human rights, of growth and progress, not simply from the perspective of the dominant cultures—but from the perspective of others as well.[18]

16. M.W. Janis, preface to M.W. Janis (ed.), *The Influence of Religion on the development of International Law* p. ix (Dordrecht: Martinus Nijhoff, 1991).
17. A.A. An-Na'im, 'The right to reparation for human rights violations and Islamic culture(s)' in T. van Boven, C. Flinterman, F. Grünfeld and I. Westendorp (eds.), *Seminar on the Right to Restitution, Compensation and Rehabilitation for Victims of Gross Violation of Human Rights and Fundamental Freedoms, Maastricht, 11-15 March 1992* p. 177 (Utrecht: Studie-en Informatiecentrum Mensenrechten, and Maastricht: University of Limburg Human Rights Project Group, 1992).
18. K. Mitra, 'Exploring the Possibility of Hindu-Muslim Dialogue' in Swidler *supra* note 3 p. 116.

Longstanding human rights activists shy away from such projects with the understandable fear of unsettling hard-won converts to the cause of human rights. They are overly suspicious about the prospect of feeding into the hands of callous dictators who rely on feeble excuses of 'cultural relativism' in order to defend their extreme policies and practices. Such a project, however, has nothing to do with those who want to compromise the basic tenets of humanity and core and irreducible values of human rights. Its only concern is the medium through which such values are disseminated, the expansion of the language through which they are now being proposed, and the genuine engagement of other cultures, peoples and religions. Such engagement aims to widen human rights and make its language, medium and standards accessible to far-flung cultures; to village dwellers who may not want to know anything of the 'achievements' of western philosophical debates but who may, nevertheless, have an intuitive respect for the dignity of human life.

Though scepticism may exist about such high levels of optimism regarding the accessibility of human rights, increasing support has meant that its norms are emerging as a key means for upholding the dignity of all human beings. 'Human rights rest on an account of a life of dignity to which human beings are "by nature" suited.'[19] As religions are also involved in the provision of universal ethical norms for the dignity of the individual and betterment of society, it is not surprising that religious leaders and believers have, at times, considered human rights as a threat to the sanctity and uniqueness of their voice in social relations. With both human rights and religion regulating some of the same 'turf' in so far as normative loyalties are concerned, competition has sometimes dominated over collaboration.

In this clash of normative loyalties, proponents of human rights put it forward as a unique language of morality, to be contrasted sharply with the self-referential subjectivities of specific belief systems. They emphasise that human rights is a non-ideological moral currency and is therefore singularly positioned for the moral dialogues necessitated in our times. Within such readings of human rights one detects a widespread rejection of religion and the overt positioning of human rights within an ideology of secularism.[20] The

19. J. Donnelly, *International Human Rights*, 2nd ed., p. 21 (Boulder: Westview Press, 1998).

20. Bryan Wilson distinguishes between the terms 'secularisation' and 'secularism' by defining the former as 'that process by which religious thinking, practice and institutions lose social significance, and become marginal to the operation of the social system', and the latter as 'an ideology … it denotes a negative evaluative attitude towards religion, and might even be appropriately seen as a particular "religious" position, in the sense that secularism adopts certain premises *a priori* and canvasses a normative (albeit negative) position about supernaturalism'. B. Wilson, '"Secularisation": Religion in the Modern World' in S. Sutherland and P. Clarke (eds.), *The World's Religions, The Study of Religion, Traditional and New Religion*, 2nd ed., p. 196 (London: Routledge, 1991).

assumptions underlying this perspective seem to be that the only way human rights norms and standards can ever hope to be 'universalised' is through such secularism. Some have argued that the modern human rights movement itself was brought into existence as, 'an attempt to find a world faith to fill a spiritual void',[21] thus denying the necessary manoeuvrability for the continuing involvement of religious values in its development[22] (based, as it was, on secularism's negative evaluation of the religious). Another significant reason for this rejection of religion has been due to the problematic consequences of religious claims of exclusivity in an increasingly heterogeneous world. As diversity is the phenomenon of our time, the more neutral setting of the discourse of human rights is being utilised to channel our response to it. Human rights has attempted to seek consensus in a complex world of believers and non-believers, and a variety of cultures, religions and races; through replacing God as the foundation of the law with that of the inborn dignity of each and every human being. Its assets are seen to be its severance from particularities attached to individual belief systems. Nevertheless, there is much controversy about this suggestion of neutrality for human rights.

A closer focus on the emergence of human rights enables us to realise its historical and socio-political underpinnings more vividly. Human rights, like individual religions, are not timeless categories in so far as their social manifestation in this world is concerned. The political voices and power structures lurking behind the emergence of particular human rights discourses can similarly not be underestimated. As Luf has argued, 'Human rights have not been a feature of all periods and all cultures. They are a phenomenon of the modern world, bearing the marks of its experience of reality and its normative ethical notions.'[23] In their societal manifestation, rather than their inner essence, both rights and religion are historical constructs. This bond of historical relativity actually unites, rather than distinguishes between, the social norms of religion and human rights. Both aspire towards universality in their validity and discourse, whilst actually bearing the marks of the historical circumstances of their emergence.

Furthermore, whilst a sketchy look at the bloody conflicts in history seems to justify some scepticism about the viability of basing international human

21. Witte, *supra* note 10 p. 9.

22. This view is voiced by Kennedy, 'Religion is what we had before we had law. Religion is the domain of irrationality and charismatic authority, law the realm of reason and the bureaucratic. International law understands its birth as a flooding forth from the darkness of religious strife, antidote to the passions of faith, on guard against their re-emergence as ideology'. D. Kennedy, 'Losing Faith in the Secular' in M.W. Janis and C. Evans (eds.), *Religion and International Law* p. 313 (The Hague: Martinus Nijhoff, 1999).

23. Luf, *supra* note 3 p. 236.

rights standards on the foundations of religious belief, basing it on secularism does not necessarily alleviate the problems either. Though such an approach may have the potential to unite the atheists, agnostics and some western-educated elites from the various religious groups to a nominal commitment; it seems to have had the effect of alienating still larger sectors of the world population and whole civilisations whose worldviews are closely intertwined with religion. Even of those who have not been overtly alienated, association with a man-made standard has not inspired the most committed of followings. International legal norms often inspire little more than tokenism, superficial governmental statements made only to attract attention to limited and short-term policy objectives rather than any profound concern for those outside the orbit of their immediate political agendas. By trading in the foundation of 'God' for its humanist alternative of 'human dignity', it could be argued that depth of commitment has been replaced by an elusive breadth of appeal that has not been entirely successful. It is not clear that such problematic foundations will ever be able to lead to genuine and whole-hearted participation by the (especially religious) masses, thus putting the whole project of bringing about a universal culture of human rights into jeopardy. It is not clear, for example, how it may be able to lead to genuine and whole-hearted participation by the leaders of the Jewish homeland, Buddhist followers, Southern Baptists, or the Shi'i multitudes of Iran. Many believers have felt alienated by secularisation, and share Mitra's sentiment that we, 'communicate in sharing our spiritual insights … in order to counteract the dangers of secularisation, which leads to dehumanisation'.[24]

Whilst acknowledging the modern day desire for a neutral[25] and universal standard of norms, one can nevertheless acknowledge that it is not absolute neutrality that is implied, or even possible, but that of the identification of, 'a set of *neutrally formulated* common human rights'.[26] Since human rights, too, represent a specific value system the purpose is to make it non-discriminatory towards the 'other', to, 'reconcile commitments to diverse normative regimes with a commitment to a concept and set of universal human rights'.[27] It therefore emerges that although many have associated the neutrality of human rights with its separation from religion such absolute neutrality from religious, cultural or ideological motivations is altogether illusory and indeed counter-productive. Religions, instead, should be encouraged to pour their visions and

24. Mitra, *supra* note 18 p. 123.

25. 'Neutral' here means impartial or unbiased.

26. A. A. An-Na'im, 'Toward an Islamic Hermeneutics for Human Rights' in A. A. An-Na'im, J.D. Gort, H. Jansen, H.M. Vroom (eds.), *Human Rights and Religious Values, An Uneasy Relationship?* p. 229 (Michigan: William B. Eerdmans Publishing Company, 1995).

27. *Ibid.* p. 229.

moral resources into the progression of human rights, whilst allowing, 'room for neutral norms and values independent of such traditions'.[28] If either a human rights ideology or religious commitments are interpreted in a totalising manner they will exclude one another—to the detriment of both projects in the long term.

On What Basis to Co-operate?

If we agree on the need for an engagement between religion and human rights, the question then arises of the basis on which such an engagement should proceed. What is the framework under which this dialogue is to occur? What is the collaboration to look like? To vaguely picture such co-operation is relatively unproblematic, as many documents and compilations outlining the commitment of various religious groups to the cause of human rights bear testament to. Indeed, boiling down the essence of both religion and human rights to that of the upkeep of human dignity and the enrichment of human life and society puts them in a synonymous light. There is also little doubt that there are numerous aspects of human rights and of various beliefs that are quite separate, and do not impinge on one another. The determination of state reporting obligations at UN treaty monitoring bodies, or decisions on prayers for the dead, do not require any collaboration between religions and human rights. However, there are many aspects of overlay between the two worldviews where both come into focus: the question of limits of the right to evangelise or proselytise, the status of religious minorities and political involvement on the basis of religious symbols or loyalties. All these demand some kind of negotiation or prioritisation of norms between human rights and various belief systems. The question is whether, and in what circumstances, the two will either clash, enrich, inform or dismiss one another? Although these parallel forces may often act in harmony, inevitably situations of serious dissension do and will also arise. Resignation to, 'a process of osmosis' and 'eventual absorption'[29] between the two, leading to the resolution of *all* clashes may prove overly optimistic, sidelining questions about how disagreements are to be resolved and which system is to trump the other. When the two systems clash,

28. P. de Silva, 'Human Rights in Buddhist Perspective' in A. A. An-Na'im, J.D. Gort, H. Jansen, H.M. Vroom (eds.), *Human Rights and Religious Values, An Uneasy Relationship?* p. 133 (Michigan: William B. Eerdmans Publishing Company, 1995).

29. S.A. Arjomand, 'Religious Human Rights and the Principle of Legal Pluralism in the Middle East' in J.D. van der Vyver and J Witte Jr. (eds.), *Religious Human Rights in Global Perspective, Legal Perspectives* p. 346 (The Hague: Martinus Nijhoff Publishers, 1996).

which is to act as the corrective against which the other is to be judged? How are the essential paradoxes between such universalist principles and particularist positions to be reconciled?

Approaches to Religion-Human Rights paradoxes

A range of options exist, each relying on varying assumptions about the role of both human rights and religion in human life and society. These are neither exhaustive nor necessarily mutually exclusive.

A strict demarcation of the public-private divide may sideline religion to the private domain and assign priority to human rights in the public sphere. Such a position may wish to leave religious matters to each individual to decide, occasionally recognising the right of religious representatives to mediate within and on behalf of their own communities. Such a position has the advantage of clarity. The correlating disadvantage is its simplicity in ignoring societal complexities and the arbitrary power implications behind its subjective public-private categorisations. Such distinctions also rely on a heavy demarcation between the sphere of influence of both religion and human rights. Assumptions are being made about the 'positivist concepts of law and the privatist concepts of religion that tend to dominate the modern Western academy'.[30] It is such perceptions that seriously resist the involvement of religion in the human rights debate, and tend to minimise areas of mutual interest between them. As the world report on Freedom of Religion and Belief suggests, despite the aim of some secularists to 'wish religion away' in the public sphere, 'The idea that religion belongs only to the private sphere is meaningless to the vast bulk of believers of all religions in the world.'[31]

Another position is that of making decisions about the role of religion dependent on the will of the majority. This makes perspectives on the outcomes of religion-human rights clashes dependent on the democratic will of the majority[32] within the community concerned. Whilst on the face of it this seems to resolve the dilemma, the preference attached to the majority clearly falls short of the whole spirit of the human rights regime. As Donnelly argues, 'Human rights are fundamentally nonmajoritarian. Human rights are concerned with each, rather than all. They aim to protect every person, against

30. Witte, *supra* note 10 p. 3.

31. K. Boyle and J. Sheen (eds.), *Freedom of Religion and Belief, A World Report* p. 10 (London: Routledge, 1997).

32. What is being discussed here is a simple calculation of the preference of the majority. The ideal of Liberal Democracy, however, is careful to protect minorities as well.

majorities no less than against minorities.'[33] In fact, the project of human rights would become meaningless if it did not extend to the protection of the vulnerable, often minority, position. This position is not able to extend its protection to the vulnerable and, in fact, would tend towards the consistent rejection of the minority position.

Much of the history of modern human rights has prioritised the legal over the religious. Whilst a number of the original 'fathers' of international law, such as Saint Thomas Aquinas, were theologians there has been a strong move away from the theistic strand in some of those natural law roots.[34] Davidson explains how the theistic tone in natural law was challenged by a concerted effort to secularise the basis of the law and, 'make it a product of enlightened secular rational thought'.[35] Grotius, for example, assisted in natural law's replacement of the Deity with 'right reason' and the secularity of the law has been a key feature of its recent development. Historically it is believed that secularisation and positive law was crucial in providing, 'a definite and systematic statement of the actual rights which people possessed'.[36] Some have continued this line of argument in suggesting that the foundation of respect for rights has to be secular. As Halliday suggests in relation to human rights in the Middle East,

> The central issue is not ... one of finding some more liberal or compatible, interpretation of Islamic thinking, but of removing the discussion of rights from the claims of religion itself. Unless this step is taken, the multiple levels of limitation ...—text, culture, instrumentality and religious hegemony—will prevail.[37]

However, the disadvantage of this strong stance of prioritising the legal over the religious in the discussion about human rights is that of the ensuing frustration and alienation it leads to amongst the religious. Is it not possible to, instead, remove the discussion of rights from the *exclusive* control and claims of one particular religion whilst also nurturing the collaboration of religions and the religious in the realisation of human rights?

In contrast, religious norms may be clearly positioned over human rights. As Mohideen reminds us, the simple exclusion of religion from the public sphere is far from palatable from the Islamic perspective.

33. Donnelly, *supra* note 19 p. 155.
34. See Hilaire McCoubrey's chapter: 'Natural Law, Religion and the Development of International Law' in M.W. Janis and C. Evans (eds.), *Religion and International Law* (The Hague: Martinus Nijhoff, 1999).
35. S. Davidson, *Human Rights* p. 27 (Buckingham: Open University Press, 1993).
36. *Ibid.* p. 29.
37. F. Halliday, *Islam and the Myth of Confrontation* p. 157 (London: I. B. Tauris, 1995).

> The Qur'an makes it clear that religion cannot confine itself to one segment of human life, nor can it choose to abstain from exercising any decisive influence over everyday life. Religion is not a private matter for each individual. The moral dimension of human activity ... is the concern of religion ... Islam is a total and integral code and way of life and is concerned with every aspect of human well-being.[38]

Another writer has complained of 'religious apartheid' in the United States and other Western states. He defines this as, 'the systematic exclusion of religious persons from public life and the resulting exclusion of religious belief as a significant factor in governmental policymaking or legislation'.[39] Whilst proponents of such positions are often condemned with derogatory terms such as 'fundamentalist' the position is no different, if a lot less popular, than the previous one. (Interestingly, Falk does also use the term 'secular fundamentalism',[40] which he recognises as potentially being just as repressive as the religious variety.) Dialogue is necessary to challenge the assumptions and barriers that exist with regard to the role of religion or belief in the human rights debate. Whilst there is much scope for the role of inter-religious dialogue, there is also the need for dialogue between religious and secular communities. This need goes beyond the discussion of human rights, but is critical to it nevertheless. The world report on Freedom of Religion or Belief suggests,

> Just as there is a need for inter-religious dialogue, so there is also a need for the secular and the religious to meet on common ground and learn to articulate a respect for each other. Frequently secular groups have fashioned themselves through the rejection of religion and this constitutes an obstacle to dialogue which needs to be overcome without threatening the underlying nature of secular belief ... there is a need to encourage ... people to examine the nature of their own secular beliefs, and to articulate them in positive terms, not just as a rejection of the beliefs of others ... Respect for the concept of belief itself is a prerequisite for acceptance of a plural society in which all beliefs are held to be inherently worthy of respect.[41]

This inherent respect for other beliefs, whether stemming from religious or secular thought, needs also to permeate any underlying assumptions with regard to the foundations of human rights, in order to ensure it does not inherently appear alienating to religious believers.

---

38. M. Mazzahim Mohideen, 'Islam, Nonviolence and Interfaith Relations' in G.D. Paige, C. Satha-Anand (Qadar Muheideen) and S. Gilliatt (eds.), *Islam and Nonviolence* p. 136 (Honolulu: Center for Global Nonviolence Planning Project, 1993).
39. P.C. Moreno (ed.), *Handbook on Religious Liberty Around the World* p. 1 (Charlottesville: The Rutherford Institute, 1996).
40. R. Falk, 'Cultural Foundations for the International Protection of Human Rights' in A.A. An-Na'im (ed.), *Human Rights in Cross-Cultural Perspectives, A Quest for Consensus* p. 58 (Philadelphia: University of Pennsylvania Press, 1992).
41. Boyle and Sheen, *supra* note 31 p. 14.

However, distinctions may indeed need to be made between those that have a genuine desire to engage in the human rights debate whilst maintaining its fundamentals, and others who are trying to thwart and undermine its very purpose. Though the line between the two cannot be easily drawn, the distinction *is* necessary for religion-human rights reconciliations not to obliterate the very contribution provided by human rights. The problem, however, is that human rights (in its popular rather than legal usage) has come to mean all things to all people. Nevertheless, perhaps the distillation of a most basic tenet of human rights—that of 'non-discrimination'—could at least serve as an initial guiding principle. Howard, for example, strongly condemns fundamentalists and traditionalists who try to engage in the human rights dialogue whilst attempting to hide that they are actually, 'against human rights; that they disagree with the ideals of equality, autonomy, and respect for all; and that they prefer societies in which certain categories of people are considered unequal and undeserving of respect, in which the assertion of human rights would be punished'.[42] It is certainly hard to imagine that accommodating those holding such attitudes could possibly prove fruitful to the long-term enhancement of the realisation of human rights.

Others may sideline the problem by arguing that any clashes between religion and human rights need to be negotiated on a case-by-case basis. The assumption is that genuine and open negotiation will always be possible between co-existing and parallel systems of religion and human rights. With priorities not being determined, this dual system has the strength of maintaining the breadth of universal human rights and the depth of rooting it in individual belief systems. However, the question of which trumps the other and in which circumstances remains unanswered. In the deeply held passions that questions—such as blasphemy—may give rise to, does this position not just attempt to make the subjective basis of such negotiations appear objective?

Another factor that needs to be kept in mind is that negotiations about the agenda and content of human rights, in the legal sense, are largely determined by, and dependent on, states. Are states really in the best position to make such normative decisions between religion and human rights? Can such state-centred processes really lead to the community engagement that such issues deserve? The systemic realities of human rights negotiations at the international level, unfortunately, often perpetuate conspiracy theories of great power monopolisation and continued imperialism. Such impressions also aggravate East-West tensions between states on the religion versus human rights question. If one takes the problem of the state-centred nature of cur-

42. R.E. Howard, *Human Rights and the Search for Community* p. 98 (Boulder: Westview Press, 1995).

rent human rights decision-making to its logical conclusion, however, what scenario does one envisage as replacing it? Whilst the benefits of community engagement on such questions are clear, what kind of structure would replace or complement current human rights decision-making and enforcement processes? These are certainly complex questions that need thorough examination, but they cannot be entered into here. What is suggested here, however, is that whilst international human rights law assigns primary responsibility for the realisation of human rights to states, the role of non-state actors is critical as the eyes and ears on the ground and as the scaffolding that can prop up the primary responsibilities assigned to states. Religious communities are a crucial part of this.

Some writers propose the determining factor in cases of debate between religion and human rights as being the issue of suffering. 'Taking suffering seriously is the Archimedes point for intermediation between the universal claim and the particular practice when it comes to resolving antagonisms between widely endorsed human rights norms and culturally ordained patterns of behavior'.[43] The logic of this position, however, is problematised when one is faced with circumstances where suffering exists on both sides. Does one then resort to utilitarian interpretations of greater versus lesser suffering, once again sidelining the minority position?

Several variants of the 'essential unity' thesis exist claiming that with free and open dialogue within and between religious and human rights cultures one would arrive at 'cultural reconstruction'[44] and the emergence of a unity of understanding. It relies on its emphasis that both, ultimately, aim for the inherent dignity of human beings. This chapter conceives of religion and human rights as parallel universes: evolving and being reinterpreted in relation to themselves and to each other. Whilst this dignity may be assigned either to the inner spiritual nature, or just the vision for the creation of a good life, both would agree on the end of dignity if not the basis of such dignity. This position certainly presents a way out of the position on the inevitability of conflict between the two, though it may be based more on the hope for a self-fulfilling prophecy than a description of present realities. Witte endorses this 'essential unity' thesis in creating a vivid picture of the compatibility between religion and human rights law. 'Law and religion stand not in monistic unity, nor in dualistic antimony, but in dialectical harmony ... Law and religion are distinct spheres and sciences of human life, but they exist in dialectical interaction, constantly crossing-over and cross-fertilizing each other.'[45] They are

---

43. Falk, *supra* note 40 p. 49.
44. *Ibid.* p. 57.
45. Witte, *supra* note 10 p. 5.

distinct, but Witte suggests that they are related: conceptually, methodologically, institutionally and professionally. The two are seen as seamless universes of meaning, existing in a cross-fertilising, harmonising relationship ebbing in and out of each other's realms. Thus, while 'Religions and ideologies are … called upon to make explicit how human rights commitment flows from the very spirit of their teachings',[46] presumably human rights on its part would also be obligated to effectively uphold freedom of religion or belief? This picture, however, does not respond directly to the question of how to empirically resolve conflicts and questions of hierarchy.

Interim Understandings

It seems that no ultimate solution can be found to this question of on what basis to resolve all conflicts that are to ever emerge between human rights and the endless wealth and diversity of religious or other beliefs. The underlying problem in determining a final solution to this question is in the monolithic assumptions it would have to make about both human rights and religions and beliefs. Furthermore, it would have to risk treating the two, and the whole variety of traditions and cultures they carry, as static entities not capable of change, thus rejecting the natural process of cross-cultural penetration leading to new understandings. The problematic aspect of 'freezing' worldviews is that it has the tendency of polarising positions and exaggerating difference. After all, both human rights and religions are subject to evolution and change. Religious truth has been described as an, 'ever-revolving kaleidoscope of meanings composed of a multitude of infinite perceptions',[47] and even a cursory glance at the history of human rights will demonstrate its ever-changing (perhaps ever-expanding) concerns and interpretations. A further dimension of the debate is the political context. The politicisation of the human rights debate by states has invested strong power connotations to the question of whether religion, tradition, culture (e.g. 'Asian'/'African' values) win out or universal human rights.

Whilst the ultimate answers to this complex debate cannot be given without indefensible simplification, and perhaps should not be attempted in the highly charged political and social climate of our times, the empirical strengthening of co-operation between religions and human rights should not be put on hold. We may have to satisfy ourselves with less conclusive and

46. Künnemann, *supra* note 5 p. 340.

47. D.A. Hart, *One Faith? Non-realism and the World of Faiths* p. 163 (London: Mowbray, 1995).

deterministic conclusions, submitting to Falk's observation that, 'There are no fixed points of normative reference'.[48] We may thus concede to the ongoing search for integrity on this topic within and between individuals and communities, for generations to come. Nevertheless, two interim understandings may be proposed.

The first is that believers too may appreciate that human rights can act as an interface between the system of ethics imparted to a particular faith at a specific historical period through divine revelation (in the case of theistic beliefs, or 'realised' in the case of non-theistic beliefs), and the more fluid, more immediate, more inclusive, political and legal role of minimum standards for human dignity, as supported through the system of human rights. As Künnemann reminds us, human rights can form an important function as a 'common ground for a pluralism of ideologies'.[49]

Though religions play a primary role in highlighting the moral values which followers attempt to translate into daily living, given the fact of pluralism they too will be judged by what is considered to be morally acceptable. Within the pluralism of our times *all* traditions and practices have to 'pass the test of some sort of universal moral code',[50] and religions cannot expect immunity from this process.[51] Within social and political circles, such decisions are often judged through the lens of human rights. As Mitra has stated, 'Modernity generates self-reflection and can be an antidote to the dogmatic adherence to the beliefs of the forebears and mechanical repetition of what they did. Uncritical adherence to traditions can stagnate any religion'.[52] The question is whether religious traditions will allow human rights to play this role of injecting 'modernity' (here being defined as our response to the diversity of our times) into religious thinking. Willing support for such a process rests on the expectation that religious traditions concede that the pursuit of *their* moral code necessitates prior belief in the validity of the grounds on which that code has been built, and an acknowledgement that human rights needs

48. Falk, *supra* note 40 p. 60.

49. Künnemann, *supra* note 5 p. 340.

50. Preface to A.A. An-Na'im, J.D. Gort, H. Jansen, H.M. Vroom (eds.), *Human Rights and Religious Values, An Uneasy Relationship?* p. viii (Michigan: William B. Eerdmans Publishing Company, 1995).

51. An interesting aside in this debate is that of the public accountability of churches, a discussion which arose out of the adoption of the Human Rights Act by the UK parliament in November 1998. This was explored in detail in a paper contributed by Canon Martyn Percy, 'Inclusion and Exemption of the Churches from the HRA' at a conference held at Imperial College on Taking Religious Convictions Seriously: The Impact of the Incorporation of the European Convention on Human Rights, (London, 6-7 January 1999, unpublished paper). It was also discussed in L. Ward, 'People power threatens church freedom', *The Guardian*, 17 February 1998, p. 10.

52. Mitra, *supra* note 18 p. 116.

to bypass such particularities. However, if the subject matter of human rights is the universal quest for what it means to be human, then *every* human being should be able to have a say in the answer to this question. The discussion about human rights, therefore, needs to be larger and wider than the choice of religion, belief or commitment of each individual, and yet not totally alien from it. The question remains, 'Can human rights be interpreted and justified from within religious traditions, such that they are supported, rather than undermined, as the "common core" of a universal morality among these traditions?'[53] As the UN Special Representative on the human rights situation in Iran reiterated (in relation to 'traditional culture', but equally relevant to 'religion'), 'Traditional culture is not a substitute for human rights; it is a cultural context in which human rights must be established, integrated, promoted and protected. Human rights must be approached in a way that is meaningful and relevant in diverse cultural contexts.'[54] The project for a 'culture of human rights' requires both cultures to rest on the basis of human rights values and for human rights values to be embedded into various cultures—thus giving realisation to the new amalgam of a 'culture of human rights'. Only time will be able to tell how far such projects for the support of human rights, utilising a variety of cultural and religious symbols and commitments, are able to collaborate towards the realisation and pursuit of a universal code of human rights.

The second interim understanding is the acceptance of the utility of human rights in relation to statecraft. As human rights is a manmade code its ultimate claims lie no higher than representing the latest register of agreed and negotiated standards for a decent human existence (ironically this humble claim *is* its strength). As social conditions and circumstances alter, its nuances can be adjusted to register more appropriate measures for changed circumstances. Human rights allow an in-built elasticity and flexibility in interpretation that allows them to move beyond their historical bounds.[55] Human rights are defined and concretised at certain points in history as key international legal documents such as the Universal Declaration of Human Rights and the two International Covenants bear witness to. However, the purpose of such texts is not to finalise concepts of human rights for eternity, nor limit future progress; the purpose is to chart, in a precise manner, historical developments

53. *Supra* note 50 p. xiii.

54. Doc.E/CN.4/1996/59, Commission on Human Rights, 52nd session, 21 March 1996, Report on the situation of human rights in the Islamic Republic of Iran, prepared by the Special Representative of the Commission on Human Rights, Mr. Maurice Copithorne (Canada), Introduction, section A.

55. Note here, for example, the notion of the European Convention of human rights as a 'living instrument'.

made thus far. This can be seen in the way that the Universal Declaration of Human Rights has been stretched, pulled and infused with new meanings and interpretations since 1948. As Clayton explains, 'Testing and being contested—by this means the discourse of rights creates itself afresh and the hierarchy of rights is subjected to public scrutiny.'[56] All of this can be achieved on a platform that has the potential of being recognised as being more dispassionate, bypassing particular belief systems which, 'are perceived ... as parochial or local in scope and as being grounded in context-specific commitments'.[57] However, human rights is not a secular 'religion' nor does it perform its functions, 'Human rights simply regulate state power versus vulnerable groups and individuals, without recourse to ideological statements in justifying their standards.'[58] The fact that ideological statements are not necessary (though, it needs to be emphasised, not alien either) to human rights standards, is important to its ensuing flexibility. In this manner, 'Human rights are designed to be transformed into legal or other procedures as quickly as possible'.[59]

The problem does not lie in the notional benefits that members of a particular belief may feel they have been divinely graced with, but the fear that with time this may, 'easily degenerate into hostility and antagonism towards the "them" and solidarity with the "us"'.[60] Many religious groups have put their weight behind the campaign for strengthening human rights[61] precisely because they have come to realise that the only means of ensuring non-discrimination, for example on the basis of belief, is through strengthening shared standards of human rights. In their search for particular protection, therefore, they have come to appreciate the need for its general application and protection. However, this only has a lasting impact when human rights is 'justified' and declared to be congruent with the religious norms of the group concerned, hence highlighting the indispensability of religion to the mass absorption of human rights standards. After all,

> the human rights movement itself entails struggles that must be carried on in many parts of the world in response to particular problems and conditions, with the energy and courage for such struggles coming from individuals who, while ultimately sharing

56. J. Clayton, 'Religions and Rights, Local Values and Universal Declarations' in A.A. An-Na'im, J.D. Gort, H. Jansen, H.M. Vroom (eds.), *Human Rights and Religious Values, An Uneasy Relationship?* p. 266 (Michigan: William B. Eerdmans Publishing Company, 1995).
57. *Ibid.* p. 260.
58. Künnemann, *supra* note 5 p. 340.
59. *Ibid.* pp. 339-340.
60. A. A. An-Na'im, *supra* note 26 p. 231.
61. For examples, see: Swidler *supra* note 3.

> some common goals and aspirations, often draw on religious resources that remain richly and irreducibly diverse.[62]

What is required, therefore, is this partnership of human rights with an endless richness and diversity of religious and other beliefs in support of the human rights enterprise.

Prerequisites for Reconciliation between Religion and Human Rights

The religious engagement in the human rights discourse presupposes a prior mutual commitment to the twin requirements of an acceptance to confront the past and respond to the challenges of the present.

Importance of confronting history

A major prerequisite to a mutually beneficial discourse between religion and human rights is the ability to confront the past. It is clear that religious engagement in the human rights discourse not only requires the ability to see when one has been wronged but also of when one may have wronged another. Such encounters with the past not only fuel a greater commitment to preventing a reoccurrence of collective prejudices in the future, but also allow fresh starts to be made and previous inter-communal tensions to be laid to rest.[63] Many such tensions exist between religious communities around the world, and much can be done by religions to show a commitment to a foundation of respect for human rights in future relationships. As one writer has stated in relation to Muslim/Hindu history in India: 'Knowing what we did or did not do does not alter the history of the past, but this knowledge—if accepted with courage and honesty—can lead to a different kind of future.'[64] On the part of human rights, a contempt for the role of religion and a resolute reliance on secularisation as the only approach will forbid religious engagement and ultimately weaken the foundations of human rights within communities and by

62. I. Bloom, 'Introduction' in I. Bloom, J. P. Martin and W.L. Proudfoot (eds.), *Religious Diversity and Human Rights* p. 10 (New York: Columbia University Press, 1996).

63. Examples included the pensive wait for the Vatican apology for the holocaust, which were largely disappointed. See: J. Hooper, 'Vatican disappoints Jews', *The Guardian*, 17 March 1998, p. 11.

64. R. Hassan, 'The Basis for a Hindu-Muslim Dialogue and Steps in that Direction from a Muslim Perspective' in Swidler *supra* note 3 p. 131. More necessary, in more recent times, may be the tackling of the Hindu-Christian community relationship in India.

many individuals. Whilst human rights may have traversed periods of stringent secularisation and resistance of religion, the time has now have come to weave a more mature and constructive encounter between the two.[65]

Religion and human rights as hermeneutical processes

Traditionalist conceptions of religious truth see such truth to be self-evident, explicit and not subject to any interpretation. Due to the recent nature of the modern human rights discourse and its fifty or so year old history, it is evident that no religion was historically able to comment on 'human rights' or, if it did, that the implications of the concept may be different to current thoughts surrounding it. The religious response to human rights is therefore interpretative and imaginative in nature demanding a reconsideration of religious norms in response to a recent innovation.[66] A religious response to such a development requires a particular attitude which is able to accept the assumption that,

> Religious traditions are hermeneutical processes: they do develop, change and—sometimes—improve in response to circumstances and in dialogue with their context. Critical dialogue does not mean a flight from fixed, unchanging positions but rather a mutual search for a better understanding of human life, a just and merciful society, nature, and ultimate reality.[67]

This process of interpretation involves an approach from within the traditions concerned which encourages a positive approach to responding to new social realities. A commitment to the hermeneutical role of religion is what distinguishes it distinctly from self-complacency, self-delusion and fanaticism. As Van der Vyver states, 'This mode of human experience carries with it the responsibility to continuously and critically reappraise one's perceptions of that truth in view of new knowledge and experience—that is, if one wishes to avoid the stagnation of intransigent orthodoxy.'[68] It is by this means that human rights and religion can prove to be complementary and mutually enriching.

---

65. There are many current initiatives to bridge such a reconciliation, for example the holding of the August 1998 Oslo Conference on Freedom of Religion or Belief and the May 1999 conference on 'Human Rights and our responsibilities towards future generations, An inter-religious perspective', organised by the Future Generations Programme of the Foundation for International Studies, University of Malta, in collaboration with the Mediterranean Academy of Diplomatic Studies and UNESCO.

66. The modern expression of the human rights discourse stretches back five decades to the post second world war period.

67. *Supra* note 50 p. vii.

On its part, human rights activists should also avoid becoming dogmatic about, and fixated upon, the present achievements of human rights. The whole utility of human rights relies not on it being fixed in stone and resistant to any future reconsideration. Through dialogue and negotiation reinterpretation and enrichment are made possible, as is greater commitment towards the realisation of its ideals. Indeed, without such commitment human rights can never become anything other than a dead letter and benchmark of failed dreams only ever activated through political and politicised channels.

Human Rights' Contribution to Religion

Such approaches could lead to two inter-related possibilities, one being freedom *for* religions, the other freedom *within* religions. Developments for human rights have already been discussed and those within human rights will be approached in the next section.

Importance of freedom *for* religions

As has been stated earlier, due to the 'peculiarly modern'[69] concept of human rights, the concept per se does not exist in the scripture of any religion. Despite many religions trying to claim 'fatherhood' to the concept of human rights, its modern construct—linked as it is to the role of the sovereign state for example—was not created by any religion, though many of its early proponents were undoubtedly inspired by their beliefs. An initial manner in which religions have come to be interested in human rights has been due to their experience of engagement in the cause of religious liberty for their fellow believers. Such rights have been pursued from a legal position, as 'Denial of legal recognition and entity status is denial of religious liberty.'[70] Hence, legal personality is what most religions seek in order to be able to express their beliefs effectively.

International legal personality facilitates the protection of diversity in the functioning of religious communities and ultimately the ability to pursue perceived injustices within a legal framework. The realisation that equality of

---

68. J.D. van der Vyver, 'Religious Fundamentalism and Human Rights', *Journal of International Affairs* Vol. 5, No. 1, p. 38 (Summer 1996).
69. Clayton, *supra* note 56 p. 259.
70. W.C. Durham, 'Perspectives on Religious Liberty, A Comparative Framework' in J.D. van der Vyver and J. Witte Jr. (eds.), *Religious Human Rights in Global Perspective, Legal Perspectives* p. 39 (The Hague: Martinus Nijhoff Publishers, 1996).

provision under the law does not necessarily lead to equality of treatment has been established through a number of examples such as the civil rights movement, the study of women's human rights and the continued threats against indigenous cultures around the world. This principle also applies to religious communities, which explains why legal personality and human rights needs to lead to a much fuller, ongoing and more dynamic relationship between states and their religious communities.

The implications of human rights for internal discourse *within* a religion

The religion-human rights discourse has both an internal and an external dimension: externally with other believers and communities and internally with regards to the respect guaranteed to every one of its own believers. The two are not necessarily correspondent within each belief system—perhaps in the same way that countries that are most vigorous in paying lip service to human rights on the world stage are rarely those that translate this most keenly into a true commitment at home.

A wide chasm often remains between how religions expect to be treated and how they treat others. It also emerges in relation to how religions treat members within or outside their religious community. The most interesting dilemma that emerges is that of new religions that emerge from the midst of previous religions. The reason these groups often suffer the worst fate is that they span the divide between internal schism and an independent body of belief. Such groups perceive themselves as having established a new belief community whereas the 'parent' community sees them as a distortion and blasphemous offshoot of their group. Human rights are thus often critically denied them as they epitomise the most threatening and dangerous form of the 'other'.[71] It is such circumstances that deepen the complexity of freedom of religion and belief still further. It is not just the toleration by believers of secularists, atheists, agnostics or followers of particular religions or beliefs that is at stake. The task facing believers amongst themselves is itself immense. Generally, 'The challenge remains considerable to establish an ethic of tolerance towards those who differ on religious grounds.'[72] Küng proposes the idea of an 'ecumenical theology' towards this end, 'ecumenical theology can help

71. A vivid example is that of the Bahá'í Faith as perceived by many members of the Shi'i clergy and by the Iranian Government.

72. Boyle and Sheen, *supra* note 31 p. 13.

to discover and work through the conflicts caused by the religions, confession, and denominations themselves'.[73]

Tensions between the rights and responsibilities of religious believers could also give rise to tensions in the day-to-day running of a religious community. Curran states, 'Most of the internal problems experienced in the church stem from the tension between authority and freedom. What is the proper use of authority, and what are proper roles of freedom?'[74] Human rights provide an ideal means of engaging in dialogue about such issues.

Just as freedom in the church can be a way of dealing with most of the major problems facing the internal life of the church, so the language of rights can be used as an instrument to deal with the major tensions facing the contemporary church. Rights language is the strongest ethical language that exists precisely because it makes a claim on other people to do something. Value language, for example, is not nearly as strong.[75]

The utilisation of human rights in communicating about how to resolve internal tensions is one example of how the religion-human rights engagement may be of benefit to religions.

Religion's Contribution to Human Rights

Most of our consideration thus far has considered the contribution of human rights to religion, but what of the potential impact of religion on human rights? Witte creates the backdrop to this vision in this way, 'Human rights are, by design, abstract statements of individual and associational living that depend upon the religious visions of persons and communities to give them content and coherence.'[76] He has further argued that, 'The deprecation of the special role and rights of religions … has "impoverished" the general theory of human rights'.[77] The case that religion may lead to the enrichment of aspects of the human rights discourse now requires analysis. The most likely benefits are likely to be four in number: the widening of the cultural base of human rights, promoting an understanding of the concept of duties, challenging the state-centric and individualistic basis of human rights and deepening the concept and commitment towards third generation rights.

73. Küng, *supra* note 11 p. 441.
74. Curran, *supra* note 6 p. 155.
75. *Ibid.* p. 158.
76. Witte, *supra* note 10 p. 30.
77. *Ibid.* p. 11.

The widened base

One of the major contributions that religious thought can offer the human rights movement is to allow a widening of the (perceived *and* actual) cultural base of human rights. The rigidly secular reading of human rights has caused much alienation amongst faith-based communities. Human rights is thus made culturally inaccessible to millions of people across the world, and the perception is compounded that it merely constitutes a means of perpetuating the political power hierarchies existing in the world today—that of the supremacy of Western secularism. A reassessment of this presentation of human rights will go a long way towards allowing the engagement of non-western societies and concepts into human rights.

Duties

Another reason why many religious writers reject the fundamental thrust of the human rights movement is due to its focus on rights and near silence on the issue of responsibilities or duties.[78] Examples can be given of a number of Christian writers and their dislike of the concept of 'rights'. One such writer explains,

> the Bible contains no irrefutable evidence of the idea that man, by the mere fact of his existence, is entitled to make a number of fundamental demands or claims on other members of society ... rather than rights or demands written into man's nature as such, what is involved is an attitude towards one's neighbour, not of inherent rights but of responsibility and service due to him.[79]

As with a significant number of other believers, this perspective seems to misconstrue the term 'rights' as being indicative of individualistic or egotistical tendencies. Such a deconstruction of the concept sidelines the term's political and legalistic terminology and its primary application to state-person guarantees rather than person-to-person expectations. Nevertheless, whilst upholding the political responsibility assumed by the term 'rights' by national and international legal and political bodies it may be possible to also envisage the contribution that a corresponding concept of duties may allow to the deepening role of human rights between individuals and groups. This is where the

78. Notable exceptions to this include Article 29 of the Universal Declaration of Human Rights, the Inter-American Declaration on the Rights and Duties of Man and Article 27 of the African Charter on Human and Peoples Rights.

79. J.W. Montgomery, *Human Rights & Human Dignity* p. 20 (Michigan: Probe Ministries International, Zondervan Publishing House, 1986).

contribution of religion may come in. Could such a duties dimension prove advantageous to the individual or collective enjoyment of human rights, especially considering its increased acknowledgement of the role of non-state actors in abuses of rights worldwide? Is it also possible to enhance the concept of the duty of the state towards the preservation of human rights and of ensuring the appropriate conditions for the realisation of human rights, perhaps through a more central emphasis on the due diligence principle? With the clear caveat that individuals or groups should not sacrifice the rights that they are entitled to in order to serve the state (otherwise human rights will prove meaningless), much room may yet remain for a role for duties to respect human rights. Indeed, the emergence of a culture of human rights and third generation rights cannot be won without a more integrated realisation of the interconnectedness between rights and duties—between individuals, groups, communities, families, and with the world environment in general.

Group rights

Another fruit of the religion-human rights engagement may include challenging the very individualistic reading of human rights. Group rights have long epitomised this weakness of the human rights dialogue. The resistance faced in the recognition of minority rights, the rights of indigenous peoples, social and economic rights, third generation rights in general, and even the collective dimension of religious rights as mainstream human rights exemplifies this tension between individual and group human rights. 'In such a dialogue [between religion and human rights] Western individualism will be subject to correction, and hierarchical social-religious philosophies will be questioned on the matter of the rights of individuals'.[80]

Conceptual developments

Further contributions of religion to closer collaboration with human rights could be of a conceptual nature. It is significant to note that, to date, religious views have not overtly been sought as contributions to the human rights debate. Although a number of religions have ensured that their voice be heard in the process of the codification of international human rights texts, their involvement has often been reluctantly and randomly accepted as NGOs rather than positively welcomed by the international community. It is for this

80. *Supra* note 50 p. vii.

reason that van der Vyver notes, 'no attempts were made, at least during the infancy of human rights thinking, to accommodate religious tenets in the circumscription of basic rights and fundamental freedoms to be protected by the repositories of political power'.[81] Such approaches have failed to recognise religion as, 'a powerful tool in the struggle against discrimination and repression in the social, economic, legal and political structures of a community'.[82] This includes its potentially positive role in terms of concepts, commitment, grass roots activism and role in developing a human rights culture. It is this recognition of the active community implications and attainments of religion that particularly implicate it in the emergence of third generation rights.[83] Witte has even argued that, 'Religious institutions offer some of the deepest insights into norms of creation, stewardship, and servanthood that lie at the heart of third generation rights.'[84]

Conclusion

The challenge is therefore an intricate one: that of allowing human rights to 'transcend all differences in the subjectivities and practices of peoples',[85] whilst also 'mediating international human rights through the web of cultural circumstances'.[86] 'In the final analysis, the acknowledgement and implementation of universal human rights should be seen as a co-operative process as well as ... a common objective—a global joint venture and not an attempt to universalize a particular cultural or religious model'.[87] Through such a rapprochement, religions and human rights will be able to collaborate, allowing religions to give human rights law 'their spirit—the sanctity and authority they need to command obedience and respect ... its structural fairness, its "inner morality"'.[88] This can lend a notable impetus to an appreciation of a wid-

81. Van der Vyver, *supra* note 68 p. 30.
82. *Ibid.* p. 35.
83. Under this hierarchy, first generation rights contain civil and political rights, second generation rights contain economic, social and cultural rights and third generation rights include solidarity rights such as the rights to peace and development. For a discussion of this hierarchy see: T. Meron, *Human Rights Law-making in the United Nations, A Critique of Instruments and Processes*, pp. 174-175 (Oxford: Clarendon Press, 1986).
84. Witte, *supra* note 10 p. 13.
85. Falk, *supra* note 40 p. 44.
86. *Ibid.* p. 45.
87. An-Na'im, *supra* note 26 p. 241.
88. Witte, *supra* note 10 p. 8.

ened foundation on which human rights rest. As 'obedience to a norm because of legal compulsion and not by virtue of personal persuasion loses it moral significance',[89] enhanced religious foundations for human rights could greatly strengthen its moral appeal. If one goes so far as to recognise the translation of human rights into a universal 'culture' as a necessary prerequisite for its effective survival into the next century, one may even conclude that, 'The regime of law, democracy, and human rights needs religion to survive.'[90]

89. van der Vyver, *supra* note 68 p. 40.

90. Witte, *supra* note 10 p. 31.

Chapter 6

Believing in Communities, European Style

Malcolm D. Evans

Professor of Public International Law, University of Bristol

The history of the last ten years, and more, shows that membership of the Council of Europe is a vital step on the *cursus honorum* towards political legitimacy and economic advantage within Europe. Membership currently stands at 44 States[1]—approaching a quarter of the international community—and, as far as the Council is concerned, membership is contingent upon realization of a culture of democracy, human rights and the rule of law.[2] Conformity with

1. The most recent adherent State at the time of writing (July 2002) was Bosnia and Herzegovina, which was admitted on 24 April 2002. This means that the only States upon the European Continent which are not now in full membership are the Federal Republic of Yugoslavia (which, however, has enjoyed Special Guest Status to the Parliamentary Assembly of the Council since January 2001 and is expected to have become a full member by the end of 2002) and Belarus. The Holy See has had Observer Status with the Committee of Ministers since March 1970.
2. See *Statute of the Council of Europe*, ETS 1, Article 3 (1949), 'Every member of the Council of Europe must accept the principles of the rule of law and of the enjoyment by all persons within its jurisdiction of human rights and fundamental freedoms, and collaborate sincerely and effectively in the realization of the aims of the Council as specified in Chapter I'. The Preamble to the State describes these as principles 'which form the basis of all genuine democracy'.

the provisions (and jurisprudence) of the *European Convention on Human Rights and Fundamental Freedoms* (the *ECHR*) is the touchstone by which this is judged, and all newly admitted States are routinely required to ratify the *ECHR* (and other human rights instruments) within one year of their being admitted to the Council.[3] Thus when considering matters pertaining the law and religion within contemporary Europe the approach of the Council of Europe in general, and of the European Court of Human Rights (henceforth 'the Court') in particular, it is of critical importance. If domestic policy and practice does not conform to what is required, then that policy and practice will be subject to criticism[4] and, if and when the applicant becomes a member, it will become liable to challenge before the European Court of Human Rights itself.

The freedom of religion and belief is currently accorded protection within the major international human rights instruments as an individual right. It is well understood that such an approach does not adequately address all facets of religious life, particularly its 'collective' dimensions, that is, the abilities of believers to engage with each other, and its 'group' dimensions, which concerns the manner in which the communities of believers are protected as an entity in its own right.[5] That, in large part, is a structural and textual failing, reflecting the dominant premises and prejudices of the human rights instruments at the time of their adoption. Whilst these texts, and the interpretations that have been placed upon them, may have been, and may be, appropriate for addressing the concerns of individuals who feel that their freedom of religion or belief has been trenched upon by the State against which they are bringing a claim, they are quite inappropriate for the task of settling questions concerning the position of religious groups—of religious communities—within the States where they are located. This realization now finds some reflection in a recommendation recently adopted by the Parliamentary Assembly of the Council of Europe, entitled *Religion and Change in Central and Eastern Europe*.[6] The Report accompanying the recommendation (henceforth

---

3. See the examples provided by the admission of Bosnia and Herzegovina to the Council: *Parliamentary Assembly Opinion No 234* para. 15 (2002), adopted 22 January 2002; *Committee of Ministers Resolution 2002(5)*, adopted 20 March 2002.
4. Both the Parliamentary Assembly and Committee of Ministers have established monitoring mechanisms to oversee compliance with admission undertakings. See *Parliamentary Assembly Resolution 1115* (1997), adopted 27 January 1997 and the *Committee of Ministers Declaration on Compliance with Commitments* accepted by Member States of the Council of Europe, 95th Session, 10 November 1994.
5. On this distinction and on this problem see, for example, N. Lerner, *Religion, Beliefs and International Human Rights* pp. 51-52 and p. 117 (MaryKnoll, NY: Orbis Book, 2001). For an argument in favour of a group-oriented approach to the freedom of conscience (as distinct from the freedom of religion) see L.S. Hammer, *The International Human Right to Freedom of Conscience* pp. 243-265 (Aldershot. Ashgate, 2001).
6. *Recommendation 1556* (2002), adopted 24 April 2002.

the Baciu Report) observes that 'Europe today finds itself facing a wholly new problem—that of striking the right balance between protecting freedom of belief and preserving the religious identity of communities and societies',[7] and acknowledges that the rights of communities are less well protected than those of individuals.[8]

At the same time, and, as indicated by the title of the Parliamentary Assembly Resolution just mentioned, at least partly in response to the relentlessly eastward march of the Council of Europe—the *ECHR* has become as much a tool for the regulation and control of organized religion in the interests of its own dogmas of democracy, rule of law and human rights, as it is a vehicle of the protection of religious freedom. This may or may not be a problem.[9] But it requires wary scrutiny from religious communities which ought not draw simple connections between the freedom of religion and the protection of human rights. In the following sections will consider the background to these thoughts.

Article 9: The 'Classic' approach

Article 9 of the *ECHR* sets out what might be termed a 'classical' individual right.[10] It is comprised of three limbs. Article 9(1) opens with the affirmation that 'Everyone has the right to freedom of thought, conscience and religion'. This is followed by a section which concerns the freedom to manifest 'religion or belief' in one of four ways: teaching, practice, worship and observance. Article 9(2) then provides that the freedom to manifest religion or belief can

7. *Report of the Committee on Culture, Science and Education, Religion and Change in Central and Eastern Europe*, Doc. 9399, 27 March 2002 (the 'Baciu Report') para. 37.
8. *Ibid*.
9. See, for example, the approaches to the freedom of religion in earlier Parliamentary Assembly Recommendations and Reports addressing other particular areas of concern, including: *Parliamentary Assembly Resolution 1396 on Religion and Democracy*, adopted 27 January 1999; Report, Doc 8270 of 27 November 1998 (Committee of Legal Affairs and Human Rights; Rapporteur, Mr Puig); *Recommendation 1412 on Illegal Activities of sects*, adopted 22 June 1999; Report, Doc. 8373 of 13 April 1999 (Committee on Culture and Education; Rapporteur, Mr Nastaste). For a critical appraisal of aspects of this trend see M.D. Evans, 'Religion, Law and Human Rights; Locating the Debate' in P.W. Edge and G. Harvey (eds.), *Law and Religion in Contemporary Society, Communities, Individualism and the State* p. 177 at pp. 182-184 and pp. 187-188 (Aldershot: Ashgate, 2000).
10. See, generally M.D. Evans, *Religious Liberty and International Law in Europe* (Cambridge: Cambridge University Press, 1997) and C. Evans, *Freedom of Religion Under the European Convention on Human Rights* (Oxford: Oxford University Press, 2001). See also J. Martinez-Torron, 'The European Court of Human Rights and Religion' in R. O'Dair and A. Lewis, *Law and Religion* pp. 186-204 (Oxford: Oxford University Press, 2001).

only be subject to limitations which are 'prescribed by law' and are 'necessary in a democratic society' for one of a number of purposes—in the interests of public safety, the protection of public order, health or morals, or the protection of the rights and freedoms of others'.

The essence of this approach is that it calls for an assessment of the degree to which the interference by the State with the enjoyment of the freedom of thought, conscience and religion is to be deemed acceptable. In doing so, the distinction between the two segments of Article 9(1) had acquired a critical importance and was considered to reflect a division between the 'internal' sphere of purely 'private' thought (known as the '*forum internum*') which was inviolable, and manifestations within the 'public' sphere (the '*forum externum*') which were protected under the second part of Article 9(1), but which were subject to limitation under Article 9(2).

The system of control in the 'public arena' had three elements. First, it was necessary to determine whether the patterns of thought under consideration 'qualified' as a form of religion or belief for the purposes of Article 9(1). Second, and if it did, was the action in question a form of 'manifestation' of that belief for the purposes of Article 9(1). Third, if a manifestation of a belief was in question, was any restriction placed upon it justifiable in terms of Article 9(2)? This provides three different points at which the enjoyment of the right can be circumscribed.

What forms of belief enjoy the 'freedom to manifest'?

The inclusion of 'thought and conscience' along with religion was intended to ensure that religion did not have a privileged status compared to non-theistic patterns of thought. It was not clear whether the term 'belief' in the following phrase concerning the freedom of manifestation, was co-terminate with 'thought and conscience', whether it was a synonym for 'religion' or whether it occupied a position somewhere between the two, meaning that some but not all forms of non-'religious' belief profited from the freedom of manifestation. It seems probable that, at first, religion and belief were considered to be one and the same, but over time this has yielded to a median position,[11] with the result that some but not every form of personal belief will qualify for protection under the structure of Article 9. It is, however, clear that the European Convention bodies have taken a broad, inclusive approach.[12] This flows from

11. This was probably inevitable since the lack of any accepted definition of 'religion' makes this a difficult, if not impossible, quest in any case.

12. See M.D. Evans, *supra* note 10 p. 385 at pp. 392-394; C. Evans, *supra* note 10 at pp. 51-66 (Oxford: Oxford University Press, 2001); C. Evans 'Religious Freedom on European

the decision of the Commission in the *Arrowsmith* case[13] in which it was decided that pacifism was a form of belief that was covered by Article 9 and since then it has made it clear that Article 9 embraces not only 'traditional' and 'mainstream' religions, such as Christianity, Islam, Judaism, Hinduism, etc. It has also long been clear from early decisions of the European Commission on Human Rights (henceforth 'the Commission') that it also embraced 'new' forms of religion or belief, such as the 'Moonies',[14] Jehovah's Witnesses,[15] the Church of Scientology,[16] and other diverse groups such as the 'Divine Light Centrum'.[17] It also embraces atheism.[18] In general,[19] it can be said that Article 9 is available—at least in theory—to those who can show that their beliefs 'attain a certain level of cogency, seriousness, cohesion and importance'.[20] Who is to determine whether this threshold has been reached? This is a difficult question. The Commission in the past has indicated that the burden is on the applicant to demonstrate that a set of beliefs actually exists, and does have such a significance for the believer.[21] However, even if this threshold is passed, there still appears to be room for some discretion on the part of the State—or the Court—to evaluate whether the content of those beliefs are to be counted as a 'religion or belief' for the purposes of Article 9.[22] Even this might seem too generous an approach to some, who would rather that a stricter approach

---

Human Rights Law: The Search for a Guiding Conception' in M.W. Janis and C. Evans (eds.), *Religion and International Law* p. 385 (The Hague: Martinus Nijhoff, 1999).

13. *Arrowsmith* v. *UK*, App. No. 7050/75, Comm. Rep. 1978, 19 *DR* 5.
14. *X.* v. *Austria,* App. No. 8652/79, Comm. Dec. 1981, 26 *DR* 89.
15. *N.* v. *Sweden*, App. No. 10410/83, Comm. Dec. 1984, 40 *DR* 203.
16. *X and the Church of Scientology* v. *Sweden*, App. No. 7805/77, Comm. Dec. 1979, 16 *DR* 68.
17. Omkaranadana and the Divine Light Centrum v. Switzerland, App. No. 8118/77, Comm. Dec. 1981, 25 DR 105.
18. *Angelini* v. *Sweden*, App. No. 10491/83, Comm. Dec. 1986, 40 *DR* 41.
19. But this broadmindedness needs to be compared with the approach taken towards Druids in *U Pendragon* v. *UK*, App. No. 31416/96, Comm. Dec. 1998, 27 *EHRR CD* 179 and see [1999] *EHRLR* 223-225. In this case the Court refused to pass directly on the question of whether druids 'counted' as a religion for the purposes of Article 9, but focussed on other questions that rendered that unnecessary.
20. *Campbell and Cosans* v. *U.K.*, Judgment of 25 February 1982, Ser. A, No. 48; 4 *EHRR* 293 para. 36.
21. See, for example, *X* v. *UK* App. No. 7291/75, Comm Dec. 1977, 11 *DR* 55, regarding the existence of the Wiccan religion. This particular task might now be more easily accomplished. See R. Hutton, *The Triumph of the Moon: A History of Modern Pagan Witchcraft* (Oxford: Oxford University Press, 1999).
22. See, for example, *Pretty* v. *UK*, Judgment of 29 April 2002, nyr para. 82, where the Court rejected the suggestion that the applicant's views concerning assisted suicide were forms of belief the manifestation of which was protected under Article 9. The Court '[did] not doubt the firmness of the applicant's views... but would observe that not all opinions or convictions constitute beliefs in the sense protected by Article 9(1)...'.

be taken,[23] but it has to be considered in the light of the practice regarding the remaining elements of Article 9.

What is a 'manifestation'?

Not all activities motivated by one's belief will necessarily qualify as a 'manifestation' for the purposes of legal protection. The international instruments only protect manifestations in 'worship, observance, practice and teaching'.[24] For many believers, it is the extent to which their beliefs can influence their actions in other spheres of their lives that is important, and it is possible that these might not be considered manifestations at all.

Once again, the approach is set out in the early case of *Arrowsmith* v. *UK*: the Commission was prepared to accept that pacifism was a belief for the purposes of Article 9 of the *ECHR* but thought that distributing leaflets urging soldiers not to serve in Northern Ireland, though motivated by pacifist beliefs, was not a 'manifestation' of them.[25] There is room for considerable debate regarding what is to 'count' as a manifestation. In general, the Court has taken a fairly cautious approach, focussing on those elements of observance and ritual which are central to the lives of believers, rather than on activities that are motivated by their religious beliefs.[26] Of course, much depends on what those beliefs are,

23. See, for example, C. Evans, *supra* note 10 p. 66, where she argues that the Commission and Court have, historically, taken an overly generous approach and so 'stretched the idea of belief so that there is an extra protection given to many that would be better dealt with as simply thought and conscience'.

24. See, for example, *UDHR*, Article 18; *ICCPR*, Article 18; *ECHR*, Article 9. The non-exhaustive catalogues found in Article 6 of the *1981 Declaration on the Elimination of All Forms of Intolerance and Discrimination Based on Religion or Belief* (UN General Assembly Res. 36/55, adopted 25 November 1981) and *General Comment No. 22(48)* adopted by the Human Rights Committee provide further guidance but are fairly restrictive, embracing matters connected with 'practice and observance' of rituals of belief. For a comparative analysis of these approaches see M.D. Evans 'Human Rights, Religious Liberty and the Universality Debate' in R. O'Dair and A. Lewis, *Law and Religion* p.205 at pp. 213-215 (Oxford: Oxford University Press, 2001).

25. *Arrowsmith* v. *UK*, App. No. 7050/75, Comm. Rep. 1978, 19 *DR* 5. Another example is *Choudhury* v. *UK*, App. No. 17439/90, Comm. Dec. 1991, 12 *HRLJ* 172, in which the limitation upon the scope of proceedings for criminal blasphemy to matters concerning offence to the Christian religion and its being unavailable for the protection of the sensibilities of Muslims was not seen as raising an issue of manifestation of a belief at all. It is possible that this case would not be decided in the same way today, given the need to take account of Article 14 and non-discrimination within the—expanding—scope of the right in Article 9.

26. For a detailed exploration of the cases see C. Evans, *supra* note 10 pp. 102-132, who concludes that 'manifestation of religion or belief ... has very limited scope and provides little protection to non-traditional forms of practice' (p. 132).

and, in principle, this should be a matter for the believers themselves to determine. However, in a number of instances it seems that the Court has been prepared to substitute its own views on the nature of the activity in question for that of the believers themselves. Thus in *Valsamis* v. *Greece* the Court disagreed with the applicants' view that a parade in which their child was required to participate was 'militaristic' in nature.[27] In *Cha'are Shalom* v. *France* the Court concluded that 'ritual slaughter' of animals was a 'rite', the practice of which was essential to the practice of the Jewish Religion'.[28] However, it was also decided that it was not the ability to undertake this rite, but the ability to be a 'beneficiary' of the act of ritual slaughter, that was important. Thus, provided that the applicants could acquire meat slaughtered in accordance with their religious beliefs, that was sufficient. It was not necessary that they be able to manifest their beliefs by engaging in ritual slaughter of animals themselves.[29] Both of these cases are on the margins of legitimacy as regards intrusion into the characterization of an internal religious practice. At the other end of the spectrum, the Court has taken what some might consider a generous approach to proselytism, considering it to be a legitimate form of manifesting ones religion or belief.[30]

There are two other trends, however, that need to be noticed. First, where a form of activity is clearly within the scope of a 'manifestation'—for example, a service of worship—the Court is increasingly willing to take a broad and 'purposive' approach to matters which are incidental to the effective exercise of that right. Thus the freedom of worship or observance can embrace 'the possibility of possessing premises'.[31] In addition, in the inter-State case

27. *Valsamis* v. *Greece*, Judgment of 18 December 1996, *RJD* 1996-VI p. 2312; 24 *EHRR* 294.

28. *Cha'are Shalom* v. *France*, Judgment of 27 June 2000, nyr.

29. *Ibid*. paras. 74-80.

30. See, for example, *Kokkinakis* v. *Greece*, Judgment of 25 May 1993, Ser. A, No. 260-A; 17 *EHRR* 397, although whether it is considered to be a form of 'teaching' or a form of 'practice' is less clear. The Court also distinguished between 'bearing ... witness and improper proselytism', a distinction that may well be in the eye of the beholder. For an account linking the question of proselytism with the related question of the right to change one's religion, see N. Lerner, *supra* note 5 pp. 80-118.

31. *Iglesia Bautista "El Salvador" and Ortega Moratilla* v. *Spain*, App. No. 17522/90, Comm. Dec. 1991, 72 *DR* 256. This clearly has implications for legal status, a point drawn out by the Commission in *Canea Catholic Church* v. *Greece*, *Report of the European Commission on Human Rights*, 3 September 1996 paras. 48 and 52, where the majority of the Commission thought that a degree of legal personality was necessary if the applicant church was to be able to effectively enjoy the freedom of worship. The Court did not approach the case in quite this way, its finding being made on the basis of Article 6 of the convention in conjunction with Article 14, rather than on the basis of Article 9 itself (Judgment of 16 December 1997, *RJD* 1997-VIII p. 2843, 23 *EHRR* 387). But the overall thrust of the Court's judgment is in the same direction.

of *Cyprus* v. *Turkey* the Court linked the freedom of religion to the freedom of movement, observing that:[32]

> It has not been contended by the applicant Government that the "TRNC" authorities have interfered as such with the right of the Greek–Cypriot population to manifest their religion either alone or in the company of others. Indeed there is no evidence of such interference. However, the restrictions placed on the freedom of movement of that population during the period under consideration considerably curtailed their ability to observe their religious beliefs, in particular their access to places of worship outside their villages and their participation in other aspects of religious life.

However, there is a second, countervailing trend, which denies the legitimacy of any act which runs counter to what might be called the 'higher' norms of the Convention system: thus in *Refah Partisi* v. *Turkey* a Chamber of the Court was unwilling to categorize conduct, which it considered failed to respect human rights and the rule of law, as legitimate manifestations of religious belief.[33] This is a case to which we shall return but for the moment it might be concluded that the Court is now willing to take a broad and purposeful approach towards established forms of manifestations, but is also inclined to take a close look at more novel forms of manifestation that are brought before it. This then mirrors its practice regarding the question of whether a form of belief is to attract the freedom of manifestation under the Convention system. There are, however, limits to its willingness to legitimize certain forms of religiously motivated activities as forms of manifestation protected by the Convention system.

Legitimate Restrictions

Even if an activity considered to be a 'manifestation' of a 'qualifying' religion or belief is at issue, its exercise might be restricted on the grounds that this is 'necessary' to protect a range of other 'goods', including the rights and freedoms of others. Practice under the *European Convention on Human Rights* has now yielded a number of examples of how these balances may be struck.[34] What needs to be stressed at the outset is that the first cases in which the

32. *Cyprus* v. *Turkey*, Judgement of 10 May 2001, nyr para. 245. See also 22 *HRLJ* 217.

33. *Refah Partisi (The Welfare Party) and others* v. *Turkey*, Judgment of 31 July 2001, 35 *EHRR* 5 para. 52. At the time of writing, the judgment in this case was being considered by a Grand Chamber of the Court, following hearings held on 19 June 2002.

34. See, for example, M.D. Evans, *supra* note 10 pp. 315-34; C. Evans, *supra* note 10 pp. 133-167; J. Gunn 'Adjudicating rights of Conscience under the European Convention on Human Rights' in J.D. Van der Vyver and J. Witte, Jr., *Religious Human Rights in Global Perspective: Legal Perspective* p. 305 (The Hague: Martinus Nijhoff, 1996).

European Court of Human Rights considered the application of Article 9 concerned the manner in which States responded to a 'clash of rights' between adherents of various forms of religion, or of no religion at all, rather than what might be considered as the 'classic' form of alleged violation, concerning the legitimacy of the State's own intrusions upon the freedom of religion of an individual. This had a significant impact on the manner in which these cases were handled. Rather than looking at the legitimacy of the States' *actions*, the focus is on the reasonableness of the States' *reactions* to situations which are seen as being 'not of its making'.[35] Such an approach finds a ready reflection in the language of toleration and provides a very different setting for the outworking and development of the freedom to manifest religion and belief.

The key statement which routinely underpins the approach of the Court was set out in the 1993 *Kokkinakis* case, the first to be decided by the Court on the basis of Article 9. It says that:[36]

> As enshrined in Article 9, freedom of thought, conscience and religion is one of the foundations of a 'democratic society' within the meaning of the convention. It is in its religious dimension, one of the most vital elements that go to make up the identity of believers and their conception of life, but it is also a precious asset for atheists, agnostics, sceptics and the unconcerned. The pluralism indissociable from a democratic society, which has been dearly won over the centuries, depends on it.

The role of the Court is to balance the enjoyment of these rights within this framework[37] and the underlying principle is that of *respect*, according to which believers are to enjoy the respect of those who hold to other forms of religious belief, or of no religious belief at all. This principle is to be taken into account when assessing the necessity of any interference with the manifestation of a protected form of religion or belief. At the same time, there is a reciprocal obligation upon believers to show respect for the beliefs of others, believers and non-believers alike. In short, the claim that an activity is a bona fide manifestation of religion or belief is not a 'trump' card: it is merely a factor to be taken into account when balancing up conflicting interests. Both

35. But *cf.* note 37.
36. *Kokkinakis* v. *Greece*, Judgment of 25 May 1993, Ser. A, No. 260-A; 17 *EHRR* 397 para. 31.
37. This entire conceptualization is, of course, rather disingenuous, since it is the legal framework, which is very much of the State's making, which generates the capacity for the State to intervene in the first place. Thus in the *Kokkinakis* case, for example, the Court saw its task as determining the legitimacy of the applicants' conviction under a Greek domestic law which criminalized improper proselytism. It chose not to see its task as determining the legitimacy of the law under which the applicant was convicted. Some members of the Court would have rather approached the case on that alternative basis, and had it done so the reasoning and the statements of principle that it sets out would have been very different, even if the result would probably have been the same.

the genesis and application of this idea can be identified in the following sets of circumstances.

Protecting the sensibilities of believers

First, there may be a conflict with the exercise of another Convention right, such as the freedom of expression provided for in Article 10 of the Convention. In the case of *Wingrove* v. *UK* the Court observed that the exercise of the freedom of expression carries with it duties and responsibilities amongst which, 'in the context of religious beliefs, may legitimately be included a duty to avoid *as far as possible* an expression that is, in regard to objects of veneration, gratuitously offensive to others and profanatory'.[38] This follows the earlier case of *Otto-Preminger-Institut* v. *Austria*, in which the Court upheld the right of the State to prevent an applicant from expressing views which were unpalatable to others on the grounds that 'the respect for religious feelings of believers as guaranteed by Article 9 can legitimately be thought to have been violated by provocative portrayals of objects of religious veneration: and such portrayals can be regarded as a malicious violation of the spirit of tolerance, which must also be a feature of democratic society'.[39] This idea has most recently been endorsed by the Court in the case of *Refah Partisi* v. *Turkey* when it said that 'where the offending conduct reaches a high level of insult and comes close to a negation of the freedom of religion of others it loses the right to society's tolerance'.[40] Thus it would appear that the State is justified in encroaching upon an applicant's freedom of expression when the form that such expression takes demonstrates a lack of toleration and respect for the religious views of others.

Protection from the views of believers

Does the same hold true under Article 9 itself? That is to say, if religious believers demonstrate a lack of tolerance or respect for the religious belief (or lack of religious beliefs) of others when exercising their own freedom to manifest their religious beliefs under Article 9, does the balancing act still

38. *Wingrove* v. *United Kingdom*, Judgment of 25 November 1996, *RJD* 1996-V p. 1937; 24 *EHRR* 1 para. 52, (emphasis added).

39. *Otto-Preminger-Institut* v. *Austria*, Judgment of 20 September 1994, ECHR, Ser. A, No. 295-A, 17 *EHRR* 397 para. 47.

40. *Refah Partisi (The Welfare Party) and others* v. *Turkey*, Judgment of 31 July 2001, 35 EHRR 5 para. 75.

work out in a similar fashion and justify the State restricting their ability to do so? The decisions of the Court in *Kokkinakis* v. *Greece* and *Larrisis* v. *Greece* both suggest that it does. Both cases concerned the arrest and conviction of Jehovah's Witnesses for improper proselytism (a criminal offence in Greece). The essence of these cases lay in balancing the right of the applicants to practice their religion by seeking to bring others to share in their beliefs, as their faith required them to do, as opposed to the right[41] of the State to intervene to protect others from unwanted exposure to their points of view. The role that the Court ascribes to the state is that of 'policing'—in the case of Greece, literally—the relationship between the what might inelegantly be called the proselytiser and the proselytised, 'in order to reconcile the interests of the various groups and to ensure that everyone's beliefs are respected'.[42] In *Larissis v. Greece* the applicants were officers in the Greek Air force and members of the Pentecostal church who had been convicted of various offences connected with their proselytism of junior airmen and a number of civilians. The Court decided that there had been no violation of Article 9 regarding their conviction for proselytising the airmen since 'the Greek authorities were in principal justified in taking some measures to protect the lower ranking airmen from improper pressure'.[43] As regards the civilians, however, the Court thought the convictions did breach Article 9, since 'the civilians whom the applicants attempted to convert were not subject to the pressure and constraints of the same kind as the airmen'.[44] As in the *Kokkinakis* case, the vital factor is the Court's assessment of the ability of the would be 'proselytised' to stand up to 'proselytiser'. The underlying principle appears to be that of ensuring respect for the beliefs of others, and this is given effect by ensuring that those

41. These problems are rendered even more problematic by a string of decisions in which the Commission on Human Rights seemed to suggest that Article 9 placed positive obligations upon the State *requiring* it to take action to prevent violations occurring. See *Stedman* v. *UK*, App. No. 29107/95, Comm. Dec. 1997, 89-A *DR* 104; *Dubowska and Skup* v. *Poland*, App. Nos. 33490/96 and 34055/96, Comm. Dec. 1997, 89-A *DR* 156 para. 2; *Scientology Kirche Deutschland* v. *Germany*, Comm. Dec. 1997, 89-A *DR* 163. The Court, however, seems less inclined than was the Commission prior to its disbandment in November 1999 to develop thinking concerning positive obligations under Article 9. As will be seen in the section of this chapter entitled *The State and the Religious Collective: Trends and Tensions*, the focus of the drift towards positive obligations now lies in the need to secure a culture of tolerance and pluralism, which is a quite different thing.

42. *Kokkinakis* v. *Greece*, Judgment of 25 May 1993, ECHR, Ser. A, No. 260-A, 17 *EHRR* 397 para. 33.

43. *Larissis and Others* v. *Greece*, Judgment of 24 February 1998, *RJD* 1998-I p. 362; 23 *EHRR* 329 para. 54. The Court also noted that 'the measures taken were not particularly severe and were more preventive than punitive in nature'.

44. *Ibid*. para. 59, where it was also noted that 'none of the evidence indicates that they [the civilians] felt obliged to listen to the applicant or that his behaviour towards then was improper in any way'.

who enjoy 'superiority'[45] over others, educationally or socially, are not unduly advantaged.

The State and the Religious Collective: Trends and Tensions

This 'classical' model and form of approach appears to have been quite adequate to deal with the issues facing the Commission and Court of Human Rights until quite recently. However, it is clear that it works best in situations where an individual is challenging the manner in which the state has acted in a particular case but it is also evident that, through the emergence of the principle of *respect*,[46] it can also provide an adequate conceptual framework for evaluating the response of the state to conflicts of rights between individuals, or groups of individuals. In the recent past, however, the Court has been called on to deal with questions of an entirely different order; questions concerning the compatibility of entire legal regimes regulating religious affairs within a state. The attempt to apply an essentially individual rights-oriented framework to questions concerning the rights of religious groups has revealed an entirely new dimension to the debate concerning the relationship between church and state within the European theatre. This is reflected in the blurring or abandoning of the 'internal'/'external' approach and replacing it with a much more 'holistic' approach that places the overall scheme of relationship between the state and groups of believers at its centre. In short, a more group-oriented approach is beginning to emerge, and with it another—perhaps an alternative—underlying principle, that of achieving 'tolerance and religious plural-

45. *Cf.* N. Lerner, *supra* note 5 pp. 110-116, who describes these as 'captive audience' cases. Whilst this may indeed explain the differences between the two situations in *Larissis* it is not obvious that the mere fact of being a 'captive' in the sense of being under some *de facto* compulsion to hear the 'message' would in itself be sufficient to justify a criminal prosecution. Some other elements would seem to be needed. For example, an itinerant preacher on a crowded train might have a 'captive' audience between stations but this does not necessarily mean that there is a relationship of 'superiority' for the purposes of the Court. What would seem to be needed is a nexus or relationship that places one party in a position in which they are unable, or feel themselves unable, to exercise an appropriate degree of thought or reflection before expressing adherence to the belief placed before them; or that their decision to express such adherence flows not from an assessment or response to the belief itself but from a perception that it would be prudent to agree, or to be seen to be agreeing, with the person who presented those beliefs to them.

46. See the section of this chapter entitled *Legitimate Restrictions* for a discussion and definition of this principle of 'respect'.

ism'. This is certainly reflected in the Baciu Report which, as has been seen, points to the tension between protecting the rights of the individual whilst at the same time recognizing the legitimacy of preserving the religious identities of communities and societies.[47]

At first sight, this may seem to be merely a reworking of the principle of 'respect' and, indeed, the very phrase 'tolerance and religious pluralism' comes from the standard recital in the *Kokinnakis* case which, as seen above, had given birth to the principle of respect. To that extent, it might be argued that this is a unifying principle uniting these strands of jurisprudence. It flows from this that the state *may* intervene to ensure that fundamental freedoms of others—including followers of other religions—are protected and respected. There is also the question of whether it *must* intervene in such circumstances. It should be noted that there is an issue concerning whether there is a positive obligation upon the state to ensure that these basic principles of respect and tolerance within a pluralist society are brought about, or whether it is only in those cases where the state does intervene that it is to act in accordance with these principles. It would certainly be consonant with current trends were such a positive obligation to be the case.[48] Those trends will be outlined in the following sections, but the essence of the Court's approach is that there is to be a 'market place' in religious belief, and the individuals are to be able to exercise 'choice' between competing views. The analogy with a vibrant democratic society is instructive: just as there must be a 'market place' in ideas within the political sphere, so must there be within the religious.[49] But there also must be rules, and the chief rule is that any activity which is incompatible with the existence of that 'market place' of ideas, or with the 'democratic society' that it is intended to support and sustain, will fall outside of the protection of the Convention system. As the Baciu Report puts it, 'the need to guarantee religious rights and freedoms ...[brings countries] ... face to face

47. Baciu Report, *supra* note 7. Indeed, the Report itself exhibits the same tensions. It argues that the individuals' freedom of religion includes the 'freedom to maintain one's religious identity' and suggests that if properly protected this will itself be sufficient to preserve religious traditions and practices 'as one aspect of their person identity' (para. 37). To that extent the tension appears to be resolved in favour of the individual and so 'traditional' religions 'may not be protected by restricting the freedoms of individuals' (para. 37). However, the Report subsequently argues that 'Guaranteeing religious freedoms also means protecting the existence and structures of religious communities' (para. 72).

48. See, for example: S. van Bijsterveld, 'Religion, International Law and Policy in the Wider Arena: New Dimensions and Developments' in R. Adhar (ed.), *Law and Religion* p. 163 and p. 168 (Aldershot: Ashgate, 2000).

49. *Cf.* Baciu Report, note 7 para. 31, which notes—with a voice of concern—'the traditional churches' rejection of cultural and religious pluralism, and the whole idea of a 'free market' in beliefs'.

with the highly delicate problem of deciding just how far religious freedom should be allowed to go in a democratic society'.[50]

The state as guarantor of respect and tolerance within the '*Forum Internum*'[51] of the religious organization

It has long been understood that the state does not involve itself in the internal procedures and processes of religious bodies at the request of members who claim that their freedom of religion or belief is not being respected by the body of which they form a part. Such matters of 'internal' order, doctrine, practice and discipline within a religious community are traditionally seen as matters for that community itself, unless some other Convention right is at issue for which the state can be held responsible.[52] This was emphasised in *Manoussakis* v. *Greece* when the Court said that 'The right to freedom of religion as guaranteed under the Convention excludes any discretion on the part of the state to determine whether religious beliefs or the means used to express such beliefs are legitimate'.[53]

Thus the state—and the European Court—is to distance itself from internal disputes between members of religious organizations,[54] and this is further buttressed by Article 11 of the *ECHR* which safeguards associative life against unjustified state interference. In consequence, the Court has said that 'the believer's right to freedom of religion encompasses the expectation that the community will be allowed to function peacefully free from arbitrary state intervention'.[55] Thus in two cases in which the state authorities sought to

---

50. *Ibid*. para. 73. For trenchant views of this nature from within the Council of Europe see, for example, Puig, *supra* note 9.

51. Although the language of the 'internal/external' division has been lost from the jurisprudence regarding religious groups, it should not be forgotten. Indeed, it remains perfectly apposite to call on this terminology to help differentiate the cases which have recently been considered by the court and doing so helps clarify that jurisprudence and also helps identify the dangers that need to be identified.

52. See, for example, applications such as *Knudson* v. *Norway*, App. No. 11045/84, Comm. Dec. 1983, 42 *DR* 247; *Stedman* v. *UK*, App. No. 29107/95, Comm. Dec. 1997, 89-A *DR* 104.

53. *Manoussakis* v. *Greece*, Judgment of 26 September 1996, *RJD* 1996-IV p. 1376; 23 *EHRR* 387 para. 47.

54. A point made clear in the Baciu Report, *supra* note 7, which observes that '... questions of church government and canon law lie outside the council of Europe's province' and that any strategy to deal with tensions that result from conflicts of such nature must 'exclude all possibility of governmental interference in questions of dogma, church organization and canon law' (para. 54), a point reflected in *Recommendation 1556*, *supra* note 6 para. 5.

55. *Hasan and Chaush* v. *Bulgaria*, Judgment of 26 October 2000, *34 EHRR* 55 para. 62.

resolve internal disputes concerning the leadership of Muslim religious communities, the Court concluded that there had been a violation of the freedom to manifest religion that was not legitimated by the Convention. The case of *Hasan and Chaush* concerned the alleged forced replacement of the leadership of the Muslim community in Bulgaria. The Court took the view that the forced removal of the applicants from their positions as leaders of a religious community constituted an interference with the freedom of religion and, because of the arbitrary nature of the grounds for intervention, this action was not prescribed by law for the purposes of Article 9(2).[56] The second case, *Serif* v. *Greece*, arose out of a dispute between the Muslim community in eastern Thrace and the Greek Government concerning the procedures for appointment of the Chief Mufti of Rodopi, culminating in the criminal conviction of the applicant for 'impersonating a minister of a known religion'. The Court found this to have been in violation of Article 9 since there had been no 'pressing social need', the Court noting that 'punishing a person for the mere fact that he acted as the religious leader of a group that willingly followed him can hardly be considered compatible with the demands of religious pluralism in a democratic society'.[57]

However, the Court has also stressed that internal tension and/or dissent within a religious community, as in any other form of community, 'is one of the unavoidable consequences of pluralism. The role of the authorities in such circumstances is not to remove the causes of tension by eliminating pluralism, but to ensure that the competing groups tolerate each other'.[58] This suggests that although the state is not entitled to 'sort out' the problem, it is entitled to exercise some form of oversight of the internal workings of religious organizations in the interests of ensuring pluralism and tolerance.

56. *Ibid*. paras. 84-88.

57. *Serif* v. *Greece*, Judgement of 14 December 1999, 31 *EHRR* 561 para. 51. It should, however, be noted that the Court stressed the significance of the applicant's not having been alleged to have performed any of the public law functions which were within the jurisdiction competence of the Chief Mufti. Had this been an element of the charge, the Court implies, such a need might well have been present. Strictly speaking, *Serif* concerns the protection of an individual from State action, rather than the right of the community. However, it is better understood from the 'collective' right perspective—the right of the community to choose its leader—than of the individual—the right to be chosen as leader of the religious community.

58. *Ibid*. para. 53.

The State, Religious Organizations and the '*Forum Externum*'

Beyond the role of the state with regard to the internal affairs of religious collectives, lies the role of the state with regard to the functioning of the religious collective within that state as a whole. This concerns the 'manifestation' of religion or belief and draws on the language and conceptual apparatus considered in the previous section concerning the rights of the individual. When transposed to the sphere of collective or group concerns, however, the results of its application appear to be rather different. At least two distinct approaches can be identified in the most recent caselaw of the Court.

The State as the facilitator of organizational religious freedom

The first potential approach is to see the state as charged with the task of facilitating the organization of the religious community, so as to enable it to be able to function within the broader legal and political community *for* which it, the state, is responsible; *to* which it, the state, is responsible; and *of* which they, the members of that religious community, form a part. Since the states' governance of this broader community is itself rights-bound, it follows that the contours of state action in facilitating participation will themselves be constrained by the overarching rights framework. However, this will only apply constraints at the outer limits of compatibility with the Convention framework as outlined in the previous section. Its practical application will not differ greatly from that of pursuing 'respect' between groups of believers and non-believers. It looks to the aims and interests of each religious community on a 'case by case' basis in order to identify their particular needs and is not interested in questions of relative status or equal enjoyment of rights within the legal and political community. It is enough if believers are able to function as a religious community within the state in a fashion that accords to them, as believers, the rights which flow from Article 9 and subject only to the limitations that are legitimate within that framework. 'Pluralism and tolerance' are realized by the state through providing a regulatory framework which facilitates the enjoyment of the freedom of religion and belief within the broader constructs of the domestic legal system, whilst retreating from the sphere of regulatory involvement and activity to the maximum degree compatible with protection of the rights and freedoms of others.

Such an approach is illustrated by the stream of thought that has emerged from the caselaw, according to which it is inherent in the notion of 'practice' of religion that religious believers must be entitled to have access to the requisite degree of legal personality to make the enjoyment of this freedom possible—by enabling them to acquire premises and objects for worship, for example.[59] The precise form that this will take will depend upon the legal framework in the country concerned, but it seems clear that the general provisions concerning the freedom of association under Article 11 are as applicable to religious organizations as to any other, and all religions are to be treated on a non-discriminatory basis.[60] It is certainly not the role of the state to place barriers upon this, unless it is in accord with the Convention framework regarding legitimate restrictions.[61]

Such an approach also seems to underpin the view that the existence of a state church is not incompatible with the Convention system.[62] Although the Court has been clear that it is neither the role of the state nor the role of the Court to privilege one religion at the expense of another, the key issue is whether the privileging of one religious community in this fashion has negative consequences for the enjoyment of the freedom of religion or belief by adherents of other beliefs or traditions. There is no need for a rigid separation of church and state provided that the state also facilitates participation of other belief communities within the broader legal and political community in a fashion which enables them to enjoy the freedom of religion.[63]

---

59. These propositions would seem to flow from *Manoussakis* v. *Greece*, Judgment of 26 September 1996, *RJD* 1996-IV p. 1376, 23 *EHRR* 387; *Canea Catholic Church* v. *Greece*, Judgment of 16 December 1997, *RJD* 1997-VIII p. 2843, 27 *EHRR* 521; and *Sidiropolous* v. *Greece*, Judgment 10 July 1998, *RJD* 1998-IV p. 1594, 27 *EHRR* 633.
60. *Hasan and Chaush* v. *Bulgaria*, Judgment of 26 October 2000, 24 *EHRR* 55 para. 62; *Metropolitan Church of Bessarabia* v. *Moldova*, Judgment of 13 December 2001, nyr para. 118. See also *United Communist Party of Turkey* v. *Turkey*, Judgment of 30 January 1998, *RJD* 1998-I p. 1, 26 *EHRR* 121 but *cf.* now *Refah Partisi (The Welfare Party) and others* v. *Turkey*, Judgment of 31 July 2001, 35 *EHRR* 5 which seems to trace the outer limits of this approach. See also J. Martinez-Torron, *supra* note 10 p. 197 and the discussions of that case in the following section.
61. *Cf. Parliamentary Assembly Recommendation 1556* para. 8 (ii) (2002) which recommends that the Committee of Ministers of the Council of Europe call on member States of the Council, and the EU, 'to guarantee all churches, religious associations, centres and communities the status of legal entities, if their activities does not violate human rights or international law'. The concluding caveat is open to objection, since it tends to confuse legitimate restrictions upon the activities of religious communities with the legal recognition of groups—a vice that is rife in domestic legislation in many parts of Europe.
62. A view which was endorsed in the Baciu Report, *supra* note 7 para. 71, which reflects the view that church–State relations 'can take various forms in a democracy' (separation of church and State, established churches, recognised churches, co-operation, agreement, etc.).
63. Article 14 of the *ECHR* prohibits discrimination in the enjoyment of a convention right on grounds of religion, rather than prohibiting discrimination between religions per se. However, it may be that the expanding notion of the ambit of a convention right is reducing the space for this form of reasoning, and with it the plausibility of this approach to established churches. It is certainly the practical logic of non-discriminatory provisions to require more interventionist and regulatory approaches than that outlined in this section.

The State and the Promotion of Pluralism

This, then, leads to the most recent pronouncements of the Court on the role of the state in relation to religious organizations. These seem to place a degree of obligation upon the state to ensure a culture of tolerance and pluralism. In *Cha'are Shalom* v. *France* the Grand Chamber of the Court would have justified an interference with a manifestation of religion on the basis of the protection of public health and public order, 'in so far as organization by the State of the exercise of worship is conducive to religious harmony and tolerance'.[64] The seven dissenting judges took a more interventionist approach, referring to the role of the public authorities as being 'not to remove the cause of tension by eliminating pluralism but to take all necessary measures to ensure that competing groups tolerate each other'.[65] The Court went further in *Refah Partisi* v. *Turkey* by referring to the State's role as 'the guarantor of individual rights and freedoms and the impartial organizer of the practice of the various beliefs and religions in a democratic society'.[66]

The practical implications of conceptualizing the role of the state in this manner are significant. For example, bearing in mind that the Court has also accepted that the 'organizational life of the religious community' is to be safeguarded under the terms of Article 9, it becomes apparent that laws regarding the legal status of religious organizations are now considered to be quite appropriate, and, indeed, necessary.[67] Whereas the case for such laws was previously thought to be that they were necessary to facilitate the manifestation of

64. *Cha'are Shalom* v. *France*, Judgment of 27 June 2000, nyr para. 84. The case concerned the refusal of the French authorities to grant an association of Jewish butchers access to slaughterhouses to enable them to conduct the ritual slaughter of animals in accordance with their ultra-orthodox views. The Court considered it sufficient that they were able to obtain supplies of meat slaughtered in accordance with their dietary requirements from elsewhere (in this case, Belgium). See para. 81.

65. Quite how this is to be achieved generally is perplexing, but it is interesting that the minority of the judges expressed their disagreement with the actual decision—which upheld the French authorities' actions—for 'its failure to secure religious pluralism...'. However, what the dissent sees as pluralism is really a question of non-discrimination and it is therefore appropriate that the dissent resolved itself into the proposition that there had been a violation of Article 9 in conjunction with Article 14 of the Convention.

66. *Refah Partisi (The Welfare Party) and others* v. *Turkey*, Judgment of 31 July 2001, 35 *EHRR* 5 para. 70: see also para. 52 where there is a reference to its role as a 'neutral and impartial organizer'. See also *Metropolitan Church of Bessarabia* v. *Moldova*, Judgment of 13 December 2001, nyr paras. 115, 118 and 123.

67. *Hasan and Chaush* v. *Bulgaria*, Judgment of 26 October 2000, 34 *EHRR* 55 para. 77: this remains so despite the manner in which the question was left open in that case, which was thought to cast doubt on the legitimacy of such laws. The state as guarantor of respect and tolerance within the *'Forum Internum'* of the religious organization.

religious freedom by the groups concerned,[68] recent judgments also point to the prospect of registration laws being used to restrict freedom of religion in a fashion that is considered to be compatible with Convention rights. This was always implicit in cases such as *Serif* v. *Greece* but is most clearly illustrated in the case of the *Metropolitan Church of Bessarabia* v. *Moldova*. The applicant church was of the Orthodox rite but looked to the Romanian rather than the Russian Patriarchate. The Moldovan authorities refused to register the church, though registration was subsequently given to the Moldovan Orthodox Church. Subsequent requests for registration were also denied, it being argued that it was not for the state to offer its support through recognition to a group that was attempting to 'break away' from a recognized church. The Court rejected this argument, taking the view that the refusal to register the applicant church did amount to an interference with the freedom of religion, and a refusal on these grounds revealed a lack of neutrality and impartiality.[69] The Court did, however, consider questions concerning the threat to the territorial integrity of the state that were said to be implicit in the claim to recognition and took the view that if a church did foster secessionist tendencies then it could in principle be appropriate to refuse recognition.[70]

Unsurprisingly, it was also prepared to accept that the refusal was capable of justification on the grounds of the protection of public order and safety but concluded that the consequences for the applicants on the facts of the case—the inability to practice their religion within an established legal framework, the alleged 'tolerance' of the state notwithstanding—were not proportionate to the 'legitimate aim' pursued.[71] What is significant about the case is that it makes it clear that erecting a legal framework within which a state can make such determinations appears to be well within the scope of Article 9, even if the manner in which such a framework is applied remains subject to scrutiny from a Convention perspective.

The question then becomes one of assessing the legitimacy of state intervention. The *Bessarabian Church* case shows that, in principle, territorial integrity can be a legitimate ground for restricting the freedom of religion. Preserving the integrity of internal democratic structures is clearly another. The contours of this limitation can be traced through the jurisprudence of the Court concerning Article 11 of the Convention concerning the freedom of association. In a series of cases the Court had rejected the claims of Turkey that

68. See the discussion earlier in this chapter under the heading 'The state as guarantor of respect and tolerance within the '*Forum Internum*' of the religious organization'.

69. *Metropolitan Church of Bessarabia* v. *Moldova*, Judgment of 13 December 2001, nyr para. 123.

70. *Ibid*. para. 125. On the facts, such tendencies were, however, unproven.

71. *Ibid*. paras. 129-130.

it was justified in banning a number of political parties because their policies were allegedly antithetical to the political construction of the Turkish state. The Court's general approach is well reflected by the following statement (emphasis added):[72]

> The fact that such a political project is considered incompatible with the current principles and structures of the Turkish state does not mean that it infringes democratic rules. It is of the essence of democracy to allow diverse political projects to be proposed and debated, even those that call into question the way in which a State is currently organized, *provided that they do not harm democracy itself*

The highlighted phrase is the key: it is only those who do not respect the underlying values of human rights, rule of law and democracy which are beyond the reach of the Convention's protections, and the only limit to the legitimacy of democracy is the refusal to recognize democratic abandonment of democracy itself. Thus, in the controversial judgment in *Refah Partisi (The Welfare Party)* v. *Turkey*, the Court says that 'there can be no democracy where the people of a State, even by a majority decision, waive their legislative and judicial powers in favour of an entity which is not responsible to the people it governs, whether it is secular or religious'.[73]

Does this present a problem for religious organizations and for their regulation by the state? It appears that it might. To the extent that the role of the state is to promote religious tolerance and pluralism, it is possible that the Court would consider a single confessional state to be at the very least suspect. Even if this were not the case, the nature of the argument underpinning the *Refah Partisi* case is disquieting. In the 1995 General Election the Welfare Party had secured 22% of the popular vote, making it the most popular political party in Turkey, and in local elections the following year attracted around 35% of the vote. In 1996 it became a partner in the ruling coalition government. An application to the Constitutional Court in May 1997, however, resulted in the dissolution of the party by Court order in 1998, primarily on the grounds that prominent members of the party had called for the introduction of Sharia law, and that was incompatible with the principles of secularism which undergirded Turkish democracy. The Court in Strasbourg agreed, arguing that 'a State may reasonably forestall the execution of such a policy, which is incompatible with the Convention's provisions, before an attempt is made to

72. *Socialist Party* v. *Turkey*, Judgment of 25 May 1998, *RJD* 1998-III p. 1233 para. 47; 27 *EHRR* 51; *Freedom and Democracy Party (OZDEP)* v. *Turkey* [GC], Judgment of 8 December 1999, *RJD* 1999-VIII p. 293; 31 *EHRR* 27 para. 41. See also *United Communist Party of Turkey* v. *Turkey*, Judgment of 30 January 1998, *RJD* 1998-I p. 1; 26 *EHRR* 121.

73. Refah Partisi (The Welfare Party) and others v. Turkey, Judgment of 31 July 2001, 35 EHRR 5 para. 43.

implement it through concrete steps that might prejudice civil peace and the country's democratic regime'.[74] This builds in the Court's earlier statement that, along with the Turkish Constitutional Court, it considered that

> sharia, which faithfully reflects the dogmas and divine rules laid down by religion, is stable and invariable. Principles such as pluralism in the political sphere or the constant evolution of public freedoms have no place in it.... introduction of Sharia [is] difficult to reconcile with the fundamental principles of democracy... it is difficult to declare one's respect for democracy and human rights while at the same time supporting a regime based on sharia, which clearly diverges from Convention values, particularly with regard to its criminal law and criminal procedures, its rules on the legal status of women and the way it intervenes in all spheres of private and public life in accordance with religious precepts....In the Courts view, a political party whose actions seem to be aimed at introducing Sharia in a State party to the Convention can hardly be regarded as an association complying with the democratic ideal that underlies the whole of the Convention[75]

Setting aside for the moment the rather embarrassing caricature of Islamic legal reasoning, it is difficult to see how this approach is compatible with the idea that the Convention organs are to remain neutral in the face of competing dogmas. The Court seems to believe that secularism is in line with human rights ideology but that Islam (or, at least, Islamic law) is not. Whilst it is for individuals—or, indeed, communities—to decide whether they wish to believe in and act upon principles incompatible with human rights thinking in the private sphere, they are not to enjoy such latitude in the public sphere, since the 'stable and invariable' nature of Islamic legal thinking is incompatible with the vibrant exchange of views with are the hallmark of a democratic society. One might pause to ask whether Christianity and Christian values—or indeed, any form of religious belief which is based upon revealed scripture—is not equally open to such charges. But the more general point is that if religious communities[76] are to be welcomed as participants in the public life of the State, it is on the condition that they respect the principles of democracy

74. *Ibid*. para. 81.

75. *Ibid*. para. 72.

76. It should be noted that this approach is not limited to religious communities and organizations. In *Gorzelik* v. *Poland*, Judgment of 20 December 2001, nyr, the Court upheld the refusal of the Polish authorities to register a cultural association which it suspected of attempting to gain credence for the existence of a Silesian 'national minority' which might then be in a position to profit from the Polish electoral laws: the Court observed that 'pluralism and democracy are, by the nature of things, based on a compromise that requires various concessions by individuals and groups of individuals. The latter must sometimes be prepared to limit some of their freedoms so as to ensure the greater stability of the country as a whole' (para. 66).

and human rights; of tolerance and pluralism.[77] And if they threaten either, then the State may take steps—indeed, might be obliged to take steps—to ensure that those values are protected: what the Baciu Report rather indelicately refers to as 'the highly delicate problem of deciding just how far religious freedom should be allowed to go in a democratic society'.[78]

Conclusion

Drawing these ideas together, the result is as follows: instead of the thrust of recent caselaw from the European Court of Human Rights concerning the freedom of religion under Article 9 being primarily focussed on the idea that the individual believer is to be protected in the enjoyment of his or her religious beliefs and their manifestation, it has been primarily concerned with the legitimacy of the manner in which the State involves itself in the organization of the life of religious communities. It is a task that is now required of it to ensure that tolerance and pluralism are maintained—both as between groups of believers and as between believers and non-believers. In short, there is both legitimacy in, and arguably a need for, the State to engage with the organization of religion at both levels.

It may well be that the manner in which the State carries out its interventionist functions are ultimately considered inappropriate from a Convention standpoint, but the legitimacy of that task cannot itself be disputed within this approach. Thus, although the actual results of the most recent cases seem to be 'victories' for religious bodies which are seeking redress for illegitimate interventions by the State[79] or for non-recognition by the State,[80] they do in fact underline the extent to which the State may involve itself in these matters in the interests of securing public order or the rights and freedoms of others.

77. It is worth noting that the Baciu Report, *supra* note 7 para. 29 draws the important distinction between diversity and pluralism, defining the latter as meaning 'not simply that numerous beliefs are held in a given area, but also that those beliefs are recognized in law and by the community as valid expressions of the religions life… , and that friendly—or at least peaceful—relations exist between churches and between people with different beliefs'.

78. Baciu Report, *supra* note 7 para. 73. Although it does not spell it out, the final logic of the Report is that it should sidestep the issue altogether, since 'guaranteeing religious freedoms is more a matter of respecting human rights and effecting democratic reforms' than of adopting a given pattern for the inter-relationship of religious communities and the State (para. 70). For the formulaically minded, one might conclude that FR = HR+D.

79. *Serif* v. *Greece*, Judgment of 14 December 1999, 31 *EHRR* 561; *Hasan and Chaush* v. *Bulgaria*, Judgment of 26 October 2000, 34 *EHRR* 55.

80. *Metropolitan Church of Bessarabia* v. *Moldova*, Judgment of 13 December 2001, nyr.

The issue seems to involve pitching 'respect' against 'pluralism'. In short, 'respect' coupled with tolerance suggests that the State 'stays out' of the business of the organization to the maximum extent possible, whereas 'pluralism' coupled with tolerance seems to open up the pathway to a more interventionist approach. In what has been termed the *'forum internum'* of religious collectives, the case for the 'respect' and 'tolerance' approach seems to be accepted by the Court and reflected in the cases considered above—*Serif* and *Hasan and Chaush* both appear to be cases in which the court took the view that the role of the State was to be guided by 'respect'. This would seem entirely appropriate.

However, it appears that very different approaches vie with each other as regards what might be called, for shorthand, the *'forum externum'* of the organization; the manner in which the organization relates to the broader legal and political community as a whole. The older and more established approach is to restrict the role of the State to that of facilitating participation in accordance with the requirements of Article 9 itself. From the perspective of the religious collectives themselves, this is a relatively benign approach (and, indeed, probably as much as could legitimately be offered to them within the constraints of the human rights framework). This must now be contrasted with the approach taken by the Council of Europe Parliamentary Assembly and the Court in the *Refah Partisi* and *Bessarabian Church of Moldova* cases which are far more interventionist and regulatory in nature and, I would argue, raises serious questions concerning the trajectory which the quest for religious freedom within contemporary Europe appears to be taking. What is absolutely clear is that these more variegated approaches outlined in the latter sections of this chapter and which relate to the situation of religious *groups* need not, nor should be, projected back into the caselaw concerning the protection offered to *individuals* by Article 9. Even when protected by the same forms of words, individual rights and collective rights are conceptually very different things, and should be treated as such.

Chapter 7

Religious Discrimination in Britain: new opportunities and fresh challenges within employment

Peter Cumper[1]

Lecturer in Law, University of Leicester

These are testing times for mainstream religious organisations in Britain. With many facing a range of problems such as falling numbers,[2] low clergy morale,[3] allegations of sexual abuse,[4] and serious financial difficulties,[5] even

---

1. Peter Cumper is a Lecturer in Law at the University of Leicester. He has also lectured at the University of Hull and at Nottingham Law School. He is the joint editor of *Minority Rights in the 'new' Europe* (Kluwer, 1999). His research interests lie in the area of human rights and constitutional law.
2. R. Becker, 'Spiritual care on the rocks', *The European Journal of Palliative Care*, Vol. 8, No.4, (2001).
3. S.H. de Vogel, 'Clergy Morale: the ups and downs', *Christian Century*, 1149, 17 December 1986.
4. S. Bates, 'Faithful shamed by scandals as church appears slow to act', *The Guardian*, 6 December 2000.
5. 'Sexual abuse hits church finances', *BBC News On Line*, 11 April 2002.

the Archbishop of Canterbury has spoken of the western church 'bleeding to death'.[6] Yet rumours of the church's death are, as Mark Twain might have put it, greatly exaggerated. In spite of the challenges facing many religious organisations at the start of the 21st century, it is important not to overlook the significance of religion and belief in the lives of many citizens.[7] Far from the popular stereo-type of spiritual devotion being restricted to the occasional act of worship, religion for many people continues to embrace every aspect of life.[8] In particular, for members of Britain's ethnic minority communities, religion is often an important part of their very identity.[9] Notwithstanding the growth of secularism in contemporary Europe, the European Court of Human Rights has accepted that, for a significant number of people, religion remains 'one of the most vital elements that go to make up the identity ... and ... conception of life'.[10] Accordingly, considerations such as these appear to explain why, at a time when the Churches' influence on society appears to be at an all time low, unprecedented measures have recently been proposed to protect individuals from discrimination on the grounds of religion or belief.

The most significant of these measures is Council Directive 2000/78/EC. Passed on 27th November 2000, the Directive outlaws workplace discrimination on the grounds of sex, race, age, religion or disability. The Government has agreed to implement this Directive by December 2003 and, at the time of writing (September 2002), a consultation paper has been published inviting the public to comment on the ways in which the Directive should be incorporated into British law.[11] The Directive is particularly significant because, for the first time, it will be unlawful to discriminate at the workplace on the grounds of 'religion' or 'belief'. In this chapter I will focus on the challenges and opportunities that will arise from the incorporation of the Employment Directive, in so far as it will extend to discrimination based on 'religion and belief'.

My chapter will be divided into four parts. First, I will examine the aims and objectives of the Directive, what it provides for and how it will operate. Secondly, I will comment on the opportunities created by the Directive and explain why its introduction is to be welcomed. Thirdly, I will focus on some

6. *The Daily Telegraph*, 12 December 1998, p. 7.

7. For example, one recent survey found that three quarters of the population regard themselves as belonging to a Christian denomination: 'Christian Britain', *The Times*, 19 December 2001, p. 4.

8. B. Parekh, 'Religion and Public Life' in T. Modood (ed.), *Church, State and Religious Minorities* p. 21 (London: PSI, 1997).

9. T. Modood, 'Culture and Identity' in T. Modood *et al*, *Ethnic Minorities in Britain* p. 297 (London: PSI, 1997).

10. *Kokkinakis* v. *Greece* 17 EHRR 397 p. 17 para. 31 (1994).

11. *Towards Equality and Diversity. Implementing the Employment and Race Directives*, http://www.dti.gov.uk/er/equality/consult.pdf (2001).

of the challenges that will be posed by the Directive's implementation. And fourthly I will consider the likely impact of the Directive on the law relating to freedom of religion and belief in Britain.[12]

The thesis of this chapter is that the Employment Directive is an important measure which will have a significant impact on the protection of religion or belief at the workplace. However, it must also be emphasised that one should also not lose sight of its relatively narrow ambit. Consequently, notwithstanding the incorporation of the Employment Directive, it should be remembered that discrimination on the grounds of religion or belief will continue to be sanctioned in a number of areas in contemporary multi-faith Britain.

The Employment Directive

The origins of the Directive can be traced back to the Treaty of Amsterdam (1997) which gave the Council of the European Union unprecedented powers to 'take appropriate action to combat discrimination based on sex, racial or ethnic origin, religion or beliefs, disability, age or sexual orientation'.[13] The European Commission used this authority to issue two new directives: Council Directive 2000/43/EC, relating to the principle of equal treatment for people irrespective of racial or ethnic origin[14] and Council Directive 2000/78/EC, establishing a general framework for equal treatment in respect of employment and occupation. Each of these Directives prohibit direct[15] and indirect[16] discrimination, as well as outlawing harassment[17] as a form of discrimination.

12. The focus of this chapter will be on Great Britain and express reference will not be made to Northern Ireland in view of the unique circumstances that exist in that region.

13. The Treaty of Amsterdam 1997, Article 13.

14. On the Race Directive generally see G. Moon (ed.), *Race Discrimination. Developing and Using a New Legal Framework* (Oxford: Hart, 2000).

15. Direct discrimination covers the situation when one person is treated less favourably than another person is, has been, or would have been treated: (a) on the grounds of religion and belief, sexual orientation, disability or age (Article 2(2)(a) of the Employment Directive) or (b) on the grounds of ethnic or racial origin (Article 2 (2)(a) of the Race Directive).

16. Indirect discrimination, under the Employment Directive, will be assumed to have occurred where an apparently neutral provision, criterion or practice has the effect of putting people of a particular religion and belief, sexual orientation, disability or age at a disadvantage compared to others unless the relevant provision, criterion or practice is objectively justified by a legitimate aim and the means of achieving it are appropriate and necessary: Article 2(2)(b). See Article 2(2)(b) for the equivalent test of indirect discrimination under the Race Directive.

17. Harassment covers conduct that 'has the purpose or effect of creating an intimidating, hostile, offensive, or disturbing environment'. See Article 2(3) of both the Employment and the Race Directives.

Furthermore, once an applicant has put forward a prima facie case of discrimination, the burden of proof under both Directives rests with the respondent to rebut the allegations that have been made.[18] However, one important difference between the two directives is that the Employment Directive (2000/78/EC) is limited in scope to matters relating to employment and occupation so that, unlike the Racial Discrimination Directive,[19] it does not cover state benefits or the provision of goods and services to the public.[20]

The overall purpose of the Employment Directive (2000/78/EC) is to ensure recognition of 'the principle of equal treatment as regards access to employment and occupation ... irrespective of racial or ethnic origin, religion or belief, disability, age or sexual orientation'.[21] However, the Directive accepts that a difference of treatment will not constitute discrimination where a genuine occupational qualification is necessary for a particular position,[22] while a specific exemption also exists in relation to the genuine, legitimate and justified occupational requirements of religious organisations.[23] The extent to which the Directive should restrict the freedom of religious organisations in matters of employment was a matter of concern for a number of church leaders[24] and I will return to examine this controversial issue in more detail later in section four of this chapter.

In implementing the Employment Directive the Government has expressed a desire to be guided by three principles. First, to 'develop practical, workable and effective legislation' that will 'have a real impact in removing unfair discrimination ... without stifling business with unnecessary burdens'.[25] Secondly, to 'seek greater coherence ... between strands (e.g. race, religion, age, etc) so that rights and obligations are easier for individuals and employers to understand'.[26] And finally, that 'sufficient time' should be given to 'employers, employees and other interested parties to consider [the Government's] proposals for implementing the Directive'.[27] Mindful of the fact that the provisions of the Employment Directive must be implemented in the United

18. Article 10 of the Employment Directive and Article 8 of the Race Directive.
19. On the wide ranging scope of the Race Directive generally see Article 3 of Directive 2000/43/EC.
20. On this generally see Article 3 of Directive 2000/78/EC.
21. Article 1.
22. Article 4(1). For example, an 'authentic Indian restaurant' will be permitted to give priority to applicants of Indian origin.
23. Article 4(2).
24. The Christian Institute, *European Threat to Religious Freedom* (The Christian Institute, 2000).
25. *Supra* note 11 chp. 3, para. 3.1.
26. *Ibid.*
27. *Ibid.*

Kingdom by 2nd December 2003, these time constraints seemingly explain why the Government has indicated that the Employment Directive will be incorporated by means of secondary (rather than primary) legislation. The Government's rationale for this policy is that it will allow 'sufficient time for consultation and preparation ... without missing important deadlines'.[28] Yet, notwithstanding such considerations, it is regrettable that such important and symbolic legislation will not be subject to the scrutiny of primary legislation. In spite of one Minister's recognition of the need to 'get the law right in this area ... to move the cause of equality forwards and not backwards',[29] some may suspect that the Government's main priority is to minimise Parliamentary debate on some of the controversial elements of the Directive. Ultimately time alone will tell whether the resulting legislation has been properly scrutinised in Parliament. At this stage however one thing is beyond dispute: the Employment Directive will create as many opportunities as it shall present challenges, and I will now proceed to consider some of these in more detail.

Opportunities

It is axiomatic that the Employment Directive creates a number of opportunities for those who claim to have been subject to discrimination and harassment at the workplace. In particular I will focus on two ways in which it can be said that the Directive makes an important contribution. First, the Directive rectifies the long-standing anomaly that discrimination on the grounds of race, but not religion, is prohibited in Great Britain.[30] And secondly the Directive compensates for a number of the shortcomings of the Human Rights Act 1998.

Rectifying an anomaly

Previously, in the absence of legislation prohibiting religious discrimination, those who claimed to have suffered unequal treatment on the grounds

28. *Ibid*. para. 3.2.

29. Tessa Jowell, Minister for Employment, 'A General Framework for Equal Treatment in Employment and Occupation', House of Commons European Standing Committee C, 24 July 2000.

30. Northern Ireland has, traditionally, been the only region of the United Kingdom where discrimination on the ground of religion or belief has been expressly prohibited by law. On this generally see the Fair Employment (Northern Ireland) Act 1989 and the Fair Employment and Treatment (Northern Ireland) Order 1998.

of religion or belief could only avail themselves of a legal remedy if they were able to show that they had been victims of indirect racial discrimination.[31] Accordingly successful litigants had to prove that they were members of a 'racial' (as opposed to a 'religious') group whose members enjoyed a long shared history and possessed their own cultural tradition.[32] This meant that faiths such as Sikhism[33] and Judaism,[34] whose members tended to share both religious and ethnic ties, fell within the remit of the Race Relations Act. However, this arrangement failed to offer protection to a wide range of other faith organisations, whose membership was defined primarily by religious rather ethnic or racial factors. This created a series of bizarre anomalies. For example, since Muslims were not, per se, covered by the Race Relations Act,[35] a Pakistani Muslim was only protected from discrimination in so far as their 'ethnic origin' brought him/her within the confines of the Race Relations legislation, while a white indigenous British convert to Islam enjoyed no such protection. The injustice of this state of affairs was also vividly illustrated by the case of *Dawkins* v. *Crown Suppliers (PSA) Ltd*,[36] where a Rastafarian (Dawkins) had been refused a job as a van driver with the Crown Suppliers (PSA) because he had refused to cut his dreadlocks. Although Dawkins' motives were not exactly clear, it appears reasonable to assume that, as with other Rastafarians, his locks were a manifestation of his religious beliefs.[37] The Court of Appeal, however, held that since Rastafarians were a religion rather than a racial group, Dawkins could not bring himself within the remit of the Race Relations Act and his application failed.

Had the Employment Directive (and the Human Rights Act 1998) been in force at the time of the Appeal Court's ruling in *Dawkins*, the case would arguably have been decided differently. In the light of the Employment Directive and the Human Rights Act, there would have to be an objective rationale for a policy that prevented a Rastafarian from wearing his dreadlocks at work. This would have to be based on matters such as health,[38]

---

31. Race Relations Act 1976, s.1(1)(b).
32. *Mandla* v. *Dowell Lee* [1983] 2 AC 548, p. 562 (Lord Fraser).
33. *Ibid.*
34. *Simon* v. *Brimham Associates* [1987] IRLR 307 and *Seide* v. *Gillette Industries* [1980] IRLR 427.
35. *Nyazi* v. *Rymans* (EAT., 10 May 1988, unreported) and *JH Walker Ltd* v. *Hussain* [1996] IRLR 11, EAT.
36. [1993] IRLR 284.
37. On Rastafarian beliefs generally see E. Cashmore, *The Rastafarians*, Report No 64 (Oxford: The Minority Rights Group, 1984).
38. *Panesar* v. *Nestle Co Ltd* [1980] ICR 144: the Court of Appeal held that a rule forbidding the wearing of beards in the respondent's chocolate factory was justifiable on the grounds of hygiene.

safety,[39] public order,[40] morals,[41] or the rights of others.[42] In the absence of such justification there would, on the face of it, appear to be a prima facie case of unlawful religious discrimination. It therefore follows that the incorporation of the Employment Directive will ensure that those who allege discrimination on the grounds of religion and belief, and fail to come within the parameters of the Race Relations Act, are no longer left without a legal remedy.

Of course, even prior to the incorporation of the Employment Directive, those who complained of discrimination on the grounds of religion or belief, and failed to avail themselves of domestic remedies, still had the option of seeking redress under the European Convention on Human Rights (ECHR). But it would be unwise to overestimate the influence of this remedy since very few applicants have managed to invoke the ECHR successfully in the area of religious discrimination. Thus, a second reason why the Employment Directive should be welcomed is that its incorporation will compensate for the limitations of the European Convention, the bulk of which has been incorporated in the form of the Human Rights Act.[43]

Limitations of the Human Rights Act

At first sight it appears that the Human Rights Act could be of real significance in terms of combating discrimination on the grounds of religion or belief. After all, Article 9(1) guarantees an individual's 'freedom of thought, conscience and religion'[44] and Article 14 expressly forbids religious discrimi-

39. It has been suggested that conditions may be imposed on the wearing of steel bangles by Sikhs at the workplace, since they may cause accidents by getting caught up in fast moving machinery: A. James, *Sikh Children in Britain* p. 51 (Oxford: Oxford University Press, 1974).
40. An example of this would be conditions imposed under s. 137 of the Highways Act 1980 prohibiting Hare Krishna members from marching through busy town centres.
41. This could cover the hypothetical situation where a naturist employee argued that his belief demanded that he go to work naked.
42. An example of this would be restrictions on the electrical amplification of the Muslim call to prayer, so as to avoid disturbing non-Muslims: S. Poulter, *Asian Traditions and English Law* p. 116 (London: Runnymede Trust, 1990).
43. For a complete list of the Convention rights which are incorporated into UK law see Schedule 1 of the Human Rights Act 1998.
44. Article 9(1): 'Everyone has the right to freedom of thought, conscience and religion; this right includes the freedom to change his religion or belief, and freedom, either alone or in community with others and in public and private, to manifest his religion or belief, in worship, teaching, practice and observance'.

nation.[45] Accordingly, during the passage of the Human Rights Bill one peer even went so far as to claim that the 'ECHR is one of the most powerful weapons for the protection of religious freedom which has ever been created.'[46] However, on a closer examination, it is unwise to exaggerate the significance of the Convention in this area. There are at least four reasons why the Human Rights Act is only likely to be of *limited* value in tackling religious discrimination.

To begin with the rights guaranteed in Article 9(1) are not absolute, but are subject to a number of limitations that are provided for in Article 9(2). On receipt of a complaint that an individual has been discriminated against on the grounds of religion or belief, a court must consider whether the restrictions on the exercise of these rights are justified. If it is shown that the interference with the complainant's rights are 'prescribed by law', 'necessary in a democratic society' and justified on a number of other wide-ranging grounds, the application will fail.[47] As will be argued later in this chapter, the interests of the commercial and business sector often take precedence over those of individuals and religious organisations in such cases.

Secondly, the limited remit of the Human Rights Act reduces its effectiveness as an instrument for tackling discrimination on the grounds of religion or belief at the workplace. The Act only provides that it is 'unlawful for a public authority to act in a way which is incompatible with one or more of the Convention rights'.[48] Unlike the Employment Directive, which covers both the public and private sectors, the activities of private bodies are not expressly covered by the Human Rights Act. Thus, until the Human Rights Act is interpreted as having horizontal effect,[49] it will fail to offer remedies to individuals who complain of discrimination on the grounds of religion or belief in the private sector.

---

45. Article 14: 'The enjoyment of the rights and freedoms set forth in this Convention shall be secured without discrimination on any ground such as sex, race, colour, language, religion, political or other opinion, national or social origin, association with a national minority, property, birth or other status'.
46. Lord Goddard, HL Hansard, Vol. 585, Col. 751, 5 February 1998.
47. Article 9(2): 'Freedom to manifest one's religion or beliefs shall be subject only to such limitations as are prescribed by law and are necessary in a democratic society in the interests of public safety, for the protection of public order, health or morals, or for the protection of the rights and freedoms of others'.
48. The Human Rights Act 1998 requires that the actions of public authorities must be compatible with the Convention (s. 6) and that '[s]o far as it is possible to do so, primary and secondary legislation must be read and given effect in a way which is compatible with the Convention rights' (s. 3(1)).
49. On this generally see W. Wade, 'Horizons of Horizontality', Vol. 116 *LQR* p. 217 (2000) and G. Phillipson, 'The Human Rights Act, 'Horizontal Effect' and the Common Law: A Bang or a Whimper?' Vol. 62 *MLR* p. 824 (1999).

A third factor that militates against the effectiveness of the Human Rights Act relates to the very narrow way in which Article 9 of the Convention has been interpreted by the European Commission and Court of Human Rights. In particular, the Commission's restrictive interpretation of Article 9 demonstrates why it took 40 years before the European Court was called upon to hear a case specifically on Article 9 of the Convention.[50] Noting the paucity of case law under Article 9, Harris, O'Boyle and Warbrick have commented, rather caustically, that 'it may be complacent to think that Article 9 has seldom been successfully invoked for lack of need'.[51] Certainly the Strasbourg-based institutions have seldom upheld the complaints of those alleging discrimination on the grounds of religion or belief at the workplace. For example, applicants seeking time off work to pray[52] or celebrate religious holy days[53] have been denied redress. This approach has led to the claim that it is appropriate to measure progress 'in inches rather than miles'[54] in terms of way in which Article 9 has been interpreted with regard to the protection of workers' rights.

A final reason why the Human Rights Act on its own is poorly equipped to assist those claiming unfair treatment at work on the grounds of religion or belief relates to the fact that the non-discrimination provisions of the ECHR are woefully inadequate. A number of obstacles face any applicant who seeks to rely on Article 14 in the context of a submission on the grounds of religious discrimination. For example, it has long been recognised that Article 14 is not a free-standing equality clause.[55] Since Article 14 is a 'parasitic provision',[56] any applicant needs to bring his/her complaint within the remit of Article 9 of the Convention. This is in marked contrast to the equivalent non-discrimination provision of the International Covenant on Civil and Political Rights, Article 26, which not merely has an independent existence but also extends to a wider range of activities than Article 14 of the European Convention.[57] The limitations of Article 14 explain why a new free-standing anti-discrimination provision, Protocol 12, was opened for signature in November 2000.

50. *Kokkinakis* v. *Greece* 17 EHRR 397 (1994).

51. D. Harris, M. O'Boyle and C. Warbrick, *Law of the European Convention on Human Rights*, p. 370 (London: Butterworths, 1995).

52. *Ahmad* v. *UK* 4 EHRR 126 (1982).

53. *Steadman* v. *UK* 23 EHRR CD 168 (1997).

54. K.D. Ewing, 'The Human Rights Act and Labour Law' Vol. 27 *Industrial Law Journal*, p. 275 at 288 (1998).

55. *The Belgian Linguistic Case* (No.2) 1 EHRR 252 (1968).

56. Harris, O'Boyle and Warbrick, *supra* note 51 p. 463.

57. On this generally see Lord Lester, 'Obligations of Non-Discrimination' in D. Harris and S. Joseph (eds.), *The International Covenant on Civil and Political Rights* pp. 563-596 (Oxford: Clarendon, 1995).

The British Government has not, as yet, chosen to ratify or incorporate this Protocol into UK law[58] and until such a decision is taken the Convention will only offer modest assistance to those who claim to have suffered discrimination on the grounds of religion or belief.

It is in this context that one can appreciate the potential significance of the Employment Directive in British law. However, it is equally important not to lose sight of the challenges that will be posed by the incorporation of the Directive.

Challenges

The fact that the Employment Directive is not limited to 'religious' discrimination, but also prohibits unequal treatment on the grounds of 'belief', clearly creates a number of opportunities for members of certain organisations that would not normally be thought of as 'religions'. Were it not for the inclusion of the word 'belief', such groups would otherwise fall outside the remit of the Directive. Paradoxically, however, this 'opportunity' for litigants also presents a serious 'challenge' for those who will be charged with implementing and interpreting the Employment Directive, particularly since the Directive fails to offer any guidance on the definition of the phrase 'religion or belief'.

Defining religion and belief

Wary perhaps of getting embroiled in acrimonious theological disputes, the Government has indicated that it does not intend to provide a definition of the words 'religion or belief' in the legislation that will be enacted to incorporate the Directive.[59] This course of action is prudent because there is no doubt that it would be very difficult to draft a statutory definition of either term. A working definition would need to be flexible enough to satisfy a broad cross-section of faiths, yet also sufficiently precise for a practical application in specific cases. Since such a balance would be practically impossible to strike it is best to let the courts determine, on a case-by-case basis, the meaning of the words 'religion or belief'. In spite of the fact that the relevant human rights jurispru-

58. See submission of the UK's representative Mr de Pulford to the Human Rights Committee, CCPR/C/SR.1961, para. 27, 23 October 2001. For a criticism of the Government's policy see M. Bharania, 'Who's afraid of Protocol Twelve', *New Law Journal*, 19 January 2001, pp. 65-66.

59. *Supra* note 11 para. 13.4.

dence will clearly be of assistance to judges when they come to carry out this task, the judiciary will continue to face a number of formidable challenges.

For a start, the courts will have to determine the parameters of 'belief' for the purposes of the Directive. Policy reasons indicate that not every 'belief' is worthy of protection. For example, the complaint of a devotee of a long-established faith wishing to visit a holy shrine and celebrate the most holy day of their religion should be distinguished from that of an Elvis Presley fan who claims that their 'belief' entitles them to have paid leave of absence to make pilgrimages to Graceland or to dress like Elvis at work. In seeking to distinguish meritorious from unmeritorious cases limited guidance may be found from the jurisprudence of the European Court. In *Campbell and Cousans* v. *UK*, a case that was decided by reference to Article 2 of the First Protocol rather than Article 9 of the Convention, the European Court held that the 'term beliefs … denotes a certain level of cogency, seriousness, cohesion and importance'.[60] Even the most devoted Elvis fan would have difficulty satisfying this test and similar considerations led the Human Rights Committee to reject a claim that a belief consisting primarily in the worship of a narcotic drug could be brought within Article 18(1) of the International Covenant on Civil and Political Rights (ICCPR).[61] Spurious claims aside it is inevitable that there will always be disputes, particularly at the margins, as to what characterises a 'belief' for the purposes of the Employment Directive.

A second challenge will be the extent to which controversial and newly established religious organisations come within the remit of the Directive. Concern has already been expressed in some quarters that the Employment Directive will offer protection to groups such as the Moonies and Satanists.[62] Irrespective of whether these fears are justified what is clear is that, under international human rights law, new religious movements are accorded the same rights as mainstream religious organisations. For example, in its interpretation of Article 18 of the ICCPR[63] the Human Rights Committee warned that 'it views with concern any tendency to discriminate against any religions or beliefs for any reason, including the fact that they are newly established'.[64] The Committee has made it clear that the principles of thought and conscience are synonymous with freedom of religion,[65] and that the words 'reli-

60. 4 EHRR 293 (1982).

61. *M.A.B, W.A.T. and J-.A.Y.T.* v. *Canada* (570/1993).

62. The Christian Institute, *supra* note 24 p. 24.

63. 'Everyone shall have the right to freedom of thought, conscience and religion …': Article 18(1) of the ICCPR.

64. CCPR/C/48/CRP.2/REV1.

65. ICCPR General Comment no. 22(48) (Article 18) Adopted on 20th July 1993, CCPR/C/21/Rev.1/Add.4, September 27th 1993, para. 1.

gion and belief' should be 'broadly construed'.[66] The equivalent provision to Article 18 under the ECHR, Article 9, has also been given an expansive interpretation. For example, the absolute guarantees of freedom of 'thought, conscience and religion' under Article 9(1) of the Convention have been extended not merely to long-established religions (e.g. Buddhism,[67] Christianity,[68] Islam,[69] Judaism,[70] and Sikhism[71]) but also to newer faiths (e.g. the Jehovah's Witnesses,[72] the Divine Light Zentrum,[73] and the Church of Scientology[74]), as well as a wide range of philosophical and ideological convictions (e.g. Veganism[75] and Pacifism[76]). Consequently there seems little doubt that the term 'religion and belief' will cover theistic, non-theistic and atheistic beliefs and that members of new religious movements will have the same status (at least in theory) as longer established religious groups under the Employment Directive. Yet not everyone is likely to welcome such a wide interpretation of the term 'belief'. Some are likely to take the view that it is wrong, in principle, to equate 'religious belief' with 'ethical or philosophical convictions',[77] while others may object, in practice, to members of organisations that have been accused of racism,[78] brainwashing[79] and even murder[80] being accorded protection from discrimination on the ground of belief. Thus, one of the greatest challenges facing those charged with interpreting the Employment

66. *Ibid*. para. 2.
67. *X* v. *UK*, No 6886/75, 5 DR 100.
68. *Steadman* v. *UK*, Application No. 29107/95, 23 EHRR CD 168 (1997).
69. *Ahmad* v. *UK*, Application No. 8160/78, 4 EHRR 126 (1982).
70. *D* v. *France*, Application No. 10180/82, 35 DR 199.
71. *X* v. *UK*, Application No. 8160/78, 22 DR 27.
72. *Kokkinakis* v. *Greece*, Application No. 14307/88, (1994) 17 EHRR 397.
73. *Omkarananda and the DLZ* v. *Switzerland*, Application No. 8118/77, 25 DR 105 (1981).
74. *X and the Church of Scientology* v. *Sweden*, Application No. 7805/77, 16 DR 68 (1979).
75. *X* v. *UK*, Application No. 18187/91 (10 February 1993).
76. *Arrowsmith* v. *UK*, Application No. 7050/75, 19 DR 5 (1978).
77. For example in *Re South Place Ethical Society: Barralet* v. *Attorney General* [1980] 3 All ER 924, Dillon J defined religion as being 'concerned with man's relations with God' and contrasted it to ethics that 'are concerned with man's relations with man'.
78. For claims of a link between the Neo-Nazi movement, Satanism and the occult see N. Goodrick-Clarke, *Black Sun: Aryan Cults, Esoteric Nazism and the Politics of Identity* (New York University Press, 2002).
79. On this generally see J. Richardson and M. Introvigne, ''Brainwashing Theories' in European Parliamentary and Administrative Reports on 'Cults' and 'Sects' ', *The Journal for the Scientific Study of Religion* No. 2, Vol. 4, pp. 143-168 (2001).
80. Groups accused of murder include Aum Shinrikyo (sarin gas attack in Tokyo), the Solar Temple (murder suicides in Switzerland and Canada), the Heaven's Gate (collective suicides in the USA) and the Branch Davidians (violence and death in Waco, Texas).

Directive will be how they respond to allegations of discrimination from groups that are synonymous with controversy.

The final challenge in this area is whether 'belief' should cover 'political' as opposed to 'religious' beliefs? When the UN Declaration on the Elimination of Religious Intolerance and Discrimination (1981) was being drafted, some governments argued that theories such as racism, nazism and apartheid should be excluded from the ambit of protected belief.[81] Certainly the scenario of the Directive protecting the rights of a Fascist employee who demands time off to celebrate Hitler's birthday is anathema to most people. Perhaps mindful of this danger the Government has indicated that, for the purposes of the Employment Directive, belief 'should be taken to refer to a religious or similar belief, and not a political belief'.[82] However, there are at least three problems with restricting the term to non-political beliefs.

First, there is no clear distinction between what the Government has called 'profound philosophical convictions similar to religious beliefs which deserve society's respect'[83] and political beliefs. If we look to Strasbourg for guidance one notes that an equivalent distinction has been drawn between conduct that is *motivated* merely by religion or belief and that which is a direct *manifestation* of it. Only the latter has received the protection of Article 9 of the Convention, but the challenge of drawing this distinction has been formidable. For example, in *Arrowsmith* v. *UK*,[84] where the applicant had distributed leaflets at an army camp calling on British soldiers to refuse to serve in Northern Ireland, the European Commission accepted that 'public declarations proclaiming generally the idea of pacifism and urging the acceptance of a commitment to non-violence' would be a 'normal and recognised manifestation of pacifist belief'.[85] However, whilst it was beyond dispute that *Arrowsmith* was a 'convinced pacifist',[86] the fact that her leaflets 'did not express pacifist views'[87] meant that they would not come within the remit of Article 9(1) of the Convention. Controversial and challenging distinctions of the kind that the European Commission had to make in *Arrowsmith* will have to be drawn by British judges should political beliefs be excluded from the remit of the Directive.

A second problem is the fact that 'belief' has been broadly construed under both the ECHR and the ICCPR, and *if* the Government specifically excludes

81. A/C3/L 2033 (1973).
82. *Supra* note 11 para. 13.6.
83. *Ibid.* para. 13.5.
84. *Arrowsmith* v. *UK*, Application No. 7050/75, 19 DR 5 (1978).
85. *Ibid.* p. 20.
86. *Ibid.* p. 19.
87. *Ibid.* p. 20.

'political' beliefs[88] from the remit of the Directive once it has been implemented, the resulting legislation could be successfully challenged. After all, the European Court of Human Rights has accepted that Article 9 of the ECHR is a 'precious asset for atheists, agnostics, sceptics and [most significantly for these purposes] the unconcerned'[89] while the Human Rights Committee has stressed that the ambit of Article 18 of the ICCPR is 'far reaching and profound'.[90]

Thirdly, there is evidence that both the Strasbourg human rights organs and the Human Rights Committee have recognised that 'political' beliefs can, on occasion, be synonymous with the principles of thought, conscience and religion. For example, Article 9 of the ECHR has been extended to cover both pacifist philosophies[91] and membership of the Turkish Communist party,[92] while an Italian's conviction for involvement in the re-organisation of a banned Fascist party was held to violate his right to profess his beliefs under Article 18(1) of the ICCPR.[93] Thus Ministers (and judges) will face a formidable challenge in determining the extent to which 'political' beliefs should be brought within the remit of the Employment Directive.

In view of the fact that British judges are required to take the case law of the Strasbourg human rights institutions into account when interpreting legislation,[94] it is likely that the phrase 'religion and belief' will be defined widely. In cases of doubt domestic courts can always refer difficult cases to the European Court of Justice while unsuccessful litigants will retain the right to complain to the European Court of Human Rights. Yet if, as expected, the courts interpret the words 'religion and belief' generously, there is a danger that, as a corollary, they will adopt a more restrictive approach to the manifestation of religion or belief at the workplace. This brings us to the next challenge that the Employment Directive will present—the problem of balancing the interests of employers and employees.

Balancing Competing Interests

The representatives of a number of well-established minority faiths have long complained about the reluctance of many employers to tolerate and accom-

88. L.S. Hammer, *The International Right to Freedom of Conscience* (Aldershot: Ashgate, 2001).

89. *Kokkinakis* v. *Greece* 17 EHRR 397 para. 31 (1993).

90. General Comment 22, para. 1.

91. *Arrowsmith* v. *UK* 19 DR 247 (1980).

92. *Hazar, Hazar and Acik* v. *Turkey* (Application Nos 16311/90, 16312/90 and 16313/90). A friendly settlement was reached in these cases.

93. *M.A.* v. *Italy* (117/1981).

94. The Human Rights Act 1998 s.2.

modate religious practice at the secular workplace.[95] The manifestation of religion or belief may certainly have a serious impact upon an individual's working life. Employees can manifest their faith in a range of ways, including refusing to work on particular days,[96] celebrating important religious festivals,[97] adopting a distinctive appearance,[98] wearing certain clothes,[99] demanding particular food,[100] and seeking leave of absence to make pilgrimages to holy places of worship.[101] Yet to what extent should the Directive impose a duty on employers to take account of the religious sensibilities of their employees?

Clearly the Government is aware of the fact that a fair balance must be struck. In implementing the Employment Directive the Government's avowed aim is to 'develop effective legislation which will have a real impact in removing unfair discrimination—but without stifling business by imposing unfair burdens'.[102] But there is, at present, little guidance on what is meant by the phrase 'unfair burden'. Certainly the burden imposed on employers under the ECHR is anything but onerous. For example in *Steadman* v. *UK*[103] a practising Christian, who was the assistant manager of a travel agency, was dismissed because of her refusal to work on Sundays. The European Commission regarded Steadman's complaint as one of contractual liability rather than religious freedom, and held that she had been dismissed as a result of her failure, 'to agree to work certain hours rather than for her religious belief as such'.[104] The Commission justified its decision on the basis that Steadman 'was free to resign and did in effect resign from her employment'.[105] This interpretation of Article 9 echoes that of *Ahmad* v. *ILEA*,[106] where a Muslim teacher was refused paid leave to attend Friday prayers at his local Mosque that over-ran the lunch-break by 75 minutes. Having refused a four and a half day weekly contract, Ahmad resigned and claimed unfair dismissal. The Court of Appeal

95. UKACIA (UK Action Committee on Islamic Affairs), *Muslims and the Law in Multi-faith Britain: Need for Reform* pp. 8-10 (London: UK Action Committee on Islamic Affairs, 1993).
96. For example, Saturdays for Jews, Sundays for Christians, and Fridays for Muslims.
97. For example, Christmas for Christians, Diwali for Hindus, Eid for Muslims, and Passover for Jews.
98. For example, growing a beard for some Sikh and Muslim males, or the decision to wear one's hair as locks by Rastafarians.
99. For example, the wearing of a Turban by Sikh males or the hijab by Muslim women.
100. For example, halal food for Muslims and Kosher food for Jews.
101. For example, the hajj for Muslims or visits to Lourdes for some Catholics.
102. *Supra* note 11 para. 3.1.
103. *Steadman* v. *UK* 23 EHRR CD 168 (1997).
104. *Ibid*. p. 169.
105. *Ibid*.
106. [1978] 1 All ER 574.

held that this dismissal was fair and this decision was upheld by the European Commission on Human Rights.[107] The Commission emphasised the binding nature of Ahmad's contractual obligations and was even unwilling to find a violation of Article 9(1) since 'the applicant remained free to resign if and when he found that his teaching obligations conflicted with his religious duties'.[108] The right of the applicant to resign in these circumstances has been described by the European Commission as, 'the ultimate guarantee of ... freedom of religion'.[109] However this interpretation of Article 9 of the Convention is unduly restrictive since it presupposes that the market will be sufficiently healthy for an applicant to move on to another job of comparable worth without unnecessary hardship.

In view of the fact that the courts will employ Article 9 in tandem with the Directive when considering allegations of discrimination on the grounds of religion or belief it is unlikely, in the short term, that the Employment Directive will have a dramatic effect on working practices. However, in the medium to long term, it is inevitable that British judges will need to strike a much fairer balance between the interests of employers and employees than has hitherto been evident in Strasbourg. In approaching cases in this area a distinction should be drawn between the introduction of measures that can easily be incorporated into the workplace and those that are likely to have serious financial or administrative implications. With regard to the former, subject to the restrictions on the manifestation of one's faith under Article 9(2) of the Convention, there are a number of ways in which employers will be able reasonably to accommodate the religious practices of their workers. For example, the Directive is likely to ensure that if a Christian employee is permitted to wear a cross, a Sikh man will be entitled to wear his turban, a Rastafarian his dreadlocks, a Jew his yarmulke and a Muslim woman her veil at the work place. Already there is evidence of many businesses relaxing strict dress codes in the interests of inter-faith harmony. For example, the fast food chain Domino's Pizzas has recently dropped a ban on its employees wearing beards following complaints from a Sikh applicant, while United Airlines have also recently made it possible for their staff to wear turbans, yarmulkes and hijabs as part of the company uniform.[110] But, in contrast to this good practice, most employers are likely to remain wary of changes that will impose burdensome obligations on them. For this reason it is clear that, due to enforced absence from the workplace, religious holidays and festivals will be a particular source of acrimony once the Directive has been implemented.

107. *Ahmad* v. *UK* 4 EHRR 126 (1982).

108. *Ibid.* p. 133.

109. *Konttinen* v. *Finland*, Application No. 24949/94, 87A, DR, 68.

110. D. Waldmeir, 'What to wear to the office', *The Financial Times*, 26 July 2001, p. 12.

One logical consequence of the Directive is that if a Christian employee is entitled to celebrate the most important festivals of his/her faith (e.g. Christmas and Easter), members of other religions should also be accorded equivalent rights. Accordingly, there is a prima facie case for Muslims being given time off work for Eid and Ramadan, Jews for the Passover and Yom Kippur, Buddhists for Vesak and Magha Puja Day, Hindus for Diwali, Sikhs for Baisakhi, Bahá'ís for their nine holy days and so on. There will certainly be pressure on the courts to adopt such an approach. Those campaigning for greater freedoms at the workplace will not merely call for a generous interpretation of the Directive, but will point to the fact that the Dutch High Court has, in the past, recognised that an employee has the right to be excused from work to celebrate important religious holidays.[111] There are a number of reasons, however, why it is unlikely that such an approach will be adopted in Britain. For a start, to permit *every* employee time off to celebrate his/her faith would, in a multi-faith workplace, impose an unreasonable burden on employers. Secondly, any such attempt to accommodate workers' holy days would inevitably lead to disputes as to whether the followers of new religious movements should have the same rights as those belonging to well-established religions. Even if agreement could be reached on this issue a third problem might be a lack of consensus within various faiths as to which holidays and festivals should be classified as being the most worthy of celebration. Fourthly, any extension of the holiday rights of minority religious employees could, paradoxically, hinder rather than advance inter-faith unity by fostering resentment amongst the majority of employees.[112] And finally, there will always be the danger that a minority of employees could abuse the system, by claiming to follow more than one religion or feigning 'conversions' so as to enjoy additional holiday entitlements.

Notwithstanding these considerations, it would be contrary to the spirit and the letter of the Employment Directive if British judges were to interpret its provisions in an unduly restrictive way. The challenge facing the courts will be to ensure that a reasonable balance is struck between the interests of employers and employees. There are, however, no clear guidelines as to what constitutes reasonable accommodation with regard to the religiously inspired practices and beliefs of employees. As we have already seen, Strasbourg jurisprudence is less than helpful while the lessons to be learnt from Northern Ireland are limited in view of the fact that there is not a multi-faith workforce in that region. The courts will no doubt look to North America for some assis-

111. *Nederlandse Jurisprudentue* No. 350, March 30, 1984.

112. One could argue that such resentment contributed to the emergence of the far right party Pim Fortuyn's List in the Netherlands.

tance in difficult cases,[113] but what is really needed is a set of guidelines that are designed to reflect local conditions. Thus, it is hoped that the Government will introduce a Code of Practice, perhaps building on existing local codes,[114] that will help employers to be sensitive to the faith requirements of their workforce.

Even with the introduction of such a Code one should not underestimate the challenge facing judges of striking a fair balance between the interests of employers and employees. They will need the proverbial wisdom of Solomon in determining the extent to which religion and belief can be manifested at the workplace. Yet, ironically, this was not the subject that attracted the most controversy when the Employment Directive was in the process of being drafted. As we will now see, the most contentious issue was the extent to which the Directive would affect the right of religious organisations to discriminate in the field of employment.

Genuine Occupational Qualifications

The third challenge posed by the incorporation of the Employment Directive is the extent to which religious organisations should be free to discriminate in order to preserve their unique status and character. This problematic issue has generated controversy in the past. For example, during the Parliamentary stages of the Human Rights Act 1998, there were a number of acrimonious debates focusing on the extent to which religious organisations should be affected by the ECHR.[115] These were only resolved by the late inclusion of s. 13 to the Act, which states that the courts must have 'particular regard' to the importance of freedom of thought, conscience and religion when considering cases involving religious organisations.

As was the case when the Human Rights Act was enacted, alarm bells were set ringing in a number of faith-based organisations by the spectre of the Employment Directive eroding religious autonomy. Concern was initially expressed that, as a result of the Directive, church schools might be forced to employ atheists and practising homosexuals.[116] Some of these fears may be assuaged by the Government's pledge that, notwithstanding the implementation of the Directive, schools of a religious character will retain their existing

113. On this generally see D. Gregory, 'The role of religion in the secular workplace', *Notre Dame Journal of Law, Ethics and Public Policy* Vol.4, p. 749 (1990).

114. See, for example: Code of Practice for Managers on Religious and Cultural Needs (City of Bradford Metropolitan Council), June 1995.

115. See, for example, HL Hansard, Vol. 306, Cols. 845-1062, 16 February 1998.

116. The Christian Institute, News Release 25 May 2000.

statutory powers to employ teachers who are members of a particular faith or denomination.[117] Nevertheless, a number of religious leaders continue to have concerns about how they and their organisations will be affected by the Employment Directive.[118]

The drafters of the Directive, in apparent anticipation of such fears, inserted Article 4 as an exception to the general principle of non-discrimination. Article 4(1) permits states to make provision for genuine occupational requirements insofar as their objective is legitimate and the requirement for them is proportionate. In addition, Article 4(2) provides that:

> Member States may maintain national legislation in force at the date of adoption of this Directive or provide for future legislation incorporating national practices existing at the date of adoption of this Directive pursuant to which, in the case of occupational activities within churches and other public or private organisations the ethos of which is based on religion or belief, a difference of treatment based on a person's religion or belief shall not constitute discrimination where, by reason of the nature of these activities or of the context in which they are carried out, a person's religion or belief constitute a genuine, legitimate and justified occupational requirement, having regard to the organisation's ethos. The difference of treatment shall be implemented taking account of Member States' constitutional provisions and principles, as well as the general principles of Community law, and should not justify discrimination on another ground. Provided that its provisions are otherwise complied with, this Directive shall thus not prejudice the right of churches and other public or private organisations, the ethos of which is based on religion or belief, acting in conformity with national constitutions and laws, to require individuals working for them to act in good faith and with loyalty to the organisation's ethos.[119]

The Government, in a deliberate effort to assuage the fears of faith groups, has indicated that it plans to insert 'a provision based on the wording of Article 4(2)' in the legislation that will incorporate the Directive into British law.[120] However, in view of the fact that Article 4(2) has been described as 'an awful provision which is impossible to read',[121] the challenges posed by its interpretation are considerable. There are at least three reasons why its remit is unclear. First, there is uncertainty over what is meant by the phrase 'genuine, legitimate and justified occupational requirement'. For example, whilst

117. *Supra* note 11 para. 13.20.

118. See, for example, Lord Bishop of Bath and Wells, HL Hansard, Vol. 625, Col. 294, 25 April 2001.

119. Article 4(2) of the Employment Directive.

120 *Supra* note 11 para. 13-14.

121. *EU Proposals to Combat Discrimination: Ninth Report of the Select Committee on the European Union*, HL Paper 68 (1999-2000) para. 109.

there would not be a problem for the Church of England to insist that ordination was an occupational requirement for admission to the Anglican priesthood, it remains unclear whether the Church could insist on appointing, say, only a Christian gardener to one of its parishes. The Church could argue that since there might be occasions when a gardener would be called upon to exercise a counselling or pastoral role (e.g. his/her contact say with grieving relatives after a bereavement), the post should only be held by a person who is a practising member of the faith. However, it would appear that those who drafted Article 4(2) intended that this exemption should be available only in 'very limited circumstances'[122] and, by implication, restricted only to the position of clergy, priests and ordained religious leaders. Assistance is unlikely to come from the legislation incorporating the Employment Directive, since the Government has indicated that it intends to define neither the organisations nor the posts that will fall within Article 4(2).[123] Ultimately, therefore, the exact parameters of Article 4(2) must be determined by the courts, and it is inevitable that there will be heated discussion over the extent to which the service staff of religious organisations (e.g. gardeners, secretaries, cleaners and to some extent cooks[124]) come within its remit and are exempt from the principle of non-discrimination.[125]

A second problem with Article 4(2) is that it is unclear what is meant by the requirement for employees 'to act in good faith and with loyalty' in the light of the organisation's ethos. For example, confusion surrounds the extent to which religious organisations will be entitled to place restrictions on the private lives of their employees. In the past religious schools have often dismissed teachers on the ground that certain aspects of their lifestyles are incongruous with the Church's official teaching.[126] However, many of these employment practices will have to change as a result of the Directive. For example, in the context of the Head teacher of a religious school who is gay, it has been suggested that Article 4(2) would only apply 'to overt conduct affronting the ethos of the institution concerned'.[127] Accordingly, the mere disclosure of the Head teacher's homosexuality would not justify his/her dismissal, although it would perhaps be different if s/he were to flaunt their sex-

122.Recital (23) to the Employment Directive.

123.*Supra* note 11 para.13-14.

124.The position of cooks may be special in so far as some faiths (e.g. Islam and Orthodox Judaism) have strict rules relating to diet and the preparation of food.

125.For a discussion of some of the principles that the courts may apply see R. Crasnow, 'Religious freedom and equal treatment', *New Law Journal*, Vol.152 p. 513, 5 April 2002.

126.See, for example, *O'Neill* v. *Governors of St Thomas More RCVA Upper School and Bedfordshire CC* [1996] IRLR 372.

127.House of Lords Select Committee on European Union, *The EU Framework Directive on Discrimination*, 4th Report, Session 2000-2001 para. 20.

uality in front of the pupils. This interpretation of the Directive would appear to be consistent with the right to privacy under the Human Rights Act,[128] but is likely to be opposed by a number of faith organisations for whom such distinctions between one's identity (e.g. a private matter) and one's conduct (e.g. a public matter) are artificial.[129]

Finally, it is unclear which organisations under Article 4(2) will be considered to have an 'ethos [that] is based on religion or belief'. As noted earlier, the legislation that the Government plans to introduce in this area will not include a list of the organisations that would fall within Article 4(2). Accordingly, a wide range of conflicting opinions have been expressed. Some have warned that the employees of religiously run hostels, hospices or old people's homes could justify the dismissal of non-believers on the ground that their employees' beliefs or lifestyles were incompatible with the religious ethos of the organisation.[130] In direct contrast, others have expressed fears that religious-based businesses, charities and hospices may be forced to employ atheists, and that 'secular courts will be given teeth to wreak havoc with the ethos of churches and non-Christian denominations'.[131] Accordingly, the challenge facing the courts, of interpreting Article 4(2) so as to reconcile the conflicting principles of non-discrimination at the workplace and the autonomy of religious organisations in the field of employment, is formidable.

With this in mind one of the few things that can be said with any certainty is that, once Article 4(2) has been enshrined in British law, the judges will have to balance a number of powerful competing interests. For a start they will have to weigh the right of religious organisations to discriminate in the fields of occupation and employment against the general principle of non-discrimination. In addition, they will be required to strike a balance between the interests of organisations with a religious ethos as *groups* and the rights of unsuccessful applicants as *individuals*. Problems also arise with the need to reconcile what some have called '2,000 years of church homophobia'[132] with the right of organisations with a religious ethos to make appointments in line with their sacred texts.[133] And finally, the judges will have to set the general principle of non-discrimination against the valuable philanthropic functions that many organisations with a particular religious ethos perform.

---

128. Article 8(1) and (2) of the European Convention on Human Rights.

129. 'EU Equal Treatment Directive', The Scottish Catholic Media Office, Press Release, November 2000.

130. See the National Secular Society, http://www.secularism.org.uk/nss/callaction2.htm.

131. C. Hart, Director of the Christian Institute quoted in *The Independent*, 30 June 2000.

132. P. Tatchell, 'End the Church's war on gay and lesbian people', *The Independent*, 2 August 2001.

133. For an example of a text that condemns homosexuality see Leviticus 20:13.

With regard to the latter it would be most regrettable if such organisations (e.g. religious charities, hospices, etc.) felt compelled by the fear of litigation to cut back on their initiatives in the community. Such considerations have prompted the European Parliament's Committee on Employment and Social Affairs to suggest that Article 4(2) should be extended to cover institutions and organisations with a religious ethos that provide social services and health care.[134] Equally it would be wrong for the employment practices of churches and similar bodies to fall beyond the remit of the law since, as Lord Lester has observed, 'even religious bodies are capable of breaching convention rights'.[135]

Therefore there are a range of important considerations that will have to be taken on board by those who will be vested with the power to determine the extent to which organisations with a particular religious ethos may discriminate. Much will depend on the way in which the Directive is incorporated into British law and it is to be hoped that the Government will choose to introduce a Code of Practice that could be based on one that has been drafted by the Northern Ireland Fair Employment Commission.[136] Useful guidance may also be sought not merely from relevant international human rights standards but from the way in which other common law[137] and EU states[138] exempt religious bodies from their anti-discrimination legislation. Ultimately, however, the courts will have the formidable challenge of balancing the interests of religious organisations and the general principle of non-discrimination. With this in mind it should be remembered that relatively few cases are likely to be brought in this area. It is likely that modest remuneration and exacting conditions of service will tend to dissuade all but the faithful from seeking employment in organisations with a religious ethos. Nevertheless some pressure groups, whose members have traditionally been denied employment by organisations based on a particular religion or belief, may, as a matter of principle, encourage the initiation of legal proceedings. Whilst much of this is pure speculation the suspicion remains that it might only take a few high profile cases for Article 4(2) to become a battleground for the church and the state in the 21st century.

134. RR\421406EN.doc, 48/98, para. 6.

135. HL Hansard, Vol. 593, Col. 2091, 29 October 1998.

136. JUSTICE, *Towards Equality and Diversity: Implementing the Employment and Race Directives —responding to the Government's Consultation Paper* p.18 (JUSTICE, March 2002).

137. For example, whilst the New Zealand Human Rights Act 1993 prohibits employment discrimination (s. 22), discrimination is permitted to 'comply with the doctrines or rules or established customs' of a religion (s. 28(1)), or where the employee is a 'clergyman, priest, pastor, official, or teacher among adherents of that belief' (s. 28(2)).

138. For example, in the Republic of Ireland, notwithstanding the general prohibition of discrimination under the Employment Equality Act 1998, the legislation recognises a number of exemptions in relation to religious, educational and medical institutions (ss. 36 and 37).

The Employment Directive and Religious Freedom

In the immediate aftermath of the atrocities of 11th September 2001 Tony Blair spoke of the need to bring, 'faiths closer in [an] understanding of our common values and heritage'.[139] To some extent the incorporation of the Employment Directive into British law should realise this aim. Its introduction will certainly have a number of benefits. For example, the long-standing anomaly that it was unlawful to discriminate on the grounds of sex,[140] race[141] and disability[142] but not religion has now been rectified. In addition, the Directive will be welcomed by those who have expressed concern about inequalities in the labour market,[143] and the under-representation of minority groups in key areas of public life generally.[144] Finally, the Directive will be of great symbolic value for the nation's faith communities. As a Muslim peer noted, prior to the drafting of the Directive, 'a religious anti-discrimination law would be a powerful symbol of public policy and would convey the important message that religious identities are valued and respected throughout society'.[145] This may be so but whilst the incorporation of the Directive is undoubtedly a measure of considerable significance, there are a number of reasons why one should be cautious about exaggerating its likely impact.[146]

First, the scope of the Employment Directive is limited. In the past those calling for legislation to prohibit discrimination on the grounds of religion or belief anticipated that such a law would cover the provision of goods, services and facilities.[147] Unfortunately, the remit is of the Directive is much narrower than might have been the case. Unlike both the Race Directive[148] and Protocol

139. *The Times*, 3 October 2001, p. 10.

140. Sex Discrimination Act 1975.

141. See the Race Relations Act 1976 and the Race Relations (Amendment) Act 2000.

142. See the Disability Discrimination Act 1995 and the Disability Rights Commission Act 1999.

143. E/C.12.1997/SR.37, Committee on Economic, Social and Cultural Rights, 29 January 1998, para. 6.

144. CERD/C/SR.1420, 15th periodic report of the UK, Committee on the Elimination of Racial Discrimination, 8 September 2000, para. 58.

145. HL Hansard, Vol. 606, Col. 456, 28 October 1999.

146. The Government itself has recognised that the employment and race directives 'will not be the end of the road on equality': Barbara Roche, Minister for Women, quoted in *supra* note 11 p. 2.

147. Lord Lester, HL Hansard, Vol. 613, Col. 1203, 7 June 2000.

148. The Race Directive (2000/43/EC) goes further than the Employment Directive in that it covers matters such as healthcare, social security, education, housing and other services available to the public.

12,[149] Directive 2000/78/EC only extends to matters that are connected with employment.[150] Accordingly the Employment Directive is likely to have a modest impact in areas synonymous with allegations of religious discrimination such as education,[151] the media,[152] the criminal justice system,[153] the prison service,[154] social services[155] and even sport.[156] Nor will the Directive remove the 'glass ceiling' that some have claimed restricts the advancement of minority groups in key areas of public life such as the civil service, the judiciary and the government.[157]

Secondly, the Employment Directive fails to rectify the constitutional anomalies that enshrine religious discrimination within the British constitution. It neither ensures that the representatives of faiths other than the Church of England have the right to sit in the House of Lords,[158] nor does it extend the protection of the blasphemy law to religions other than Christianity.[159] The latter anomaly is likely to remain in spite criticism from members of the ICCPR's Human Rights Committee,[160] the Law Commission,[161] various peers,[162] and a number of academic writers.[163] Finally, the Employment Directive will not affect what is perhaps the most obvious example of institu-

---

149. The Employment Directive can be compared to Protocol 12 of the European Convention on Human Rights which prohibits discrimination with regard to 'any right set forth by law', thereby covering discrimination in respect to a wide range of civil and political rights.

150. For some examples of the scope of the Employment Directive see *supra* note 11 para. 2.2.

151. See, for example, P. Weller, A. Feldman and K. Purdam *et al*, *Religious Discrimination in England and Wales* chp. 3 (London: Home Office Research Study 220, 2001).

152. For allegations of religious discrimination in the media see CERD/C/SR.1420, Committee on the Elimination of Racial Discrimination, 15th periodic report of the UK, 8th September 2000, para. 37.

153. Weller, Feldman and Purdam, *supra* note 151 chp. 5.

154. J. Beckford and S. Gilliat, *Religion in Prison. Equal Rites in a Multi-Faith Society* (Cambridge: Cambridge University Press, 1998).

155. Weller, Feldman and Purdam, *supra* note 151 chp. 7.

156. Whilst the captain of the England cricket team (Nasser Hussain) is a Muslim, it is noticeable that there are few minority faith players and administrators in the higher echelons of sports such as football, rugby, golf, tennis and cricket.

157. Lord Parekh, HL Hansard, Vol. 632, Col. 1395, 20 March 2002.

158. The Bishoprics Act 1878. See P. Goodrich, 'A Bishop in the House of Lords', *Law and Justice* 63 (1997).

159. *R* v. *Metropolitan Stipendiary Magistrate ex parte Choudhury* [1991] 1 All ER 306.

160. CCPR/C/SR 1050, para. 3 (see point made by Sadi).

161. The Law Commission, *Offences Against Religion and Public Worship*, Law Commission Report No. 145 (1985).

162. See, for example, Lord Lester, HL Hansard, Vol. 555, Cols. 1891-1909, 16 June 1994.

163. See, for example, S. Poulter, 'Toward Reform of the Blasphemy and Racial Hatred Laws' *PL* 375 (1991).

tionalised religious discrimination—the fact that succession to the crown is limited to those who are of the Protestant Christian faith.[164] A reigning monarch who marries a Catholic or converts to Catholicism will lose the crown, a sanction that awaits any incumbent who refuses to, 'join in communion with the Church of England as by law established'.[165] In spite of the fact that it has been claimed that the ban on the monarch marrying a non-Protestant contravenes the Human Rights Act;[166] and it has been acknowledged by both the Attorney General[167] and the Prime Minister[168] as being discriminatory; reform has, as yet, not been forthcoming.[169] Paradoxically, therefore, once the Directive comes into force the Sovereign will be a member of only a small group of people whose continued 'employment' is dependent on them not changing their faith.

Thirdly, notwithstanding the incorporation of the Employment Directive, there are a number of other measures that the United Kingdom could take to enhance its powers to deal with religious discrimination. For example, the Government has, so far, refused to heed calls, at both the international[170] and domestic level,[171] to ratify and incorporate Protocol 12 to the European Convention. The incorporation of this Protocol would provide for a free-standing right to protection from discrimination by public authorities and would compensate for the limitations considered earlier in Article 14 of the Convention. Such a change of policy would certainly make it easier for those complaining of discrimination on the grounds of religion or belief to rely on the Human Rights Act. Alternatively, the Government could recognise the right of individual petition under the International Covenant on Civil and Political Rights, thereby giving citizens an opportunity to avail themselves of the Covenant's non-discrimination clause.[172] A similar proposal has also been put forward with regard to the rights of individuals to invoke the International

---

164. The Act of Settlement 1700, s. 1.

165. *Ibid.* s. 3.

166. This claim has been made by Geoffrey Robertson, *The Guardian*, 6 December 2000.

167. Lord Williams, *The Daily Telegraph*, 10 March 2001, p. 1.

168. Tony Blair, *The Guardian*, 5 June 2001.

169. A ten-minute rule Bill that would have repealed the provisions in the Act of Settlement prohibiting Catholics from succession to the throne was unsuccessfully proposed by Labour MP Kevin McNamara: *The Guardian*, 11 February 2002.

170. CERD/C/SR.1420, 15th periodic report of the UK, Committee on the Elimination of Racial Discrimination, 8 September 2000, para. 38.

171. Lord Lester, HL Hansard, Vol. 624, Col. 288, 25 April 2001.

172. This has been advocated by the Human Rights Committee, CCPR/CO/73/UK;CCPR/CO/73/UKOT, para. 7, 6 December 2001 and by R. Higgins, The Foreword in D. Harris and S. Joseph (eds.), *The International Covenant on Civil and Political Rights* p. xvii (Oxford: Clarendon, 1995).

Convention on the Elimination of All Forms of Racial Discrimination.[173] And finally, perhaps the most radical solution would be the enactment of a single Equality Act. In the absence of such legislation it has been claimed that it is necessary to refer to 30 Acts, 38 statutory instruments, 11 codes of practice and 12 EC Directives to get a comprehensive overview of British discrimination law.[174] A positive recent development has been the Government's promise to establish a single Equality Commission that will, *inter alia*, have jurisdiction over discrimination on the grounds of religion or belief.[175] Yet more could be done and it is to difficult to avoid the conclusion that the campaign to eliminate discrimination generally, and religious discrimination in particular, will not be successfully waged until the Government chooses to equip itself with all of the legal tools at its disposal.

Fourthly, even if the Government complements the Employment Directive by initiating further legal reform, it is important to remember that 'discrimination cannot be tackled by law alone'.[176] A Government Minister recently acknowledged this by noting that, with regard to the challenge of implementing the Employment Directive, 'legislation alone is not enough'.[177] After all, as a Special Rapporteur of the Commission on Human Rights has observed, '[I]t is on the minds of men that all forms of intolerance and discrimination based on religion or belief take form and it is at this level, much more than others, that action should primarily be taken'.[178] Mindful of the limitations of law as a vehicle of social reform, Lord Parekh has recently called, *inter alia*, for 'a sensitive blend of popular education [and] voluntary self-regulation by industries and other institutions'.[179] In order to realise Lord Parekh's bold vision the Government must adopt measures over and above its incorporation of the Employment Directive, such as the promotion of inter-community projects[180] and the introduction of educational policies designed to tackle religious discrimination.[181] If the Government is serious about tackling religious dis-

173. Lord Lester, HL Hansard, Vol. 600, Col. 1276, 12 May 1999.

174. B. Hepple, M. Coussey and T. Choudhury, *Equality a New Framework – Report of the independent review of the enforcement of UK anti-discrimination legislation* p. 21 (Oxford: Hart, 2000).

175. *The Times*, 15 May 2002, p. 9.

176. Lord Parekh, *The Daily Telegraph*, 18 October 2000, p. 26.

177. Angela Eagle, HC Hansard, Vol. 370, Col. 82W, 26 June 2001.

178. A. Amor, *Implementation of the Declaration on the Elimination of All Forms of Intolerance and of Discrimination Based on Religion Or Belief*, E/CN.4/1994/79 para. 98 (1994).

179. *Ibid.*

180. See, for example, The Runnymede Trust, *Islamophobia A Challenge For Us All* Chp. 8, pp. 50-55 (1997).

181. The UN Special Rapporteur on Freedom of Religion or Belief, Abdelfattah Amor, has commented on the 'decisive contribution' which the education system can make to the 'emergence of attitudes and behaviour which reflect tolerance and non-discrimination', E/CN.4/1999/58, 11 January 1999, p. 3, para. 8.

crimination and harassment it must allocate sufficient resources to tackle the problem. It is interesting to note that proper funding was seen as an essential prerequisite of the extra-legal measures which were referred to in the White Paper that preceded the first Race Relations Act in 1965.[182] Some may argue that efforts to tackle discrimination both nationally[183] and internationally[184] have been undermined by inadequate financial support. Irrespective of the truth of such claims it is clear that the old adage, 'you get what you pay for', applies equally to efforts by the state to fight discrimination on the grounds of religion and belief, as it does to all other aspects of life.

Conclusion

The Prime Minister has stated that he would like to see Muslims (and presumably members of other religious groups) not merely accorded equal rights as citizens of this country but also '*seen* as an integral part of British society'.[185] There is little doubt that the incorporation of Employment Directive, alongside the Human Rights Act 1998 and the recent decision to establish a single Equality Commission, will give official recognition to the fact that 'religious communities and their members have a significant contribution to make to local and national life'.[186] Yet it would be unwise to be complacent. Continued vigilance is necessary, particularly in the light of the resurgence recently of a number of far right groups in both Britain[187] and Europe[188] that are avowedly hostile to certain religious groups.[189] Thus, it is to be hoped that the incorporation of the Employment Directive is the start and not the end of a process

182. Cmnd. 6234, para. 26.

183. C. McCrudden, D. Smith, C. Brown, *Racial Justice At Work* p. 277 (London: PSI, 1991).

184. The UN Special Rapporteur on Religious Intolerance has previously complained of the 'paucity of resources allocated to his activities', *supra* note 178 p. 25, para. 119.

185. *The Muslim News*, Issue 118, 28 February 1999.

186. Council of Europe, *Preliminary Conclusions: Seminar on Religion and the Integration of Immigrants* p. 169 (Strasbourg, 1999).

187. On this generally see F. Bodi, 'Call this monster by its name', *The Guardian*, 14 May 2002, p. 16.

188. On the growth of the Far Right in Europe and their particular hostility to Islam see P. Finn, 'A Turn from Tolerance', *The Washington Post*, 29 March 2002, A01.

189. Although the Far Right in Europe have recently targeted Judaism and Islam, one should not ignore the warning that in recent years there has been '[a]n upsurge of State policies directed against 'sects' or new religious movements': Report submitted by A. Amor, Special Rapporteur on Freedom of Religion or Belief, E/CN.4/1999/58, 11 January 1999, p. 22, para. 104.

which will ensure that the Prime Minister's fine words are more than mere rhetoric.

Chapter 8

Freedom of thought, conscience and religion or belief in the context of recent social and political changes in the Netherlands

Cornelis D. de Jong[1]

Special Adviser on Human Rights, Netherlands Ministry of Foreign Affairs

This article contains an analysis of the rather turbulent political and social developments which took place in the Netherlands in the first half of 2002 and the role of the freedom of thought, conscience and religion or belief in that context. The sudden rise of a political movement whose spokesman called Islam a rather 'backward religion' and wanted to abolish the right of non-discrimination on the basis of race or religion, followed by the murder of that spokesman, sent an almost unprecedented shockwave throughout all layers of Dutch society. Although it would fall beyond the scope of this article to provide an in-depth analysis of the social background of these events, an attempt

1. This article represents the personal views of the author only.

has been made to confront existing rules of national and international law concerning the freedom of religion or belief with the recent developments[2] in the Netherlands. In particular, the question will be addressed of whether the time has come to restrict the freedom of religion or belief or the right of non-discrimination in view of the social tensions that are sometimes attributed to too extensive an interpretation of these freedoms.

The article consists of three parts. Firstly, a brief general description of the recent developments in the Netherlands will be given. Secondly, the main elements of the freedom of religion or belief and the right of non-discrimination, as developed in international law, will be analysed against the background of the various policy proposals made by the political movement referred to above.[3] Finally, an attempt has been made to address the concerns that gave rise to the recent turmoil in the Netherlands in a manner which is consistent with international law.

Social tensions in the Netherlands during the first half of 2002

During the second half of the 20th century, the Netherlands could be stereotyped as a politically and socially stable country.[4] Traditional tensions between various Christian groups (particularly between members of the Protestant Churches and those belonging to the Roman Catholic Church), as well as tensions between socialists and capitalists had been absorbed through a model which has been referred to as the 'pillar model'. In accordance with this model Protestants, Catholics, Socialists and Liberals organised themselves separately not only in politics, but also in all sorts of social and educational organisations. If you were a Protestant, you belonged to a Protestant trade union, a Protestant football club, went to a Protestant school and voted of course for a Protestant party. These organisations provided the various groups with a home base which provided necessary protection. Co-operation with other groups was possible, but was in practice confined to those areas where it could not be avoided. Politics was such an area, since due to the prevailing system of proportional representation none of the existing parties was likely to have a

2. This article is current as of the end of August 2002.

3. i.e. 'List Pim Fortuyn'.

4. For a recent description of the social history of the Netherlands in the 20th century, see: C. van Eijl, L. Heerma van Voss and P. de Rooij, *Sociaal Nederland, Contouren van de twintigste eeuw* (Amsterdam: Aksant, 2002).

majority in parliament and governments could not but consist of coalitions between various parties.

From the 1960s onwards, the 'pillar model' became ever less applicable to the social situation in the Netherlands.[5] The tensions between Protestants and Catholics had largely become a thing of the past and, moreover, a strong secularisation process[6] had made religion less important, or at least important for ever fewer people. In politics, this led to the merger of the two main Protestant parties and the Catholic party, and to a more general and less Christian emphasis by the new political party. The Netherlands Labour party, representing most of the socialist voters, went through a similar process. Since most of the original workers' demands had been met by the creation of an extensive social welfare system, differences between the Labour party and other parties on such socio-economic issues became gradually less apparent. Between August 1994 and July 2002 differences between the Labour party and its traditional opponent, the conservative Liberal party, had diminished to such an extent that a coalition between these parties became viable.[7]

A second development that should be mentioned here is that the traditionally monolithic (predominantly white) Dutch society became far more diverse through an increase in immigration since the 1970s. Originally, these immigrants came from either the former Dutch colonies or from Turkey and Morocco. The latter two countries were so-called 'recruitment countries', from which government officials selected (groups of) immigrants who could work and stay in the Netherlands, filling the jobs that the indigenous population could not or did not want to do. When the need for this type of labour persisted, and the stay of these immigrants was extended, eventually it was accepted that these immigrants (and the members of their families) could stay indefinitely and hence should be considered part of the Netherlands society. Finally, since the late 1980s the Netherlands also faced an increasing number of asylum applications and a growing immigrant population as a result of this. Although the nationalities of asylum applicants varied over the years, many

5. An extensive analysis of the processes of 'pillarisation' and 'depillarisation' has been made by P. Pennings, *Verzuiling en Ontzuiling: de lokale verschillen: opbouw, instandhouding en neergang van plaatselijke zuilen in verschillende delen van Nederland na 1880* (Kampen: Kok Agora, 1991).

6. A description of the secularisation process can be found in the following study of the Social and Cultural Planning Office of the Netherlands: J.W. Becker and R. Vink, *Secularisation in the Netherlands, 1966-1991: changing opinions, changing behaviour* (The Hague: SCP, 1994).

7. Although written from a liberal perspective, the following publication contains much information on the relationship between the Labour and Liberal Parties in the 20th century in the Netherlands: P.G.C. van Schie (ed.), *Tussen polarisatie en paars: de 100-jarige verhouding tussen liberalen en socialisten in Nederland* (Kampen: Kok Agora, 1995).

of them originated from an Islamic country or adhered to the Islamic faith. This was also true for the Turkish and Moroccan immigrants[8] as well as for a minority of immigrants from the former Dutch colonies. As a consequence, Islam became the second major religion in the Netherlands, second only to Christianity.

Immigration therefore led to a completely new social situation. Whereas the traditional, Christian organisations had either gone through some kind of remodelling of their identities, often along more secular lines, or had diminished in importance, the new Islamic immigrants generally stuck to the importance of their religion. The Islamic religion is not secularised in the sense that its tenets determine almost every facet of life and are not confined to the realm of spirituality. The secularisation process which the Netherlands had gone through, to the contrary, had reinforced the separation of Church and State that had been developed in the 19th century.

Although these differences were prevalent from the very beginning, the first official policy reaction was optimistic. It was believed that the differences would diminish over time, as they had diminished among Protestants and Catholics. As pointed out by the Netherlands Scientific Council for Government Policy,[9] originally the attempts of the Netherlands Government focused on eliminating any discriminatory provisions in Dutch legislation and on the enhancement of the legal rights of immigrants. This followed the familiar pattern of strengthening the position of minority groups so that they would become full (and integrated) members of society. Furthermore, one of the basic principles was that immigrants should be able to maintain and develop their own cultural and religious identity. From the indigenous population, respective governments expected a positive attitude towards the immigrants irrespective of their culture, or at least a non-discriminatory attitude.

In the beginning there were very few developments tempering this optimism. The numbers of Islamic immigrants were so low that the latter's visibility in society was confined to a few neighbourhoods within the larger cities. When, in the late 1980s and 1990s these figures rose considerably, and with

8. According to the official statistics of the Netherlands Central Statistical Office, the number of Moroccans rose from around 20,000 in 1972, 72,000 in 1980, and 168,000 in 1990 to 284,124 in 2002; the number of Turks rose from around 30,000 in 1972, 120,000 in 1980, and 206,000 in 1990 to 330,709 in 2002.

9. *The Netherlands as Immigration Society*, (The Hague: WRR, 2002). The original policy document of the Netherlands Government was called the *Memorandum on Ethnic Minorities* and was issued in 1983; for the most recent policy document, see *Kansen krijgen, kansen pakken – Integratiebeleid 1999-2002* which was submitted to the Netherlands Parliament on 2 November 1998. An analysis of Islamic institution-building in Europe can be found in J. Rath, R. Penninx, C. Groenendijk and A. Meijer, *Europe and its Islam: the Netherlands, Belgium and Britain react to an emerging religious community* (Leiden: Brill, 2001).

them also the visibility of Muslims in Dutch society, the differences became much more apparent. At the same time, due to changing conditions in the labour market, unskilled labour was less in demand and unemployment figures among the immigrant population rose. Moreover, throughout the 1990s reports of high crime rates among the immigrant population[10] came to the fore. Of course these crime rates do not in themselves say anything about the possible relationship between ethnic or religious factors and crime since other factors, such as the social position of delinquents, may be more important. However, relatively high crime and unemployment rates coupled with a concentration of immigrants in the bigger cities, did not provide a fertile soil for integration. At the same time, an increase in cultural clashes could also be noted: certain religious tenets of Islam, such as the wearing of headscarves by Muslim women, were very visible and led to an increasing unease among the rest of the population.

Although in the late 1990s the integration policies of the respective governments became ever tougher, the basic premise of non-discrimination and respect for the culture, including the religion or belief, of immigrants remained predominant. In retrospect, one cannot but conclude that the gap between the authorities developing such integration (and immigration) policies, and large segments of the Dutch society, became ever wider.

Since World War II, the Netherlands has never known any major fascist or nationalist parties. Whereas in other European countries anti-immigrant parties started to become more important, comparable parties in the Netherlands did not gain any significant support. However, in 2001 the political landscape in the Netherlands began to shift. On 25 November 2001 Pim Fortuyn was elected party leader of a newly established national party called 'Leefbaar Nederland' (livable Netherlands). This party brought together a number of independent local parties and aimed at bridging the gap between the national politicians in The Hague and the population at large. Before his election, Fortuyn had been active as a columnist, as a private consultant and as an academic. Although he had voiced opinions on many policy issues, it is his statements on religion, culture and immigration that are particularly relevant in the context of this article. In this respect, reference can be made to his book *Tegen de islamisering van onze cultuur, Nederlandse identiteit als fundament* (Against the Islamization of our culture, Dutch identity as the basis) published in 1997,[11] and to several of his columns.

10. For a nuanced, yet realistic view of crime among immigrant populations, see: F. Bovenkerk, 'Crime and the Multi-ethnic Society: A View from Europe' in *Crime, Law and Social Change* (19) pp. 271-280.

11. P. Fortuyn, *Tegen de islamisering van onze cultuur, Nederlandse identiteit als fundament* (Uithoorn: Karakter Uitgevers, 1997).

From the moment of his election, Fortuyn received wide-spread public attention. His style was new and he was not averse to raising many controversial issues. On 9 February 2002, however, he gave an interview to one of the national newspapers[12] which went too far even for his own party—his observations with regard to Islam and the right to non-discrimination based on race or religion were found to be shocking and not in line with the general policies of his party. As a consequence, he had to resign as party leader of 'Leefbaar Nederland'. But on 1 March 2002, Fortuyn was able to announce the creation of a new national political party, built around him and carrying his name—the LPF (List Pim Fortuyn) was born. His public appearances were increasingly successful with the viewers, and many people who had turned their backs on politics developed a new interest in it, since Fortuyn seemed to address the issues that had been largely ignored by existing political parties. On 6 May, on the eve of the national elections, Fortuyn was murdered—an event that horrified the country and led to an almost complete halting of all election activities. Eventually the LPF obtained 26 out of 150 seats in parliament, which was an all-time high for a new party, and in August 2002 a new government was installed consisting of the Christian-Democrats, the LPF, and the Conservative-Liberals.

It is difficult to say why people voted so massively for the LPF. The murder of a national politician was unprecedented in the Netherlands and many must have given their vote as a sign of protest against such a barbaric act. However, even before the murder of Fortuyn, the opinion polls showed an equally large and even increasing measure of support for his party. Apart from his confrontational and in that sense refreshing style, his message must obviously also have had a direct appeal to large segments of the Dutch society. It therefore seems justified to examine these in rather more detail.

For a brief analysis of his ideas, especially with regard to the freedom of religion or belief and the right to non-discrimination, I have examined the revised 2002 edition of his book on Islamization,[13] together with his interview on 9 February 2002 and a couple of his columns on this issue.[14] In these publications Fortuyn expressed his concerns with any form of fundamentalism, particulary with Islamic fundamentalism.

In Fortuyn's view, the 1960s and 1970s in the Netherlands had not only done away with the pillar-model as described above, but had also introduced a stron-

12. *De Volkskrant*.

13. P. Fortuyn, *De Islamisering van onze cultuur: Nederlandse identiteit als fundament* (Uithoorn: Karakter Uitgevers BV, 2002).

14. P. Fortuyn, *Hoofddoekjes en tulbanden*, http://nu.nl/fortuyn (28 January 2000); P. Fortuyn, *EU immigratiegebied?*, http://nu.nl/fortuyn (11 February 2000); P. Fortuyn, *De dreiging van de Islam*, http://www.lijstpimfortuyn.info/news.php?goto=columns&column_id=27 (18 September 2001).

ger emphasis on the individual (the individualisation of society), and had given equal rights to women and homosexuals. Due to the individualisation process, younger people especially had lost their interest in collective cultural and social values. In addition, the end of the basically partriarchal and hierarchical family structure meant that the passing on of old values to the younger generation was no longer assured. The strengthening of the rights of women and homosexuals was, in the opinion of Fortuyn, a purely positive development which made a full development of man's talents possible irrespective of sex or sexuality.

By way of contrast, the orientation of (especially Islamic) immigrant communities had not followed a similar development. Fortuyn went so far as to say that religious fundamentalism, especially Islamic fundamentalism, might not yet be widespread among the Muslims in the Netherlands but that the danger for its growth existed and that certainly the adherence to religious tenets by Muslims was much stronger than with most of the Christians in the Netherlands. In Fortuyn's view, the best way of countering the growing influence of Islam was a revival of respect for the national traditions based on Judaism, Christianity and Humanism. On the basis of these traditions, the Netherlands had developed its parliamentary democracy, which filtered various ideologies and made it possible to develop and implement policies which reflected the general values but also respected the position of minorities. Due to the developments mentioned above, the indigenous Dutch population was hardly aware of these assets anymore and was therefore not well protected against any fundamentalist tendencies threatening its democratic system.

Although Fortuyn did not give many concrete examples of what he saw as wrong behaviour amongst (many) Muslims, the following elements were mentioned. Firstly, Fortuyn accused Islam of not respecting the fundamental principle of separation of Church and State and went as far as to call Islam a 'backward religion'.[15] In this respect he referred to existing legislation in Islamic countries where, for example, matrimonial and inheritance rights were governed by religious instead of secular legislation. He also mentioned the example of the conviction of an Egyptian professor[16] for having violated the official interpretation of the Qur'an in his academic work. After his conviction his marriage was declared null and void and eventually he had to seek asylum in the Netherlands. Without the separation of Church and State, Fortuyn argued, it was impossible to have a viable parliamentary democracy, since obviously the rights of dissenting minorities would not longer be protected.

Secondly, Fortuyn criticised the manner in which women were allegedly treated by their Muslim husbands. Although he admitted that nobody knew

15. In the interview with the *Volkskrant*.

16. That being the case of Nasr Abu Zaid.

exactly what happened behind the closed doors of Muslim homes, he suspected the worst by just looking at the public behaviour of Muslim women. Their clothing (headscarves, long dresses or raincoats) and their aversion of any eye contact with other people (especially men) in the streets made him fear that in reality they were scared to have any outside contacts. Instead of promoting women's rights those Muslim girls who did climb up the social ladder persisted in their own culture and happily wore headscarves themselves as a means of identifying themselves as 'Muslimas'.

Thirdly, Fortuyn criticised the persecution of homosexuals in Egypt and the generally hostile attitude of the Muslim community in the Netherlands towards homosexuals. In particular, he referred to the intimidation of homosexual teachers by their Muslim pupils. Furthermore, he regretted the limited possibilities for homosexual Muslims to be open about their homosexuality and yet live a normal life.

Finally, Fortuyn analysed the position of Muslim youth. Whereas the general climate in the Netherlands had evolved from an authoritarian, family-oriented society, to a society based on negotiation even within the family between parents and their children, Muslim families were still largely based on the traditional, authoritarian system. This meant, Fortuyn argued, that Muslim children were confronted with an authoritarian upbringing at home and an open and free society outside. This led to the exploitation of this freedom to its fullest. Dutch girls were seen as possible outlets for sexual desires that with the strict Islamic codes could never be fulfilled with Muslim girls before marriage. It also explained to Fortuyn the poor academic achievements of Muslim youth at schools and the high crime rates among the immigrant population at large.

As referred to above, Fortuyn suggested the revival of traditional Dutch values. He certainly did not advocate a return to the situation before the 1960s and 1970s and was well aware of the new situation in the information age. In particular, he accepted that a new international culture had emerged as a consequence of globalisation, especially in economic terms. That new culture, in his view, was rather superficial and consumer-oriented but could not be curbed. Instead, he saw the revival of traditional values as a possibility for redeveloping a national identity within a broader, international culture. As the cornerstone of such a process, Fortuyn emphasised respect for parliamentary democracy, separation of Church and State, and equal rights for men and women irrespective of sex and sexuality.

Fortuyn only mentioned a limited number of practical measures in dealing with Muslim communities. He welcomed a more active interest taken by the national security forces in scrutinising Islamic organisations, including mosques. As he put it, Fortuyn did not trust what was going on in the mosques. Insofar as it did not harm national society, he respected the freedom of religion, but in his opinion social issues were discussed there and he did not rule out that Muslims were also indoctrinated with fundamentalist beliefs in mosques.

Secondly, he proposed to put an end to segregation and concentration tendencies through a new housing policy which could make it impossible for people to live in areas with already high concentrations of members of their ethnic or religious group. Although this might clash with the right to non-discrimination as interpreted in the Netherlands, Fortuyn did not see this as a real obstacle. In his view, the right to non-discrimination was abused since only whites seemed to be prosecuted in this respect, and possibly discriminatory acts by others were not even examined. More generally, Fortuyn proposed widening the scope of the freedom of expression so that statements would not automatically come under the category of being discriminatory. In his interview of 9 February 2002, Fortuyn went as far as to propose the deletion of the non-discrimination article in the Constitution altogether.

Thirdly, Fortuyn did not accept religiously inspired clothing amongst public officials. In particular, he held that headscarves or turbans should not be allowable for such officials. He vehemently opposed plans to allow for such headware within the police force.

Finally, Fortuyn proposed an intensive dialogue with the Islamic groups in the Netherlands. He proposed that the basic tenets of the Dutch culture should be explained to them, and that all new immigrants would have to subscribe to these values. Insofar as the existing immigrant population was concerned, Fortuyn did not go so far as to plan to impose Dutch culture upon them, but hoped that by promoting their social and economic position the Muslim community would eventually undergo a similar process to that which the indigenous Dutch population had previously undergone.

Relevant aspects of the freedom of religion or belief as recognised in international law

The right to freedom of thought, conscience and religion or belief has been recognised in various international legal instruments. I mention in this respect the *Universal Declaration of Human Rights,*[17] the *International Covenant on Civil and Political Rights*[18] and the *Declaration on the Elimination of All Forms of Intolerance*

17. Adopted and proclaimed by GA Res. 217A(III) of 10 December 1948.
18. Adopted and opened for signature, ratification and accession by GA Res. 2200A(XXI) of 16 December 1966.

and of Discrimination Based on Religion or Belief[19] as the main UN instruments; in addition, the Netherlands are a party to the *European Convention on Human Rights* and are also committed to a range of morally binding OSCE[20]-instruments. These instruments provide an international framework, which is largely legally binding for any Dutch Government and reduces the number of policy options; however, the codification of the freedom of religion or belief has not been a straightforward process and although certain rights have been explicitly recognised, in other areas there is still room for interpretation at the national level. In this part of the article, I shall examine the various policy questions that came to the fore in the first part of the article with a view to establishing the framework imposed upon the Netherlands by international human rights law. The final part of the article will provide some indications on how a policy could be developed with respect for this framework, in order to meet the concerns among significant layers of the Netherlands society.

The freedom of religion or belief[21] is a complicated freedom. During the codification history of this freedom, there has always been a strong movement in favour of a broad interpretation of this freedom, but there has been an equally strong movement pointing out that abuse of the freedom of religion or belief is not only possible, but can also have grave consequences, since by definition religion or belief determine one's outlook on life[22] and people are therefore prone to manipulation. Throughout history, and even today, there have been numerous civil and international tensions or wars based on religious grounds. This has led to wide recognition of the freedom of religion or belief in the abstract, but it has been extremely difficult to agree on the specific elements of this freedom. The codification of the UN Declaration took more than 20 years. Although attempts have been made to elaborate a UN Convention on the freedom of religion or belief, as yet it is believed that the differences of opinion are such that the negotiations of a Convention might actually result in an international instrument that weakens rather than strengthens the protection of the freedom of religion or belief.[23]

19. Proclaimed by GA Res. 36/55 of 25 November 1981. For practical reasons I shall refer to this instrument as the UN Declaration.

20. Organisation for Security and Co-operation in Europe.

21. For practical purposes, I shall refer to the freedom of religion or belief as a shorter alternative for the freedom of thought, conscience and religion or belief. However, this should not be interpreted as an underestimation of the elements of 'thought' and 'conscience'. For an extensive analysis of the meaning of each of these terms, see: C. de Jong, *The Freedom of Thought, Conscience and Religion or Belief in the United Nations (1946-1992)* (Antwerp, 2000).

22. In this respect, reference can be made to the fourth preambular paragraph of the UN Declaration, which considers that religion or belief, for anyone who professes either, is one of the fundamental elements in his conception of life.

23. See, for example, B. Tahzib, *Freedom of Religion or Belief, Ensuring Effective International Legal Protection* pp. 423-494 (The Hague: Martinus Nijhoff, 1996).

International law is basically neutral with respect to religion or belief itself. Although in the past communist States tried, sometimes successfully, to include references to the abuse of freedom of religion or belief in international instruments,[24] these efforts have been offset by statements made by countries with, in particular, an Islamic or Catholic orientation. Instead of singling out individual religions or beliefs, the international instruments emphasise the need for non-discrimination. In principle, all religions or beliefs are equal and any government policy should be based on this consideration.

It would have been logical for the international community to have accepted the principle of separation of Church and State as a corollary to the principle of non-discrimination. Especially in the United Nations, attempts towards this position were made[25] but they failed. States with a State religion argued that it was perfectly possible to have an official national Church or belief and yet respect the principle of non-discrimination. Although the records of the Human Rights Committee show that in practice there may be various problems with such official religions or beliefs, this principle has been maintained, even by that Committee itself.[26]

Although the freedom of religion or belief needs to be respected and its protection should be offered on a non-discriminatory basis, this does not mean that the freedom is unlimited. A distinction has to be made between the freedom to have or to adopt a religion or belief of one's choice, which is generally perceived as an unlimited freedom,[27] and the freedom to manifest one's

24. For a survey of these initiatives, see de Jong, *supra* note 21 pp. 646-650.

25. E.g., the Ukrainian SSR in the informal working group of the UN Commission on Human Rights, in 1964 (E/3873, p. 77) and again in 1973 (A/9134, p. 34).

26. In its General Comment on article 18 of the Covenant, the Committee considered that: 'the fact that a religion is recognized as a State religion or that it is established as official or traditional or that its followers comprise the majority of the population, shall not result in any impairment of the enjoyment of any of the rights under the Covenant, including articles 18 and 27, nor in any discrimination against adherents of other religions or non-believers'. This does not preclude the existence of official religions. However, individual members of the Committee raised critical questions on these issues during the examination of individual country reports. For a survey of such questions, see de Jong, *supra* note 21 pp. 339-342.

27. This is often called the *forum internum*. See, for example: B. Vermeulen, 'Freedom of religion in Western Europe: Past and Present' in Jonneke M.M. Naber (ed.), *Freedom of religion: a precious human right, A survey of its advantages and drawbacks* p. 19 (Assen: Van Gorcum, 2000); in Th. Meron (ed.), *Human Rights in International Law: Legal Policy Issues* pp. 179-180 (Oxford: Clarendon Press, 1984); Th.C. Van Boven, *De volkenrechtelijke bescherming van de godsdienstvrijheid* p. 160 (Assen: Van Gorcum, 1967); J. Humphrey, in Th. Meron (ed.), *Human Rights in International Law* pp. 179-180; D.J. Sullivan, 'Advancing the Freedom of Religion or Belief through the UN Declaration on the Elimination of Religious Intolerance' *The American Journal of International Law* 82 p. 493 (1988). It should be noted, however, that especially Islamic countries have objected to the unlimited character of the right to change one's religion or belief, as Muslims are not normally allowed to convert to

religion or belief. Article 18, paragraph 3 of the Covenant makes the latter freedom subject to such limitations as are prescribed by law and are necessary to protect public safety, order, health, or morals or the fundamental rights and freedoms of others. Of these limitation grounds, I consider the last one the most important. It reflects the general principle that the manifestation of religion or belief may not encroach upon the fundamental rights and freedoms of others. There are many examples of such clashes and the previous part of this article contained a number of practical examples in this respect.

Let us now take a closer look at the various problems related to religion or belief in the Netherlands. The first development mentioned concerned the influx of Muslim immigrants and their increasing visibility in Dutch society. Although such a development may bring with it social tensions and even culture shocks, for example when Christian churches are converted into mosques, the neutrality of international law with respect to individual religions or beliefs implies that immigrants cannot be denied their rights under the freedom of religion or belief. At the same time, governments are required to promote tolerance between adherents of different religions or beliefs, and an active policy against possible social and cultural tensions is not only permitted but even called for under international law. In this respect, measures aimed at promoting dialogue between various religions or beliefs and educational measures can prove to be useful instruments in reducing tensions.

The freedom to manifest one's religion or belief includes the right to establish and maintain places of worship. Article 6, paragraph (a) explicitly recognises such a right. The same right has been recognised in paragraph 16.4 of the Vienna Concluding Document of the OSCE. This means that a government cannot deny the establishment of, for example, mosques, simply because this would cause cultural or social tensions in the area. Any such restriction should be based on one of the above mentioned limitation grounds, and none of these grounds lends itself to that. Although the tensions may endanger public safety or public order when they take violent forms, the establishment of a mosque in itself is not the cause for these tensions and its prohibition may not take away the tensions either. It should be recalled here that the European Court on Human Rights considers very carefully what is called the necessity test: an interference should correspond to a pressing social need and, in particular, it should be proportionate to the legitimate aim pursued.[28] Against this back-

---

another religion. See, for example: de Jong, *supra* note 21 pp. 34-50 and pp. 55-60. These objections make M.D. Evans conclude that although it has become generally accepted that Article 18 does embrace the right to change religion, the evidence advanced in support of this is not wholly convincing. M.D. Evans, *Religious Liberty and International Law in Europe* (Cambridge: Cambridge University Press, 1997)

28. *Olsson* v. *Sweden*, A 130 para. 67 (1988).

ground, it seems impossible to argue successfully that such a prohibition was necessary to protect public safety or public order. Nor can it be argued that any fundamental rights and freedoms were encroached upon by the establishment of a mosque. There is no fundamental right not to have a mosque in one's area, and the fundamental right to establish places of worship for other religions or beliefs is not hampered by the establishment of a mosque. Again, the national government should take its responsibility to promote tolerance among various religions or beliefs by reducing tensions, but it cannot do so by restricting the rights and freedoms of one religion or belief in particular. That would amount to discrimination and is therefore unlawful under international law. The same holds true for any attempts to revitalise any of the more traditional beliefs in the Netherlands, such as Christianity, Judaism or Humanism. In its policies, the national government is not allowed to give preferential treatment to any religion or belief.

The second issue which came to the fore in the previous part of the article is the wearing of headscarves in public. The right to wear religiously inspired clothing has not been explicitly recognised under international law. Neither the UN Declaration nor any of the OSCE texts refer explicitly to such a right. Nevertheless, the issue has come up, especially in the proceedings of the Human Rights Committee.[29] When this Committee dealt with an individual communication from a Canadian Sikh who was fired after refusing to wear safety headgear at work instead of the (religiously inspired) turban, it considered that this limitation of the freedom to manifest one's religion or belief was permissible under the limitation ground referring to public safety. By taking this line of reasoning, the Committee implicitly acknowledged that the wearing of religiously inspired clothing is one of the manifestations of the freedom of religion or belief. It means that Muslim women who want to wear a headscarf in public are in principle permitted to do so, even if this is not generally welcomed by the public at large. Again, there is no fundamental human right saying that one should be protected against the sight of headscarves or any other religious symbols. It would also be far-fetched to say that the wearing of headscarves in itself leads to social and cultural tensions for the same reasons as mentioned above in respect of the right to establish and maintain mosques. Any general limitations based on public safety or public order (*ordre public*) for this reason alone are bound to be unlawful under international law.

This may be different in specific places or under specific circumstances. Fortuyn, for example, was a declared opponent of police officers wearing headscarves or turbans. In the Netherlands there has also been the case of a

29. de Jong, *supra* note 21 p. 140.

clerk of the court wishing to wear her headscarf during sessions of the court.[30] The basic premise should remain that there is a right to manifest one's religion or belief, *inter alia*, by wearing religiously inspired clothing. Limiting this right will have to be necessary for the protection of specific interests. One such interest could be the need for State neutrality in matters relating to religion or belief. By wearing religiously inspired clothing State officials might create the impression of being biased even if they do not, in practice, discriminate. This, however, is a very delicate balance. As I have stated above, under international law it is even permitted to have an official national Church as long as in practice other religions or beliefs are not discriminated against. I would therefore be inclined to maintain that the right to manifest one's religion or belief and the fundamental rights and freedoms of others have to be carefully weighed against each other.[31] In the case of court proceedings, for example, article 14 of the Covenant states that everyone shall be entitled to a fair and public hearing by a competent, independent and impartial tribunal established by law. The question therefore is of whether a clerk of the court wearing a headscarf or any other religious symbol undermines the impartiality of the court. When this case was considered by the Netherlands Equal Treatment Commission, the latter argued that considering the position of the clerk during the court proceedings, the headscarf should be permitted, since the impartiality of the tribunal as such was not at issue. Perhaps the Commission would have come to a different conclusion in the case of a judge wearing a headscarf. In any case, the Netherlands Minister of Justice declared on 29 August 2001[32] that, if necessary, he would change the law to ensure that neither clerks nor judges were allowed to wear religiously inspired clothing. According to the Minister, the clothing prescriptions are specifically aimed at the protection of the impartial nature of the court and this holds both for judges and clerks. As these conflicting opinions show, this remains a delicate matter, especially since the same government did not seem to have any difficulties with police officers wearing either headscarves or turbans. International law only provides limited guidance in these very specific cases.

Another issue mentioned by Fortuyn concerned the position of women and homosexuals. In his opinion, the rights of these groups are undermined by the repressive nature of Islamic precepts and practices. The precise issues

30. This issue has been dealt with by the 'Commissie gelijke behandeling' (*Equal Treatment Commission*) in its judgement 2001-53.

31. B. Tahzib-Lie concludes that restrictions relating to religiously inspired clothing of public employees will generally fail to meet the necessity test. Her analysis is, however, of a more general nature and solely based on the limitation grounds of public morals or public order (*ordre public*). B. Tahzib-Lie, 'The advancement of women's equal enjoyment of the right to freedom of religion or belief' in Naber, supra note 27 pp. 57-60.

32. See, for example, De Telegraaf, 30 August 2001.

mentioned in the case of the protection of Muslim women, i.e. lack of social contacts for them due to, *inter alia*, their clothing, and explicit prohibitions concerning any such contact with unknown men, hardly lead to particular policy concerns other than dialogue. This does not come as a surprise, since for any government it will be practically impossible to adopt specific rules or regulations for the way men and women interact in private. Only in extreme cases, such as in the case of domestic violence, is there justifiable reason for public action and interference within family life. The overall principle in international law is, however, that the family should be protected against public interference. This principle is laid down in, for example, Article 23, paragraph 1 of the Covenant which states that the family is entitled to protection by society and the State. Although in accordance with paragraph 4 of the same article States shall also take appropriate steps to ensure equality of rights and responsibilities of spouses during marriage, this provision, which was even controversial at the time of its adoption, cannot be interpreted extensively: it applies to legal rights and responsibilities[33] but it cannot be interpreted as to imply, for example, the right to the same amount of social contact. From a general policy perspective it can, of course, be argued that the position of women is of concern to the authorities. But the measures that can then be considered are all of a promotional, rather than of a prescriptive, nature.

Homosexuality and Islam has become an issue of concern in the Netherlands for a number of reasons. Firstly, a major public upheaval arose when on 8 April 2002 a local court[34] acquitted the Imam of Rotterdam, El Moumni, of charges concerning the offence of homosexuals. The charges followed statements by the Imam made during a broadcast of public national television, when he had said that homosexuality was harmful for Dutch society and that it was a contagious disease. According to the local court the Imam was entitled to make these statements, insofar as they were an expression of his religion, and were therefore protected by the freedom of religion or belief and did not constitute incitement to discrimination, hostility or violence. The latter is explicitly prohibited by Article 20 of the Covenant. In its judgement, the court had taken into consideration that in parts of the interview that had not been broadcast, the Imam had clearly stated that violence against homo-

33. In this respect, it should be noted that the Shari'a rules of personal and private law contain several discriminatory elements. See, for example, A. A. An-Na'im, *Towards an Islamic Reformation: Civil Liberties, Human Rights and International Law* p. 176 (Syracuse, NY: Syracuse University Press, 1990). Despite some pressures, especially from the Moroccan community, the Netherlands Governments have not made it possible for any application of such rules in the Netherlands. The Islamic community in the Netherlands is therefore legally bound by the same – non-discriminatory – rules relating to marriage, divorce and inheritance rights, as the rest of the population.

34. Rechtbank Rotterdam, case no. 10/040070-01.

sexuals by Muslims was not permissible. Here again, it is a delicate balance between fundamental rights and freedoms, in particular between the freedom of religion or belief and the rights of non-discrimination and of physical integrity. Arguably, the Imam may not have known that his appeal not to use any violence against homosexuals would not be broadcast, but even so he should have known that his statements might be abused or misinterpreted, especially since there was already a tendency of violence by Muslim youth against homosexuals. I would not therefore be surprised if the ruling in the appeal procedure, which is still pending, is different.

Secondly, Fortuyn mentioned a specific issue that merits attention—the discrimination of homosexual teachers by their pupils. It must be admitted that homosexual teachers are an easy target for harassment by their pupils. The latter, almost by definition, try to find a vulnerable aspect to their teachers so that they can use it in the on-going power game that is often played out in schools. Most people will remember cases of harassment of teachers based on, for example, physical anomalies. In that sense, harassment of homosexual teachers could be seen as part of the same scenario. However, the situation may have surpassed this pattern—since Islamic teachings tend to be so outspoken about the negative aspects of homosexuality, the normal pattern of social control to keep harassment within acceptable limits may no longer be effective. Parents may implicitly or explicitly support their children at home and if they participate for example in the school board, even officially. In schools with a large percentage of Muslim pupils, the school boards could be so much influenced by the Muslim background of the parents that even the school authorities cannot offer effective protection for homosexual teachers. As a consequence, many teachers may decide not to show their sexuality.

In January 2002, the Netherlands government explicitly included the investigation of discriminatory practices against homosexual pupils or teachers in the mandate of the national Inspector of Education. It goes without saying that harassment of homosexual teachers cannot be tolerated when it goes beyond what can be considered 'normal' in a school situation. Especially when such harassment is not solely confined to the situation at school, the government needs to introduce appropriate criminal sanctions to deal with such harassment. It is more problematic to come to a clear-cut decision when certain school boards of private educational institutions adopt, as their policy, that teachers should not show their homosexual nature when they are teaching. In accordance with international law, it is possible to establish educational institutions based on a specific religion or belief, and if that religion happens to condemn homosexuality it is difficult for the institution to remain credible when at the same time one or more of its teachers proclaim this type of sexuality. But this is not so different from other moral issues. If a teacher is an active Muslim, the school board will probably not welcome an active profession of his or her religion if the school happens to be Orthodox Christian. At the same time, the government can undertake all sorts of promotional activities to support the social acceptability of homosexuality, even in schools, but it will not be possible to prohibit certain regulations aimed at maintaining the denominational nature of the school, even if this means that homosexual teachers cannot proclaim their sexuality at that particular school.

Finally, Fortuyn criticised the abuse of the right to non-discrimination by restricting, in particular, the freedom of expression. In his opinion, almost every reference to inter-ethnic problems resulted in accusations of discrimination. First of all, it must be reiterated that the right to non-discrimination is such a fundamental right under international law that even if, as proposed by Fortuyn, it was deleted from the national constitution it would still be binding upon the Netherlands. All relevant international instruments recognise the right to non-discrimination based on, *inter alia*, religion or belief and emphasise its paramount importance. However, the above-mentioned judgement in the El Moumni case already shows that the judge does allow for very far-reaching statements to be made. In my opinion, the freedom of expression can indeed be limited, but paragraph 3 of Article 19 of the Covenant mentions a number of conditions for accepted restrictions. Restrictions shall only be such as are provided by law and are necessary for respect of the rights or reputations of others and for the protection of national security or of public order (*ordre public*) or of public health or morals. Article 20 furthermore prohibits advocacy of national, racial or religious hatred that constitutes incitement to discrimination, hostility or violence. It would therefore run counter to international law to give an unlimited right of expression, but the limitations are themselves restricted. In my opinion, Fortuyn's criticism of the right to non-discrimination was probably more based on social and political practices than on the legal mechanisms themselves.

The way forward: A reappraisal of the freedom of religion or belief?

The second part of this article showed that international human rights law restricts many of the policy options advocated by Fortuyn. As a reaction to the ongoing challenge posed by Fortuyn's ideas and legacy, theoretically three approaches are possible. Firstly, the Netherlands could either withdraw its support from international human rights instruments or, at least, it could try to do away with any elements that are considered obstacles to the fulfilment of national policy objectives. Secondly, Fortuyn's movement could simply be condemned for not respecting existing international law. Thirdly, solutions could be sought to meet the concerns raised by Fortuyn and his followers while respecting international law.

I would not normally have mentioned the first option, as it could immediately be done away with as being both unethical and unrealistic. However, for a populist, as Fortuyn was, international law was not as sacred as it normally is. His proposal to delete the reference to the right to non-discrimination in the Dutch constitution, for example, showed that he was not even aware of the fact that this step alone would never change the overall commitment of the Netherlands to this right, since it is part of customary international law. However, such a draconian step as to rescind the ratifications of international human rights instruments was never seriously discussed by Fortuyn or his political party. This does not have to come as a surprise for a number of reasons. Firstly, the few countries in the world that have challenged international human rights law outright are either dictatorships or fundamentalist Islamic States (or a combination of both). The Islamic Republic of Iran, for example, often declared that international human rights law would only apply insofar as it did not run counter to the precepts of Islam. It would have been both cynical and incredible if Fortuyn had joined the ranks of such fundamentalist States in order to counter Islamic influences in the Netherlands. Secondly, there are strong legal arguments why such a step would be unrealistic, even for Fortuyn and his party. Especially after the entry into force of the Treaty of Amsterdam, the membership of the European Union is closely linked to respect for international human rights law. Without this, it is virtually impossible to become or remain a member of the EU. For economic reasons alone, leaving the EU is not a realistic option for any government of the Netherlands, irrespective of its political orientation. And although Fortuyn may have been critical of the EU, he certainly did not ever suggest leaving the EU altogether. Thus, even if we leave aside the argument that essential elements of international human rights law continue to be binding upon States as part of international customary law, there are political and legal considerations which indeed make it unrealistic and virtually impossible for a country such as the Netherlands to rescind its obligations under international human rights law.

Although the second option, i.e. the formal condemnation of Fortuyn's ideas as being contrary to international human rights law, may seem attractive at first sight, I think that in the long term this approach is dangerous. The wide public support for his political ideas, not only after his death but also during his active political career, points to the fact that he raised issues and advocated stands that are shared by many and, considering the intensity of support, are also deeply-felt. I do believe that if one thing has become clear throughout the Fortuyn turmoil, it is that mainstream Dutch politics had not addressed some of the most contentious issues, and that more emphasis has to be put on both the basic rights under the freedom of religion or belief and on the limitations of the freedom to manifest one's religion or belief. Not taking any action means that the Netherlands Government would fail to promote tolerance based on religion or belief, as it is required to do under international law. It is therefore an obligation under international law not to simply reject Fortuyn's ideas, and especially its underlying tendencies, but to seek solutions that will diminish tensions and will eventually lead to a harmonious society in which adherents of different religions or beliefs respect each other.

The third option, i.e. the formulation of policy options based on respect for international human rights law, is therefore the only viable one. In my opinion, oddly enough, this is possible, if instead of restricting the rights of religions or beliefs, these rights were to be promoted. To support this thesis, I refer to the beginning of this article, where the social situation in the Netherlands in the second part of the 20th century was described. Due to secularisation, individualisation and strongly increased economic welfare, the indigenous Dutch population has lost most of its traditional beliefs, as well as the organisations based on these beliefs. This made it particularly vulnerable, when it was confronted with a religion such as Islam, that did not yet show any signs of secularisation. In the policy options mentioned by Fortuyn, the emphasis rested on containing the influence of Islam in the Netherlands. However, the same result could be obtained if the indigenous Dutch population were to be made less vulnerable, in other words, if the population was actively pursuing its own values and beliefs. In a sense, Fortuyn did advocate such a policy when he stated that it was necessary to put more emphasis on the traditional values in the Netherlands based on Christianity, Judaism and Humanism. The underlying values propagated by Fortuyn were a combination of traditional Dutch values, such as thriftiness, self-discipline, and tidiness, supplemented with more recent values, such as individual freedom, and respect for the rights of women and homosexuals.

Although it is not legally possible for a State Government to advocate specific religions or beliefs while discriminating against others, it is of course not prohibited to promote certain values if these are not contrary to international human rights law. Thus, there seems nothing wrong with promoting thriftiness, self-discipline, tidiness and respect for individual freedoms. The question remains, however, of whether the indigenous Dutch population will be ready to return to these values themselves and to embrace them as part of a traditional, yet new, ideology.

At first sight, a revitalisation of the old pillar model might seem the ideal solution, but I do not believe that this will be the case. Distinctions between

Protestants and Catholics, or between Social Democrats and Liberals have effectively been blurred. I do believe that there is room for an Islamic pillar, but so far it has been difficult to unite all the various tendencies within Islamic groups in the Netherlands.

If the old pillar model cannot be revitalised, how then can values be promoted? Although I do believe that the Government can set the right example by adhering to these values itself, and by a variety of communication methods with society at large, it can only be successful if it also addresses underlying factors. In that respect, I am afraid that a Government which, on the one hand, promotes the free market at the national and international level and, on the other hand, promotes values such as thriftiness and self-discipline, will be issuing conflicting statements and will therefore be ineffective. Although I have been unable to do any social research on this particular issue, I do believe that the protest against immigrants reflects a much deeper rooted level of dissatisfaction in society. Of course, immigrants are easy targets, but in a sense they are merely the symbol of a broader trend, the effects of which are now becoming visible, and that is the ever continuing process of globalisation. If traditional Dutch society and its values have been lost, then it is easy to blame immigrants for that, but there have been more processes with perhaps an even more profound effect—and Fortuyn mentioned these as well. The massive size of schools and hospitals, for example, leads to alienation when persons are most vulnerable, i.e. as children and as sick people. Also, and more generally, the old geographical pattern of combined housing, shopping and working has been overhauled by a system of concentrated shopping areas, and dead living areas, and (at night) dead office areas. Because of endless mergers, individually owned shops have become rare and in every city or town the shopping area contains more or less the same shops. Moreover, advertising has become so pervasive and intense that people are constantly taught that they should buy to be happy and that they can forget about their traditional values of thriftiness and altruism. Everyone knows, however, that happiness bought by consumerism does not last very long. In the long run, people become restless and dissatisfied within such an ever-lasting cycle of consumerism leading to instant but momentary happiness. I would not be surprised if the votes for Fortuyn could also be considered votes against this process of globalisation and that many of the voters are actually in favour of a return to a society that is much more small-scale and humane. Fortuyn did not provide a real answer to these deeper considerations, as he never took a stand on globalisation itself and remained vague about how international globalisation could be combined with the establishment of small-scale entities, which he did propose.

A Government that takes the promotion of thriftiness, self-discipline and tidiness seriously will, therefore, have to deal with the negative consequences of a free market economy. In the end, this may lead to new political divisions. Traditional, free market-oriented parties can offer economic welfare, but they also promote a society deprived of its traditional homogeneity and of its traditional values. Parties promoting a return to those values will have to curb the free market so that the adverse effects of globalisation and commercialisation can be effectively combated. If small-scale businesses, hospitals and schools are desirable, perhaps new legislation and new policies must be developed to make this possible. To take the example of small-scale businesses, the free market itself will never produce these; only through stiffer competition rules can such a result be achieved.

The freedom of religion or belief deals with such values, as it protects all beliefs that determine one's outlook on life. Instead of trying to restrict its scope, this freedom should actually be cherished, and values should play a much bigger role in politics again. Having said this, such an approach does not, of course, take away the tensions between various religious or non-religious groups. As a first step, however, I do believe that those who feel threatened by Islam would feel a lot happier if they could instead organise around certain basic values that they could subscribe to and, in particular, if they were offered an alternative to single-minded free market theories which transform man into *Homo oeconomicus* whose behaviour is entirely determined by economic considerations.

Apart from the reformulation of basic values, and their protection against commercial and other interests, the promotion of tolerance among different ethnic and religious groups requires a most active government in other areas as well. Certain rights can be curtailed, especially when the fundamental rights and freedoms of others are at stake. But such steps can only be taken when the government shows the same amount of respect for all religions or beliefs. In my view, it is certainly counterproductive to call Islam a 'backward religion'. A dialogue between Muslims and others in the Netherlands is necessary. However, it can only be productive if it is based on mutual respect. There are certainly issues which have to be dealt with robustly, such as the basic tenet of Islam that Muslims are not allowed to convert to another religion or belief. The rights of women and homosexuals need also to be defended against possible discrimination based on religion or belief. And, of course, crime cannot be tolerated, from wherever it may stem.

For the promotion of tolerance, the government has a number of tools at its disposal. Firstly, general public information can be provided. By showing that the government is neutral towards individual religions or beliefs it sets the right example. Secondly, the government can support initiatives for dialogue between the various groups in society. In a sense, it is laudable that instead of giving financial support to single-culture organisations and events the new policy line in the Netherlands seems to be that such support will focus on organisations and events that try to build bridges between these groups. And finally, the government can require from educational institutions that they promote tolerance. Even private educational institutions based on a particular religion or belief should still pay attention to other religions or beliefs as well. In any case, schools should teach children respect for others irrespective of their religion or belief.

It should also be recalled though that the promotion of tolerance cannot be achieved by the State alone. Although the government can set the right tone and promote activities, in the end it will also depend on the role of non-governmental organisations. Fortunately, the Netherlands has a rich tradition of such organisations and, on the basis of this social fabric, it should be possible to develop permanent intercultural and interreligious dialogue based on mutual respect.

It will be fascinating to see how political movements will deal with these new challenges. The recent developments in the Netherlands show, however, that an underestimation of the need of people to identify themselves with specific, well-articulated values can lead to enormous tensions. Perhaps, politics should focus more on the benefits of the freedom of religion or belief than on its defects. If a reappraisal of the freedom of religion or belief is necessary, it is in this sense only.

Chapter 9

Fidei Defensor Revisited: Church and State in a Religiously Plural Society

Michael Ipgrave

Inter-Faith Relations Adviser,
Archbishops' Council of the Church of England

In a television documentary broadcast in June 1994, the Prince of Wales declared a preference to be known when monarch as 'Defender of Faith' rather than 'Defender of the Faith'. This remark was, of course, far more than a point of mere grammar, or of the most appropriate translation of the Latin title *Fidei Defensor*. Prince Charles' comment referred to a concept deeply rooted in the history of the relation between Church and State in Britain. More specifically, the Prince was drawing attention to one traditional motif which has related the monarchy to the Church *of England*; other parts of the United Kingdom have different histories of Church-State relations, which lie beyond my primary remit here. At the same time, the Prince's remarks pointed to a series of challenges which need to be faced in relating that historical tradition to contemporary religious plurality in British society. The question which I propose to explore, using the *Fidei Defensor* motif as a guide to structure the discussion, is therefore this: What is the most appropriate attitude to adopt to an established Church for those who wish to promote a genuinely pluralistic society which provides effective safeguards against religious discrimination?

I have framed my question in terms of 'attitudes towards an established Church', rather than 'attitudes from the established Church', and this implies an important limitation to the scope of this paper immediately, as follows. Since 'establishment' involves a relationship between Church and State, any adequate debate on the question would need to look at the effect of possible changes on both Church and State. Here, however, my only concern is the latter, i.e. the implications for the British State of either maintaining, or alternatively abandoning, a form of religion enjoying with the State the special cluster of relationships generally known as 'establishment'. I begin by briefly tracing the historical national background to the question and to the *Fidei Defensor* in particular.

The historical background

A useful point to start with will be with the observation that one party to the Church-State relationship in England predates the other by a considerable margin in its existence as an organised body. The first to record the story of the English nation, Bede (672-735), entitled his work *Historia ecclesiastica gentis Anglorum*,[1] and his choice of the adjective was not fortuitous. In Bede's lifetime, as for a further two centuries, national identity was expressed by a well-defined Church of England, but not by any State of England. Augustine's appointment as Archbishop of Canterbury in 597 had been predicated on an authority over all bishops of either the English or the British races;[2] while the Celtic bishops were initially reluctant to submit, the Synod of Whitby in 664 had effectively cleared the way for the establishment of one Church of England, and the subsequent administrative reforms of Archbishop Theodore resulted in the first Synod of the Church of England being held in 673 at Hertford.[3] At that time, the political life of the English was still deeply divided between rival kingdoms. The first king to claim a title to rule over the whole of England was Offa of Mercia in 774, one hundred years after the Synod of

1. 'An *ecclesiastical* history of the English people' [my italics].
2. *Cf.* Gregory's Letter of 601 to Augustine: 'You, brother, are to have under your subjection those bishops whom you have consecrated as well as those who shall be consecrated by the bishop of York, and not those only but also all the bishops of Britain (*omnes Brittaniae sacerdotes*)—Bede, *Ecclesiastical History*, I, 29.
3. Bede, *Ecclesiastical History*, IV, 5.

Hertford,[4] while the effective establishment of an English state really dates back only to the reign of King Edgar, 958-975.[5] Significantly, Edgar was the first to have himself crowned and anointed by the Archbishop of Canterbury in 973, indicating a reliance of his State on the Church to validate its claims to authority. Nor is this is merely a matter of ancient history; Edgar's rite is still in essence that which has been used, with some modifications, in royal coronations up to that of the present Queen.

Throughout the Middle Ages, some sense of a priority of the Church continued to be evidenced in an expressed commitment to ensure its liberty. The first stipulation of the *Magna Carta* (1215) was precisely this: 'The English Church (*Anglicana ecclesia*) shall be free, and shall have its rights undiminished and its liberties unimpaired'. That is a remarkably bold statement to set alongside the Charter's later detailed regulations about weights and measures, fee-farm, socage, and burgage, and the removal of fish-weirs from the Thames and the Medway. It can be read as an eloquent demonstration of the deep rootedness within the formative English national history of a practical concern for religious freedom.[6]

In 1521, Pope Leo X bestowed the title *Fidei Defensor* on Henry VIII of England, who had recently presented to him a theological treatise, *Assertio Septem Sacramentorum*,[7] denouncing the Protestantism of Martin Luther. Only twelve years later, Leo's second successor as Pope, Clement VII, excommunicated the same King in a dispute over his matrimonial arrangements which was to lead to a still unhealed rupture between the Church of England and the Roman Catholic Church, and to open the way for the Reformation in England. However, in 1544, the English Parliament recognised the continuing validity of Henry's title, despite its papal origins. Translated as 'Defender of the Faith', it was decreed to be a style used for the king and his heirs, and in this form it

4. In two documents of this year Offa styles himself by the alternative titles *rex Anglorum* and *rex totius Anglorum patriae*. The former, indicating the older idea of the ruler of a people rather than of a country, was more common during the rest of his reign. *Cf.* F. Stenton, *Anglo-Saxon England* pp. 211f (Oxford: Oxford University Press, 3rd ed, 1986).

5. Norman Davies remarks on the imperial overtones of this, quoting a 10th-century chronicler on the significance of the country's newly established name: 'Britain is now called England, thereby assuming the name of the victors'—*The Isles: A History* p. 229 (London: Macmillan, 2000).

6. The support of the Church for the *Magna Carta* and its derivative charters was an important factor in their consolidation within national life. Successive 13th-century Archbishops, for example, threatened excommunication against violators of their provisions—J.C. Holt, *Magna Carta* p. 284 (Cambridge: Cambridge Univeristy Press, 1976).

7. 'A Defence of the Seven Sacraments'—i.e., a reassertion of the traditional Catholic enumeration of seven sacraments, as against the Reformers' limitation of the sacraments to those rites for which a clear origin could be found in the Gospels; according to the latter, generally only two (Baptism and the Eucharist) were admitted as sacraments.

has continued to be claimed by English and British monarchs up to the present.

Since the Prince of Wales' remarks about the way in which he would like to interpret this role have attracted considerable controversy, it is worth making one or two points about the title *Fidei Defensor* in its historical context. The first is a simple linguistic point, there is no definite article in Latin, so the version Prince Charles preferred—'Defender of Faith'—is every bit as accurate a translation of Leo X's original as the Parliamentary version of 1544—'Defender of *the* Faith'. The Prince, incidentally, did not say that he would choose to be known as 'Defender of Faiths', though the plural form might be inferred as a logical consequence of his remarks about defending religious freedom for all.

It may also seem surprising that a title conferred by a Pope following publication of an anti-Lutheran treatise should still be used by monarchs committed to defending the Protestant establishment.[8] However, the grant of the title *Fidei Defensor* was not in fact a direct recognition of Henry's arguments in the anti-Lutheran *Assertio*, though the treatise did provide the Pope with an opportune occasion for honouring the King. Rather, it was meant to provide Henry with a style comparable to those enjoyed by the Kings of France and Spain—*Rex Christianissimus* and *Rex Catholicus* respectively; and in fact several other titles, such as *Rex Fidelis* or *Orthodoxus*, were canvassed before *Fidei Defensor* was agreed. This is of significance in that it detaches the title somewhat from the controversial defence of one form of faith against another, pointing rather to a more general statement of the role of the monarch in safeguarding 'authentic' religion (however such authenticity might be defined). With this wider understanding, it is much easier to understand both the 1544 Parliament's application of the title to the monarch in the new context of a reformed Church of England and also Prince Charles' desire further to explore its meaning in the changed society of modern Britain.

Henry's break with Rome of course had a major impact on Church-State relations in England, since it removed any alternative political backing for the Church in its relation with the national power structures. However, the Anglo-

8. The current Coronation Oath is in essentials that set down in the *Act Establishing the Coronation Oath* of 1689. In this form, used for the Coronation of William III and Mary II, the Archbishop asks the monarchs (among other questions): ' "Will You to the utmost of Your power Maintaine the Laws of God, the true Profession of the Gospell and the Protestant Reformed Religion Established by Law? And will You Preserve unto the Bishops and Clergy of this Realme and to the Churches committed to their Charge all such Rights and Priviledges as by Law doe or shall appertaine unto them or any of them?" King and Queene: "All this I promise to doe." After this the King and Queene laying His and Her Hand upon the Holy Gospells, shall say, "The things which I have here before promised, I will performe and Keep: Soe help me God." Then the King and Queen shall kisse the Booke.'

Saxon and medieval self-understanding of a state which saw itself as in varying degrees dependent upon, generally validated by, and at times challenged by, the spiritual authority of the Church continued as a dominant ideology across the Reformation break, and continued also to find organisational expression in constitutional arrangements—for example, the role of the Archbishop in the coronation ceremony, the continuing place of Church of England bishops in the House of Lords, or the recognised place of public worship in marking great national events. Two factors have, though, since then led to radical transformations in the social situation to which this historically formed understanding has to relate. One is the growth of religious diversity, the other the rise of an influential secular account of the state. These seem to me quite distinct, though naturally interrelated in various ways, and I want to say something about each in turn.

Attitudes to religious diversity

Despite the attempts of 16th century monarchs—Elizabeth I in particular—to keep all their subjects together in one comprehensively drawn national Church, the formation and growth of diverse and separate religious groups has been an irreversible and increasing characteristic of British life since the Reformation. There are various different ways of mapping this diversification. Sociologically, one of the key distinctions is between those faith organisations which arose within the British context and those formed by people coming here from abroad. It is important to see how far back into British religious life the roots of a multi-culturalism, which is fed by the arrival and settlement of minority groups from abroad, reach. For example, Huguenot refugees were welcomed to England from the 16th century onwards, and brought with them a French culture which contributed greatly to the life of the east end of London in particular. Jewish people, having been expelled from England by Edward I in 1290, were readmitted by Cromwell in 1655, and Anglo-Jewry has enjoyed a continuous history since then. The first Greek Church in England was opened in Soho in 1677;[9] there is some evidence of an Armenian community in Plymouth earlier in the 17th century;[10] and so on. In the last

9. Unfortunately, this church was confiscated by the authorities in 1684 and handed over to the Huguenots, to the dismay of the Greek Archbishop. This followed pressure from the strongly Protestant Bishop of London, Henry Compton, who tried to insist that the Greeks should abandon their icons and repudiate transubstantiation.

10. K. Taverdi, *A History of Armenians in Britain* (London: Centre for Armenian Information and Advice, 1988).

century, this pattern of diversification increased exponentially, resulting in a truly multi-cultural society in many parts of Britain. However, the ways in which such religio-cultural diversity affects, and is affected by, the pattern of Church-State relationships can only be understood when set in the context of a wider plurality which also includes religious groups with their origins in English society. In order to analyse this, specifically theological factors need to be taken seriously in the self-understanding of the various groups involved.

One method of providing a definitely religious map of plurality in Britain might be to begin by distinguishing between the various Christian churches on the one hand, and the non-Christian religious groups on the other. Of course, this distinction is critically important in the area of inter-faith relations, but it does not seem the most crucial factor for our question. In part, this is because of the very different histories which different groups within the same faith have experienced in their relationship with the British state. The so-called 'Toleration Act' of 1689,[11] for example, produced a large measure of legal toleration for most Trinitarian Nonconformist Protestants in England; but the majority of legal restrictions on Roman Catholics and Jews were not removed until the 1846 *Religious Disabilities Act*.[12] Religiously identical groups could also be treated differently in different parts of Britain: while Anglicans south of the Scottish border always enjoyed full civic rights except for a short period during the Commonwealth, Scottish Episcopalians until 1792 were severely restricted even in their freedom to meet for worship.[13] In terms of 'Church-State relationships',[14] a more important determinant of different patterns of religious inclusion or exclusion is perhaps the tension between two positions which I shall describe as, respectively, 'majoritarianism' and 'minoritarianism'. These two attitudes, moreover, to some extent cut across other religious divides.

11. More precisely, the *Act for Exempting Their Majesties' Protestant Subjects Dissenting From the Church of England From the Penalties of Certain Laws.*
12. This did not entail the full removal of discrimination, however; 'Emancipation' as used in Anglo-Jewish history refers to the passing of the 1858 *Jews' Relief Act*, which permitted the entry of Jewish MPs into Parliament through allowing for a variation in the form of the oath required on taking public office—*cf.* G. Alderman, *Modern British Jewry* pp. 51ff (Oxford: Clarendon, 2nd ed, 1998).
13. Toleration Acts from 1712 allowed 'qualified congregations' to meet for worship using the (English) Book of Common Prayer, but as this would involve praying by name for the King, and so repudiating the Stuart claim to the throne, most Episcopalians refused to participate, particularly in the Highlands. The restrictions on Non-juring worship were only removed following the death of Prince Charles Edward Stuart in 1788, when the Government considered that Jacobitism no longer posed a threat.
14. As is customary in this area, I am here using 'Church-State' as a convenient shorthand to indicate in general terms the relationship between the state and a variety of religious communities—many of which, of course, would not describe themselves as 'churches'.

Among the different branches of Christianity in British history of the last five centuries, two different poles can be identified in attitudes to the Church's relation with the State. Some have felt in principle that there should be a majority Church, to which most people should be assumed to belong unless there was some good reason why they chose not to; and this Church should enjoy a special relationship with the State. Conversely, such a Church is in principle obliged to fulfil a vocation of ministry and service to the whole of the nation. Such a 'majoritarian' view has traditionally been the mainstream of Anglican thinking, but it is also found in the (Presbyterian) Church of Scotland. The endorsement of such an approach in principle is also found among both the Puritans and the Roman Catholics of the 16th and 17th centuries; their quarrel was not with the idea of a national Church but with the specifically Anglican form that Church took in England.

In radical distinction to this was the 'minoritarian' stance adopted by the 17th century 'Separatists', the ancestors of the Baptists, Congregationalists, Quakers, and other smaller groups. These rejected in principle any identification of Church and State, stressing rather the gathered identity of the authentic community of faith over and against the secular authorities. It is not surprising that some of the most eloquent statements of the principle of religious freedom come out of these traditions, since their primary concern was to resist the encroachments of worldly power on the relationship between the believers and the divine. Thus, in 1612 the early Baptist writer Thomas Helwys insisted that: 'Mens religion to God is betwixt God and themselves; the King shall not answer for it, neither may the King be judge betwene God and man. Let them be heretikes, Turks, Jewes, or whatsoever, it apperteynes not to the earthly power to punish them in the least measure'.[15] It was another Baptist pioneer, Roger Williams, who first coined an image which has become celebrated as a symbol for many of the American model of Church-State relationships, when he wrote of a 'hedge or wall of separation between the garden of the church and the wilderness of the world'.[16]

Thomas Helwys extended his argument for religious freedom from Christian believers to include people of other faiths also; the minoritarian-majoritarian distinction is pertinent in a multi-faith situation as much as in the context of intra-Christian diversity. It would be natural to expect most

15. T. Helwys, *The Mistery of Iniquity* (1612), cited in N. Wright, *Public Truth or Private Option? Gospel and Religious Liberty in a Multi-Faith Society in the Light of the Resurrection* (Joppa Group Occasional Paper, 1999).

16. E.S. Gaustad, *Liberty of Conscience: Roger Williams in America* p. 207 (Valley Forge, PA: Judson, 1999). The 'wall of separation' referred to in American debates is usually taken to be derived from the writings of Thomas Jefferson ('a wall of separation between church and state'). As Gaustad observes, however, on this occasion 'the interest of both "parties"—pietist and deist—could happily coincide'.

non-Christian faiths, present in this country as minority communities, to express themselves in a minoritarian mode. The Anglo-Jewish community, for example, has tended to see the preservation of cultural and religious identity as a key goal in interaction with the State, and it was this motivation which led to their securing a range of legislative measures designed to recognise and preserve their distinctive customs and practices. Nevertheless, the core impulses of some faith traditions, despite their demographically minority position in Britain, seem to point in another direction, away from minoritarianism towards a wider responsibility for and engagement with society. For instance, it could be argued that Islam is, in many of its forms, a tradition which is essentially majoritarian in its attitude to the relationship of religious and secular authorities.

Religious freedom and religious discrimination

How do these different attitudes to Church-State relationships affect the reality of religious discrimination in Britain today? It is important at the outset to make a distinction between three questions: first, the guaranteeing of fundamental religious freedom; second, the eradication of religious discrimination; and third, the structuring of the relationship between religious communities and the State. I shall argue that the relationship between both the first two of these issues and the third is not so straightforward as it is assumed to be by those who take as self-evidently desirable a model of the state which casts it in the role of religiously neutral and secular arbitrator: 'In order to develop a theory [of religious freedom] that is more relevant ... it is necessary to consider arguments in favour of freedom of religion or belief that do not rely on strict separation between Church and State'.[17]

As to the guaranteeing of fundamental rights, the result of an initially piecemeal removal of restrictions on different religious groups, there has been an entrenching of religious freedom which now in almost every respect in Britain meets the standard enunciated in the European Convention on Human Rights: 'Everyone has the right to freedom of thought, conscience and religion; this right includes freedom to change his religion or belief and freedom,

17. C. Evans, *Freedom of Religion Under the European Convention on Human Rights* p. 22 (Oxford: Oxford University Press, 2001). As her title makes clear, Evans is writing not merely out of the British, but more widely the European context. She notes that, on one hand, 'there are a wide variety of relationships between Church and State in members of the Council of Europe', on the other hand, 'there appears to be a European commitment to the principle of religious freedom' (pp. 21f).

either alone or in community with others and in public or private, to manifest his religion or belief, in worship, teaching, practice and observance'.[18]

It could be said that these provisions now generally apply to all British subjects—except, somewhat ironically, to the monarch and heirs to the throne, who are prohibited both from becoming Roman Catholics and from marrying Roman Catholics.[19] It must be acknowledged that much of the early progress towards this achievement of fundamental religious freedoms for all was made in the face of considerable opposition from influential sectors of the established Church. In more recent years, though, the Church of England has demonstrated a firm commitment to the principle of religious freedom. In this, it has been in line with trends in the wider world of Western Christianity, and particularly with the statement of the Second Vatican Council in the declaration *Dignitatis Humanae* that 'the human person has a right to religious freedom'.[20] *Dignitatis Humanae* is significant, moreover, in that it not only enunciates the principle of religious freedom but also provides a theological justification for that principle rooted in the core Christian doctrine of the creation of human beings in the image of God.[21] At the same time, neither Anglicanism nor Roman Catholicism has abandoned its essentially majoritarian stance; nor to date have the constitutional arrangements of an established Church in either England or Scotland been significantly weakened to allow for the recognition of these freedoms on the part of adherents of minority religious groups.

In contrast to the general practice of religious freedom, the elimination of religious discrimination presents a continuing challenge to contemporary

---

18. Article 9.1—text, as amended by Protocol No. 11 of November 1998, in J. Wadham and H. Mountfield, *Blackstone's Guide to the Human Rights Act 1998* (London: Blackstone, 1999). Since 2000, the Convention has been incorporated into UK law through the Human Rights Act.

19. By the Act of Settlement 1701 and Royal Marriages Act 1772 respectively. In 1999, a motion calling for the repeal of this legislation was passed by the Scottish Parliament—James Macmillan, 'I had not thought about it like that before', in T.M. Devine, *Scotland's Shame: Bigotry and Sectarianism in Modern Scotland* pp. 267f (Edinburgh: Mainstream, 2000). Yet it could be argued that these regulations are not so much an infringement of personal freedom as a restriction imposed for the purpose of holding a particular office. As such, they would certainly constitute religious discrimination, but might be justifiable in equality jurisprudence by the claim that they were necessitated by the requirement of communicant Anglican status as a 'genuine occupational qualification' for the (English) monarch.

20. *Dignitatis Humanae* 2, in A. Flannery OP: *Vatican Council II: The Conciliar and Post-Conciliar Documents* (Dublin: Dominican Publications, 1975). This teaching dramatically reversed the earlier position of, for example Pius IX's *Syllabus of Errors*, 'that the Catholic religion be the only State religion, excluding all the other cults'—No. 2978 in H. Denzinger and A. Schönmetzer, *Enchiridion Symbolorum Definitionum et Declarationum de Rebus Fidei et Morum* (Barcelona: Herder, 36th ed, 1975).

21. *Cf.* further on the theological background of Christian opposition to religious discrimination the report by the Churches' Commission for Inter Faith Relations, *Religious Discrimination: A Christian Response* (London: CTBI, 2001).

society. At the time of writing, British law provides no protection for people against discrimination on the grounds of their religious identity, though the Government is committed to some form of legislation against discrimination on grounds of religion or belief in the area of employment through an Employment Directive adopted under Article 13 of the Treaty of Amsterdam.[22] Racial or ethnic identity, on the other hand, has for several years been accorded a strong degree of protection in British law, and there is also legislation against discrimination on the grounds of gender and disability. Attention has rightly been focussed on this disparity by the Muslim communities in particular, and the evidence suggests that in Britain Muslims[23] are among the groups most likely to experience discrimination on the grounds of their religious identity.[24]

The question then arises of what pattern of Church-State relationship can provide the best context to help in combating religious discrimination, whether this relationship be directed against members of a *specific* faith community or generally against people of *every* faith tradition. Two very different approaches seem possible at this point. Which is favoured will depend on the way in which the formative history of British Church-State relations is viewed in relation to the current situation, and in particular on the analysis that is given of the rather slippery term 'secularism'. I will outline first the approach which I would not myself choose to follow—not least because it is rather simpler to explain than the approach which I prefer.

Multiplying minoritarianism: separation of Church and State

The first approach proposes 'secularism', interpreted as the State's disengagement from support of all forms of religion, as a way of arbitrating neutrally between the claims of different and rival faith communities within society. In a multicultural, and still more, a multi-faith society, it is argued that the State's role cannot be to identify with one tradition rather than another. Such an identification, it is claimed, would imply religious discrimination, or at least religious disadvantage, for those traditions not so identified. Clearly, the argument continues, the only way effectively to maintain State neutrality is to remove *all* constitutional links with *all* faith communities—including in particular the disestablishment of established Churches—and to insist on a clear and rigorous principle of separation between Church and State. Some

22. See the chapter by P. Cumper in this book for a further discussion of this theme.

23. See the chapter by T. Modood in this book for a further discussion of this theme.

24. P. Weller, A. Feldman, K. Purdam *et al*, *Religious Discrimination in England and Wales* pp. 103f (London: Home Office Research Study 220, 2001).

protagonists of this position further add that this would be advantageous not only for the State, which would become authentically and properly secular, but also for the Church, which would find its integrity and prophetic witness restored through the severance of a compromising link with the State. In effect, this approach is therefore recommending that what I have described as the 'minoritarian' approach to Church-State relationships should be multiplied and applied across the multi-faith and multi-confessional board.

Separationism seems, at first sight, to have the not inconsiderable virtues of simplicity and lucidity as a concept. This judgement needs to be qualified, however, by a recognition that practical decisions as to precisely where to build the 'wall of separation' may not be so easy to achieve as the enunciation of the general principle. In Church-State separation in the contemporary USA, for example, there have been tangled and often bitter disputes in the educational arena over the constitutionality of prayer in public schools, or of financial relief for parents choosing to educate their children in religious schools.[25] As to claims about the likely positive effect of disestablishment on the Church, it seems that there are pointers in both directions. The majoritarian traditions of Anglicanism, emphasising a responsibility to the whole of the community, have been central to the life of the Church of England both before and after the Reformation and, in particular, they underpin the pastoral ministry of the parish system. There might be a danger that the outward-looking horizons of Anglicanism, and the generosity of spirit which it can show at its best, would be eroded if the existing constitutional expressions were removed; indeed, disestablishment might reinforce growing attitudes within the Church of England which are not so much minoritarian in the traditional Nonconformist sense as frankly sectarian.[26] On the other hand, the disestablishment of the Church in Wales in 1920 by no means led to a loss of the Anglican sense of spiritual reference to the whole of society at either a local or a national level.[27] The Church of England, and still more the Church of Scotland, possess a high degree of financial, organisational and, above all, spiritual independence which means that the description 'State Church' sometimes used of them is quite misleading;[28] and there is good reason to doubt that their essential character

25. *Cf.* S.V. Monsma and J.C. Soper, *The Challenge of Pluralism: Church and State in Five Democracies* pp. 28ff (Lanham, MY: Rowman & Littlefield, 1997).

26. I use the word 'sectarian' here to indicate an attitude within the Church which focuses entirely on internal concerns, with little or no interest in issues of wider society.

27. John Davies remarks that the Welsh Anglicans 'continued to look like an Establishment—and to a considerable extent, to be treated as one'—*A History of Wales* p. 539 (London: Penguin, Eng. ed, 1994).

28. Paul Avis, in a vigorous defence of the principle of establishment, argues that the Church of England is more appropriately described as a 'national Church' than a 'State Church'—*Church, State and Establishment* (London: SPCK, 2000).

would be modified by disestablishment.[29] It might also be the case that disestablishment could be seen in quasi-economic terms as freeing up the 'religious market' and thereby encouraging a healthy sense of competition among the churches which could benefit them all. However, my principal concern is not with the likely effects on the Church but with the State, and here there seem to be two problems with the separationist approach I have just outlined.

The first relates to the understanding of 'secularism' which is assumed by opponents of the Church-State relationship. This is an extraordinarily difficult word to handle, and there is always the danger for people of faith of falling into one of the twin extremes of paranoia or complacency in its understanding. Nevertheless, it does seem that simply to gloss 'secularity' as impartiality in matters of religion is already to slide into a particular ideological position which stands contrary to many faith perspectives, particularly those from majoritarian traditions. As a corollary of saying that the State should not enjoy a special relationship with any one faith community, one could effectively diminish the part played by *any* faith in the State's life; an ostensible concern to combat the religious disadvantage of *some* could result in the religious marginalisation of *all*. And such a consequence would express, not so much neutrality in religious matters, as the adoption of a particular belief—namely that religion has no constitutive part to play in the life of the State—a belief which also falls within the range of meanings of that slippery term 'secularism'. Such views have been powerfully expressed in the USA by those who advocate the so-called 'Equal Treatment' approach to Church-State issues in place of strict separationism.[30] Michael McConnell, for example, insists that 'secularism' can and does operate powerfully in society as a competitive alternative to all religions: 'In the marketplace of ideas, secular viewpoints and ideologies are in competition with religious viewpoints and ideologies. It is no more neutral to favour the secular over the religious than it is to favour the religious over the secular'.[31]

29. A Church which has very recently gone through a process of disestablishment is the (Lutheran) Church of Sweden. The Archbishop of Uppsala has expressed his opinion that disestablishment of the church is 'inevitable' in advanced Western nations, as the church's present established status brings 'only disadvantages'. (*Christian Century*, 16 June 1999). It is interesting to note that the Archbishop's remarks concentrated on the effect on the Church, rather than the State—and of course it must also be borne in mind that the pattern of Church-State relationships in Sweden has been rather different to that of England (or Scotland).

30. Two leading scholars of this approach define it as follows: 'governmental neutrality in matters of religion, a neutrality that is more fully attained by the equal treatment of persons and groups of all faiths—religious and secular—than by an attempt strictly to separate religion and government'—S.V. Monsma and J.C. Soper (eds.), *Equal Treatment of Religion in a Pluralistic Society* p. 2 (Grand Rapids, MI: Eerdmans, 1998).

31. M.W. McConnell, 'Equal Treatment and Religious Discrimination', *ibid*. p. 33.

This may sound rather remote from British concerns, so let me give a practical example from *The Times* of London. In an article published two days before Christmas 2000, the columnist Matthew Parris suggested that Members of Parliament who derive their ethical views from their religious faiths should, 'declare in the Register of Members' Interests that they are laying up for themselves treasures in Heaven, where moth and rust do not corrupt'. His proposal was only half serious, but the reasoning behind it was in earnest: 'An MP's doctrinal position (if he has one) on the existence of the soul, the sanctity of human life and the point at which life begins, will more or less determine how he votes on abortion, and those ethical issues raised by research into embryology which the House decided (for example) in the debate on stem-cell research ... These are real, concrete, everyday concerns upon which statute has a direct bearing'. Parris' point was that such doctrinal assumptions were not the basis for ethical decision-making for the majority either of MPs or of the electorate, and therefore should not be acted on in the public arena by legislators without their being open to severe, even hostile, scrutiny, and possible discounting, in the same way that a personal financial interest would be. Parris went on to claim that we should all acknowledge as the, 'basis for our ethics the assumption that man is good and life is good and the world is good, and that this is all we know and all we need to know'.[32]

I do not quote those words in order to question Parris' ethical principles, though they do seem extraordinarily naïve in their optimism. Rather, the significant point in his argument is that a particular form of belief—secular belief—is assumed as the norm from which any kind of religious beliefs are deviant, and action on the basis of those deviant beliefs is in some sense disqualified as inappropriately self-serving. Secularism is for Parris a norm in the double sense of being what people *should* believe and also being what they *do* believe. He says of contemporary Britain: 'That the vast majority are virtual atheists cannot, I think, be seriously disputed'. A few lines later, however, he has to admit that, 'atheism, though the term best describes the practice of the majority, is not yet as a principle widely acknowledged'. Presumably he has in mind here the repeated findings of opinion polls which show that a majority of the population, whatever their lack of religious practice, do affirm belief in God, and also do choose to describe themselves as Christians in some sense. The results of the 2001 Census, to include for the first time a question on religion, will perhaps make the dimensions of this question clearer, but in the mean time it does rather seem that Parris is promoting as a majority opinion what is in its committed manifestation a minority belief—namely secular

32. M. Parris, 'What place should the gods have in politics?', *The Times*, 23 December 2000.

humanism. Moreover, he is at least implying that this belief is the only appropriate basis for communal ethical thought or legislative decision-making.[33]

This brings me to the second problem that I have with the approach which would claim to solve the problem of Church-State relationships through a principle of separation. Secularism, whether or not it is actually a minority opinion, is a majoritarian way of thinking, in the sense that it sees itself as a body of thought to which most people should be assumed to subscribe unless there is good reason to show that they do not (unless, that is, they 'declare their religious interest' in Parris' terms). But it is a majoritarianism of a particular kind, arising out of, and to some extent still defined by, a series of minoritarian protests against religion. As such, it does not easily encourage the formation of communities of shared guidance and faith, or provide a coherent source of validating and challenging the State's life, in the way that traditional religions have done at their best. Given the weakness of 'secularism' in organisational terms, there is a real danger that the adoption of this ideology as the ultimate point of reference for the State would create a vacuum in a place that has been filled by religious authority since before the English state came into being. This would represent not so much a natural development, as a feeble abandonment of the nation's formative history. Disestablishment would of course raise very practical problems—the un-picking and the re-stitching of a Constitution, particularly an unwritten one, would be no easy matter—but the deeper anxieties must relate to how that vacuum might ultimately be filled. The history of the 20th century does not encourage unmixed faith in the blessings likely to accrue from secular ideologies.

Diversifying majoritarianism: extending the religious establishment

What is the alternative to the attempt to distance the state in equidistant separation from all religious communities? The bringing together of the formative British history with current confessional and religious plurality could result in an attempt to extend and diversify establishment, rather than to abolish it. Indeed, in an incipient way the patterns of a wider 'informal establishment' have for some years been becoming apparent in Britain among the Christian churches; the further involvement of other faith communities would in a sense

33. Parris' view that legislators should not rely on their own religious faiths to inform their decisions is probably a more widely held opinion than his explicit secular humanism, but this in turn is sharply challenged by a growing number of political philosophers—e.g., most recently, C.J. Eberle, *Religious Conviction in Liberal Politics* (Cambridge: Cambridge University Press, 2002).

be initiating another stage in a process which is already underway. However, despite this sense of a continuing evolution in the shape of establishment, it is important not to underestimate either the elements of newness, which an extended and diversified establishment would imply, or the theological challenges which this would pose to the Church of England in particular.

Whereas the conceptual basis of separationism is easy to grasp in a multi-faith society, because minoritarian approaches can easily be multiplied to accommodate a variety of religious traditions, it is more difficult to provide a logically satisfying account of how a majoritarian approach, rooted historically in one particular tradition, can embrace religious plurality without distorting the integrities of the various faiths in order to incorporate them all in a framework which expresses the preconceptions of the established Church. However, it may be that the very complexity of the intertwined nexus of Church-State relationships known as 'establishment' is helpful in this respect. Precisely because the establishment of religion is worked out in so many different situations, each with its own particular dynamics and parameters, it may prove easier to evolve contextually appropriate arrangements acknowledging plurality on a case-by-case approach, rather than drawing up an overarching theory of how the establishment should be extended. I shall suggest a few examples of the kind of approach that might be adopted in various situations.

An extended and diversified—what the Archbishop of Canterbury refers to as a 'hospitable'[34]—establishment would involve the Church of England working together with other Christian Churches and with other faith communities to ensure that the insights and values of faith can be perceived and weighed within the public life of our country—something that has already been broached, for example, in the suggestion of a wider religious representation within a reformed House of Lords. It would imply a greater visible presence and role for other communities in the great occasions of national and civic life—here too, a bank of practical experience is being collected through the multi-faith dimensions of such events as the Millennium and the Royal Jubilee. It would require robust and well-resourced organisations to bring together both different Churches and different faith communities to share common concerns and provide points of reference for interaction with Government—and developing templates for such partnerships can be found

34. G. Carey, 'Holding Together: Church and Nation in the Twenty-First Century', lecture delivered at Lambeth Palace on 23 April 2002—available on http://www.archbishopofcanterbury.org. The Archbishop went on to develop the particular role which he saw for the Church of England within such a 'hospitable establishment' in the following terms: 'Hospitality requires a host. So, it is part of our role, I believe, to seek to provide space and access, opportunity and the right atmosphere for the many dealings and interactions between faith communities and the wider society, however and wherever we can'.

in organisations such as the Inter Faith Network for the UK or the Inner Cities Religious Council. It would also need to create safe spaces where Christians of different denominations and people of different faiths could debate vigorously with one another, witnessing to the points where they differ as well as to those where they agree—but this should not be difficult to comprehend within an establishment based up to now on the Church of England, which can hardly be described as a monochrome body of opinion. Most importantly, the question of establishment in the broad sense needs to be seen as an issue which applies not only at national level but—sometimes in a more pressing fashion—within local communities and organisations also. The same fundamental challenges are present in ensuring, for example, that the provision of pastoral and spiritual care in hospitals or prisons, the availability of 'faith schools', or the contribution of religious groups to urban regeneration all take serious account of the realities of contemporary religious plurality in their particular local contexts.

Extending and diversifying establishment in these ways would thus involve much detailed and complex work. There would also be a major challenge of finding a place for the insights and values of people with secular beliefs, in a way that respected both their integrity and the overall principle of a State which acknowledged its particular relationship with religious faith. There would be a need for all faith communities to see establishment as an opportunity for service and guidance in humility, not for the advancement of sectional interests. Despite all the challenges, though, this does seem to be a way forward which is both true to the insights of the history which has formed British society and also responsive to the plurality which now marks that society. It would provide protection for religious freedom and against religious discrimination, and within such an extended and diversified establishment it is possible to imagine a very significant role for the monarch as *Fidei Defensor*, 'Defender of Faith'.

Chapter 10

The Place of Muslims in British Secular Multiculturalism[1]

Tariq Modood

Professor of Sociology, Politics and Public Policy and Director, Centre for the Study of Ethnicity and Citizenship, University of Bristol

The large presence of Muslims in Britain today (between 1 and 2 millions, more than half of South Asian, primarily Pakistani, origins) is a result of Commonwealth immigration from the 1950s onwards. This was initially male labour from rural small farm owning and artisan backgrounds seeking to meet the demand for unskilled and semi-skilled industrial workers in the British economy, with wives and children arriving from about the 1970s. The proportion of urban professionals among South Asian Muslims was small, though it increased with the arrival of political refugees from East Africa in the late 1960s and 1970s (though the majority of this group were Hindus and Sikhs).

1. Some of the work on which this paper is based was made possible by the ESRC award R000222124, for which I am grateful. Further details of this ESRC project, entitled *Ethnic Diversity and Public Policy*, are available at http://www.regard.ac.uk. This paper was originally written as a chapter in N. Alsayyad and M. Castells (eds.), *Muslim Europe or Euro-Islam: Politics, Culture and Citizenship in the Age of Globalisation* (New York: Lexington Books, 2002). A shorter French version of this paper is available in *Social Compass*, 47 (1), March (2000).

Britain, especially London as a cosmopolitan centre, has been very attractive to some of the rich and the professional classes from the Middle East, especially from the 1970s onwards, and many of them have large investments in property in the city. There have, during this period, also been waves of political refugees from other parts of the Muslim world, Somalia and Bosnia being two notable recent cases.

Racial Equality Movements

The presence of new population groups such as these has made manifest certain kinds of racisms in Britain, and anti-discrimination laws and policies began to be put into place from the 1960s. These laws and policies, initially influenced by contemporary thinking and practice in relation to anti-black racism in the US, assume that the grounds of discrimination are 'colour' and ethnicity. Not only is it in the last decade or so that Muslim assertiveness has become a feature of majority-minority relations, but indeed prior to this racial equality discourse and politics was dominated by the idea that the dominant post-immigration issue was 'colour-racism'.[2] This perspective was epigramatically expressed by the writer, Salman Rushdie: 'Britain is now two entirely different worlds and the one you inherit is determined by the colour of your skin'.[3] He, together, with most anti-racists, has come to adopt a more pluralistic perspective, and one in which the Muslim presence is seen as a fact to be ignored at one's peril. Nevertheless, in a pure or in a mixed form, the US-derived racial dualism, continues to be an influential force in British social science and radical politics.[4] One consequence of this is that the legal and policy framework still reflects the conceptualisation and priorities of racial dualism.

To date, it is lawful to discriminate against Muslims *qua* Muslims because the courts do not accept that Muslims are an ethnic group (though oddly, Jews and Sikhs are recognised as ethnic groups within the meaning of the law). While initially unremarked upon, this exclusive focus on race and ethnicity, and the exclusion of Muslims but not Jews and Sikhs, has come to be a source

2. J. Rex and R. Moore, *Race, Community and Conflict* (Oxford: Oxford University Press, 1967); CCCS (Centre for Contemporary Cultural Studies), *The Empire Strikes Back* (London: Hutchinson, 1982); A. Sivanandan, 'RAT and the Degradation of the Black Struggle', *Race and Class*, XXVI (4) (1985); P. Gilroy, *There Ain't No Black in the Union Jack* (London: Routledge, 1987).
3. S. Rushdie, 'The New Empire Within Britain', *New Society*, 9 December (1982).
4. M. Luthra, *Britain's Black Population: Social Change, Public Policy and Agenda* (Aldershot: Ashgate, 1997).

of resentment amongst Muslims. Muslims do, however, enjoy some limited indirect legal protection *qua* members of ethnic groups such as Pakistanis, Arabs and so on. Over time, groups like Pakistanis have become an active constituency within British 'race relations' (Middle Easterners tend to classify themselves as 'white', as in the 1991 Census, and are not at all prominent in political activism of this sort, or in domestic politics generally). One of the effects of this politics was to highlight race.

A key measure/indicator of racial discrimination and inequality has been numerical under-representation in prestigious jobs, public office, etc. Hence, people have had to be (self)classified and counted, and so group labels, and arguments about which labels are authentic have become a common feature of certain political discourses. Over the years, it has also become apparent that by these inequality measures it is Asian Muslims, and not Afro-Caribbeans, as policy-makers had originally expected, who have emerged as the most disadvantaged and poorest groups in the country.[5] To many Muslim activists, the misplacing of Muslims into 'race' categories and the belatedness with which the severe disadvantages of the Pakistanis and Bangladeshis has come to be recognised by policy-makers means, at best, that race relations are an inappropriate policy niche for Muslims[6] and, at worst, they see it as a conspiracy to prevent the emergence of a specifically Muslim socio-political formation.[7] To see how such thinking has emerged we need to consider the career of the concept of 'racial equality'.

The initial development of anti-racism in Britain followed the American pattern, and indeed was directly influenced by American personalities and events. Just as in the USA, the colour-blind humanism of Martin Luther King Jnr. came to be mixed with an emphasis on black pride, black autonomy and black nationalism as typified by Malcolm X, so also in the UK (both these inspirational leaders visited Britain). Indeed, it is best to see this development of racial explicitness and positive blackness as part of a wider socio-political climate which is not confined to race and culture or non-white minorities. Feminism, gay pride, Quebecois nationalism and the revival of Scottishness are some prominent examples of these new identity movements which have come to be an important feature in many countries, especially those in which class-politics has declined.

5. T. Modood *et al*, *Britain's Ethnic Minorities: Diversity and Disadvantage* (London: Policy Studies Institute, 1997).
6. UKACIA (UK Action Committee on Islamic Affairs), *Muslims and the Law in Multi-faith Britain: Need for Reform* (London: UK Action Committee on Islamic Affairs, 1993).
7. Muslim Parliament of Great Britain, *Race Relations and Muslims in Great Britain: A Discussion Paper* (London: The Muslim Parliament, 1992).

In fact, it would be fair to say that what is often claimed today in the name of racial equality, especially in the English-speaking world, is more than would have been recognised as such in the 1960s. Iris Young expresses well the new political climate, when she describes the emergence of an ideal of equality based not just on allowing excluded groups to assimilate and live by the norms of dominant groups, but based on the view that 'a positive self-definition of group difference is in fact more liberatory'.[8]

The shift is from an understanding of 'equality' in terms of individualism and cultural assimilation to a politics of recognition, to 'equality' as encompassing public ethnicity. 'Equality' as not having to hide or apologise for one's origins, family or community but requiring others to show respect for them and adapt public attitudes and arrangements so that the heritage they represent is encouraged rather than contemptuously expected to wither away. There seems, then, to be two distinct conceptions of equal citizenship, with each based on a different view of what is 'public' and 'private'. These two conceptions of equality may be stated as follows:

- The right to assimilate to the majority/dominant culture in the public sphere; and toleration of 'difference' in the private sphere.
- The right to have one's 'difference' (minority ethnicity, etc.) recognised and supported in the public and the private spheres.

These are not, however, alternative conceptions in the sense that to hold one, the other has to be rejected. Multiculturalism (as recent anti-racism has come to be) requires, however, support for both conceptions. For the assumption behind the first conception is that participation in the public or national culture is necessary for the effective exercise of citizenship, the only obstacle to which are the exclusionary processes preventing gradual assimilation. The second conception, too, assumes that groups excluded from the national culture have their citizenship diminished as a result. It offers to remedy this by accepting the right to assimilate, yet adding the right to widen and adapt the national culture and the public and media symbols of national membership to include the relevant minority ethnicities.

It may be thought that the second conception of equality involves something of a contradiction: it accepts that participation in the national or shared culture(s) is necessary for effective equality, but encourages individuals to cultivate minority identities and practices. There is indeed a genuine tension here, and perhaps it can only be resolved in practice, through finding and cultivating points of common ground between dominant and subordinate cultures, as

8. I. Young, *Justice and the Politics of Difference* p. 157 (Princeton University Press, 1990).

well as new syntheses and hybridises. The important thing is that the burden of change (or the costs of not changing) are not all on one party.

Beyond a Liberal Politics

This new, emergent notion of equality creates some dissonance with pre-existing political concepts. It does not fit in easily, for example, with a Tory British nationalism. But, more to the point, it is at odds with some of the centre-left ideas that underpinned the earlier notion of racial equality.[9] The politicisation of 'racial' and ethnic groups (but also women and homosexuals) is taken to introduce 'particularism' into 'universalistic' conceptions of justice defined by meritocratic individualism, liberal citizenship or socialist equality. (Why class solidarity or national citizenship are 'universalistic' and identification with the female half of the species or black internationalism are 'particularistic' I personally fail to understand.) The success of the new concept of multicultural equality, at least on the Left, has, however, been made possible because it was not anomalous but fitted in with wider challenges to liberal individualism. For example, it fitted in with feminist arguments that ostensible gender-neutral conceptions of the political, of citizenship, of the domain of law and of legal norms, as well as a host of substantive laws and policies, were in fact covert but systematic expressions of male perspectives and ignored the needs and capacities of women.[10] On the one hand, the abstract, rational individual of liberal politics and jurisprudence was in fact a man (as evidenced by the fact that this individual didn't seem to have any domestic or child-rearing obligations). On the other hand, the definition of the political, the activities appropriate for public discourse, political campaigns and legal control, favour male interests, leaving unchallenged male power in domestic and sexual relations. Hence, the alternative politics born out of the slogan, 'the personal is the political'.

The politics that I have just mentioned is both a theoretical, discursive politics as well as a politics of institutional reform, competition for office and social policies. My concern here—as a way of coming to approach the political-normative climate of opinion in which British Muslims can and are mounting a case for Muslim rights—is particularly with the theoretical dimension of

9. H. Goulbourne, 'Varieties of Pluralism: the notion of a pluralist, post-imperial Britain', *New Community*, 17 (2), January (1991); H. Goulbourne, *Ethnicity and Nationalism in Post-imperial Britain* (Cambridge: Cambridge University Press, 1991).

10. C. Pateman, *The Sexual Contract* (Stanford: University of Stanford Press, 1988); Young, *supra* note 8.

the politics of 'difference' as a critique of the 1960s notions of liberal equality. It is therefore worth mentioning some other theoretical sources of this politics in order to emphasise how important it has become amongst centre-left egalitarians, especially in book-writing and book-reading circles in Britain and elsewhere. It is a politics that gets considerable underpinning from the rise of philosophical anti-essentialism in the social sciences.[11] Originating from the—very different—work of thinkers such as Nietzsche, Heidegger and Wittgenstein, given a certain indeterminate radicalism in the hands of more recent theorists like Foucault and Derrida, anti-essentialism in one form or another has been used to critique hegemonic ideas such as nation-state, community, class, and even counter-hegemonic notions such as woman, black and so on.[12] This has been taken to such an extent that an appreciation of perspectivism, of the essentially contested nature of concepts, of fluidity and multiplicity of meanings, of cultural pluralism and perhaps even aporia, has quickly established itself as an orthodoxy in social theory.

Of relevance here, is how this anti-essentialism, when married to a theory of political equality as participation in a discursive public space,[13] can define inclusion into a political community not in terms of (as many European politicians do as regards Muslims) accepting the rules of the existing polity and its hallowed public-private boundary lines, but the opposite. Public space is defined as essentially contested and indeed created through on-going discursive contestation and political struggles, where the rules of what are appropriate concerns, and the terms of politics, far from being fixed in advance, are an object of political discourse.[14] Typically, on these accounts, the public-private distinction works as a 'gag-rule' to exclude matters of concern to marginalised and subordinated groups, and the political integration of these minorities on terms of equality inevitably involves their challenging the existing boundaries of publicity. Integration flows from the process of discursive engagement as marginal groups begin to confidently assert themselves in the public space, and others begin to argue with and reach some agreement with them, as well

11. T. Modood, 'British Multiculturalism: Some Rival Positions and Thoughts on the Way Forward', seminar paper to the Commission on the Future of Multi-ethnic Britain, London, July (1998).

12. D. Fuss, *Essentially Speaking* (New York: Routledge, 1989).

13. H. Arendt, *On Revolution* (New York: Viking Press, 1963); H. Arendt, *Human Condition* (London: University of Chicago, 1968); J. Habermas, *The Theory of Communicative Competence, vol. 1: Reason and the Rationalisation of Society* (Boston: Beacon, 1983); J. Habermas, *The Theory of Communicative Competence vol. 2: Lifeworld and System* (Boston: Beacon, 1987).

14. S. Benhabib, *Situating the Self* (New York: Routledge, 1992); N. Fraser, 'Rethinking the Public Sphere' in G. Calhoun (ed.), *Habermas and the Public Sphere* (Cambridge, Mass.: MIT Press, 1992).

as with the enactment of new laws, policies and so on. Indeed, laws and policies may be of lesser importance, for these theories explicitly repudiate the classical liberal identification of the political with the realms of laws and the state. A more expansive understanding of the political is more compatible with the idea of shifting boundaries and politics as debate and allows for the changing of certain attitudes, stereotypes, stigmatisations, media images, national symbols as primary political goals. Hence, it should now be clear why I believe that in the 1990s we were dealing with a new concept of equality; one in which the issues of 'representation' were not just to do with the numbers of various categories of people in certain jobs or positions of power, but with 'representation' as the public imagining of groups qua groups.[15]

Racialisation and Identity

This may seem all rather abstract, and as no more than the preoccupation of a few academics and their students. It is, in my opinion, an important part of the story of the emergent politics of Muslim identity in Britain. In any case, it is time to briefly mention some of the events that had been taking place 'on the ground'. The 'minorities' politics, the cutting-edge anti-racism that developed in Britain in the 1970s and early 1980s, first in radical activism and ultra-left corpuscles then, following the Brixton riots of 1981, in some local government, trades unions, radical public sector professional associations and the Labour Party, was based on a concept of political blackness. The British population was divided into two groups, black and white. The former consisted of all those people who were potential victims of colour-racism though, in both theory and practice, they were assumed to disproportionately have the characteristics of the Afro-Caribbean population.[16]

This political movement has played an important part in opening up the question of 'race' in Britain and has come to define the identity of many people (less so now than at its height in the mid to late 1980s). Whether, at any point, this political identity was embraced by the majority of South Asians or Muslims is an open question (I personally think not). Two things however are clear. Firstly, this identity was embraced by Asian political activists in the 1980s, especially those whose activism was concerned with mainstream British society rather than the organisation of their own communities.

15. S. Hall, 'New Ethnicities' in J. Donald and A. Rattansi (eds.), *'Race', Culture and Difference* (London: Sage, 1992).
16. T. Modood, 'Political blackness and British Asians', *Sociology* Vol. 28, no. 3 (1994).

Secondly, that from the late 1980s onwards, if not earlier, most Asians were emphasising a more particular ethnic or religious identity rather than this all-inclusive non-whiteness. Several factors were at play here. For example, time, numbers and confidence. As the Asian communities became more settled and thought of themselves less as sojourners, as they put down familial and community roots, and as some Asian groups, especially African Asians, began to acquire a prosperity and respectability that all Asians sought, they began to express their 'own' identities rather than the borrowed identity of blackness, with its inescapable Afro-Caribbean resonances. Movements outside the UK were relevant (for example, the Sikh battle for Khalistan, the growth of Hindu cultural nationalism, the rise of Islamism in various parts of the world). Additionally, the multicultural climate I have described above played an important part in encouraging people to define themselves and publicly project themselves in terms of authenticity, 'difference' and victimhood and gave them the confidence to reject opposing arguments (such as that newly-settled groups should be seen and not heard; that when in Rome do as the Romans do). This was probably especially the case with middle-class professional people who had some choice as whether to emphasise 'integration' or 'difference' in their public discourse and political persona.[17]

Political blackness was, therefore, unravelling at a grass-roots level at the very time when it was becoming hegemonic as a minority discourse in British public life (1980s). The single event that illustrated this most dramatically was the battle over *The Satanic Verses* that broke out in 1988-89. This was seen by all concerned as a 'Muslim versus The West' battle. On the Muslim side, it generated an impassioned activism and mobilisation, that no previous campaign against racism had remotely done.[18] Many 'lapsed' or 'passive' Muslims (Muslims, especially the non-religious, for whom hitherto their Muslim background was not particularly important) (re)discovered a new community solidarity. What was striking was that when the public rage against Muslims was at its most intense, Muslims neither sought nor were offered any special solidarity by any non-white minority. It was, in fact, some white liberal Anglicans that tried to moderate the hostility against the angry Muslims, and it was inter-faith fora rather than political-black organisations that tried to create space where Muslims could state their case without being vilified. Political

17. This was even truer of the Caribbeans than the South Asians. However, at least superficially, they were able to and did combine an ethnic assertiveness ('black' as pride in African roots) with a wider political solidarity ('black' as inclusive of all non-whites) without a new identity vocabulary.

18. T. Modood, 'British Asian Muslims and the Rushdie affair', *Political Quarterly* Vol. 61, no. 2, pp. 143-160 (1990); reproduced in J. Donald and A. Rattansi (eds.), *'Race', Culture and Difference* (London: Sage, 1992).

blackness—seen up to then as the key formation in the politics of post-immigration ethnicity—was seen as irrelevant to an issue which many Muslims insisted was fundamental to defining the kind of 'respect' or 'civility' appropriate to a peaceful multicultural society, that is to say, to the political constitution of 'difference' in Britain.[19]

The fundamental problem for political blackness came from the internal ambivalence I mentioned earlier, namely whether blackness as a political identity was sufficiently distinct from and could mobilise without blackness as an ethnic pride movement. This black identity movement, in a growing climate of opinion favourable to identity politics of various kinds, was successful in shifting the terms of the debate from colour-blind individualistic assimilation to questions about how white British society had to change to accommodate new groups. But its success in imposing or making a singular identity upon or out of (unlike black America or South Africa) a diverse ethnic minority population was temporary (probably at no time did a majority of Asians think of themselves as part of a positive black identity). What it did was pave the way to a plural ethnic assertiveness, as Asian groups, including Muslims, borrowed the logic of ethnic pride and tried to catch up with the success of a newly legitimised black public identity.

Let me illustrate the process I am pointing to by referring to a larger historical case, the emergence of oppositional identities in British India. Diagrams 1 to 4 (see p. 232) represent schematically the political situation at four time-periods. Diagram 1 represents the situation before the arrival of the British in India, when Muslims ruled over Hindus. Diagram 2 represents the situation when the British ruled India. Diagram 3 depicts a later time when the nationalist movement attempted to create a unified oppositional identity of Indian. The last diagram shows the failure of that movement with the assertion of a Muslim identity by the majority of Muslims, leaving some Muslims and other minorities grouped around a Hindu+ identity, a majority Hindu grouping aspiring to transcend sectarian divisions. The point of the example is that an oppositional identity depends upon emotionally welding together a disparate population; to do so one must draw upon the traditions and beliefs of the oppressed, especially in a way that is readily communicable to the ordinary mass of people. Where the relevant population embodies one or more major historical cleavage, the task is difficult. The mobilisation of the Indian masses required an appeal to past Hindu glories, to Hindu symbols and customs, in short to a form of Hindu nationalism. But the beating of that drum led through group competition and a 'me-too-ism' to a rival oppositional identity, a Muslim nationalism and eventually the creation of Pakistan, which, too,

19. Modood, *supra* note 16.

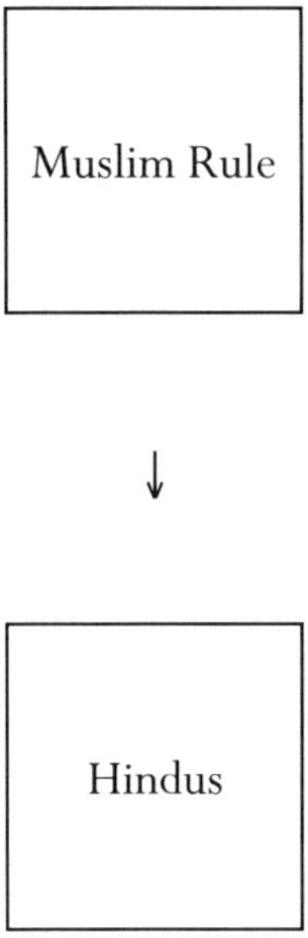

Diagram 1

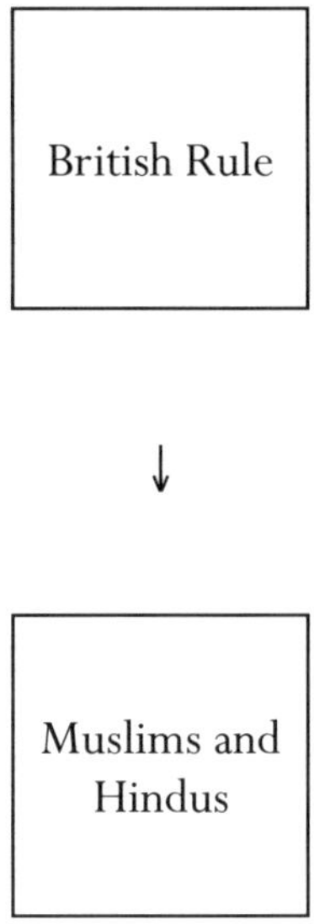

Diagram 2

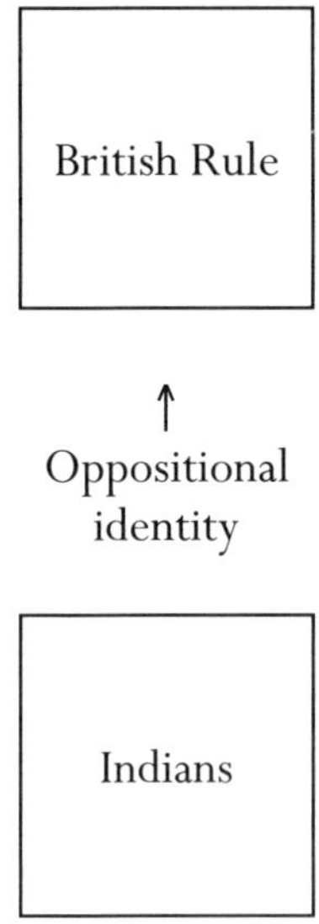

Diagram 3

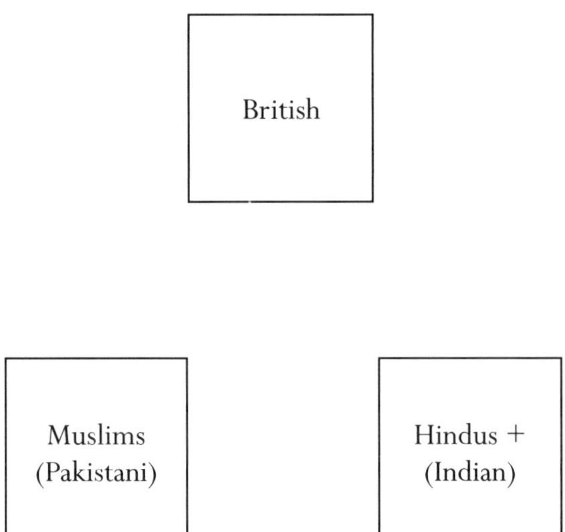

Diagram 4

the more populist it had to be, that is to say the more it had to mobilise mass action, the more religious it also became in rhetoric, imagery and so on. If the matter could have been left to an Anglicised Indian elite, communal passions would not have been aroused; but the politics of anti-imperialism required the mobilisation of the masses and the political struggle had to be couched in terms that made sense to the masses and could elicit their support and sacrifices.

I hope the point of the historical illustration is clear: just as the development of an Indian oppositional identity was confused with Hindu nationalism, so it is not surprising that the development of a contemporary British 'black' (i.e., non-white) oppositional identity was confused with the development of a black ethnic pride (African roots) movement, and triggered off other ethnic assertions such as 'Asian', 'Muslim' and so on, and reduced a political 'black' to an ethnic blackness.

Not only have British ethnic minorities not united under a single identity capable of mobilising them all, but the number of identities which generate intensity of commitment and community mobilisation grows all the time. Of course much of this is to do with context and in particular what one feels one needs to react against. Pakistanis were 'black' when it meant a job in a racial equality bureaucracy, 'Asian' when a community centre was in the offing, 'Muslim' when the Prophet was being ridiculed, 'Kashmiris' when a nationalist movement back home had taken off and blood was being spilt. These identities are pragmatic moves as well as define the field in which moves are made. And yet all this leaves unanswered the question: why is it ethnic (i.e. regional and national origins) and religious identities that have come to be politically prominent amongst South Asians in Britain instead of other group identities, most notably, a colour-based identity?

At a time when social theory and research is dominated by constructivism and anti-essentialism of various sorts, it is with some trepidation that I raise the question about whether, among alternative identities, certain ethnicities or collectivities may be more 'real' than others, have a greater durability or ability to resurface—in short whether they may not have some characteristics that cannot be accounted for by radical constructivism.

When I try to explain to myself why, say, Pakistanis mobilise around 'Muslim' with a conviction, intensity and solidarity that they do not around 'black', I use the distinction between a group's mode of oppression and mode of being. So that even if it were the case that white British society saw and treated Muslims as a 'coloured Other', it doesn't follow that Muslims accept that description of themselves. Excluded groups seek respect for themselves as they are or aspire to be, not simply a solidarity on the basis of a recognition of themselves as victims; they resist being defined by their *mode of oppression* and seek space and dignity for their *mode of being*.[20] All the identities that are being discussed here are in some sense reactive and are shaped by a situation that the minorities do not control (though I am impressed by the degree to which the minorities are active in these identity formations). I am not contrasting situationally or politically constructed identities with something primordial. My point is that a minority will respond to some forms of exclusion or inferiorisation and not to others. The ones it will respond to are those which relate in some way to its own sense of being. Again, this sense of being is not atemporal and can change, but it does mean that neither the oppressor nor the oppressed are totally free to set the terms of a reactive identity—the oppression must 'speak' to the oppressed, it must reach their sense of being.

So, part of the answer as to which identity will emerge as important to a group at a particular time lies in the nature of the minority group in question. That the Caribbeans have mobilised around a colour identity and the south Asians around religious and related identities is not chance nor just a 'construction' but based on something deeper about these groups. That Muslims in their anger against *The Satanic Verses* found a depth of indignation, a 'voice' of their own, in a way that most had not found in relation to events and in mobilisation in the previous decades, cannot be explained just in terms of issues to do with political leaderships, rivalries, tactics, etc. Certainly, some individuals and organisations exploited the situation but they could not have done so if there was not a 'situation' to exploit.

Muslim Identity Politics

Once out, the genie has not been re-corked. In a very short space of time, 'Muslim' has become a key political minority identity, acknowledged by Right and Left, bigots and the open-minded, the media and the government. It has become integral to local community politics and yet thrives through romantic, global solidarities as wars and massacres in Palestine, Bosnia, Kosovo, the Gulf, Chechnya, Kashmir and India fill our newspapers and television screens and lead some young British-born Muslims to reinvent the concept of the umma as global victims. This politics has meant not just a recognition of a new religious diversity in Britain but a new or renewed policy importance for religion. Recent empirical evidence shows overwhelmingly that the

20. T. Modood, 'Catching up with Jesse Jackson: being oppressed and being somebody', *New Community*, 17 (1), October (1990); reproduced in T. Modood, *Not Easy Being British: Colour, Culture and Citizenship* (London: Runnymede Trust, 1992).

religion of one's family is the most important source of self-identity amongst South Asian origin people, especially Muslims. The Fourth National Survey of Ethnic Minorities, a large, nationally representative survey found that rather than skin-colour, which was prominent in the self-descriptions of Caribbeans, it was religion that was prominent in the self-descriptions of South Asians.[21] This owes as much to a sense of community as to personal faith, but the identification and prioritisation of religion is far from just a nominal one. Very few Asians marry across religious and caste boundaries and most expect that their children will be inducted into their religion. At a time when a third of Britons say they do not have a religion, nearly all South Asians said they have one, and 90 per cent said that religion was of personal importance to them (compared to 13 per cent of whites). While about a quarter of whites attend a place of worship once a month or more, over half of Hindus and seven out of ten Sikhs attend once a month or more and nearly two-thirds of Muslims attend at least once a week. Even amongst the young, expressions of commitment were exceptionally high: more than a third of Indians and African Asians, and two-thirds of Pakistani and Bangladeshi 16-34 years old said that religion was very important to how they led their lives compared to five per cent of whites (though nearly a fifth of Caribbeans took this view).

There are two important points to make here about these identities, especially of Muslim identity. Firstly, they cannot be characterised as belonging to private life and irrelevant to public policies and resources. For example, half of the Muslims interviewed said that there should be state funding for Muslim schools. Secondly, religious and ethnic identities were not simply an expression of behaviour, of participation in distinctive cultural practices. For, across the generations and in relation to time spent in Britain, there was a noticeable decline in participation in the cultural practices (language, dress, attendance at place of worship and so on) that go with a particular identity. Yet the decrease in self-identification with a group label (black, Muslim, etc.) was relatively small. That is to say, there are, for example, people in Britain who say of themselves that they are Muslim but may not be at all religious. In one sense, there is nothing new or peculiar about this. In another sense, it marks a new conception of ethno-religious identities. For what we are not talking about are passive or fading identities. That would be to overlook the pride with which they may be asserted, the intensity with which they may be debated and their capacity to generate community activism and political campaigns. People may still feel passionate about the public recognition and resourcing of aspects of their community identity, even though as individuals they may not wish that resource for themselves. So for example, the demand for public funding of

21. Modood, *supra* note 5.

Muslim schools has been a source of Muslim grievance, with some secular, as well as religious Muslims highlighting the injustice of a system that funded Christian and Jewish, but not Muslim, schools. Yet in our survey only half of those Muslims who supported funding of Muslim schools said that if they had the choice they would prefer to send their own child to a Muslim school; once again, the young were not much less likely to want the funding but were much less likely to want to take up the option for their own (future) children. Muslim purists might disparage these ambivalences but in fact the success of the Muslim campaign partly depends on the political support of the non-fully-religious Muslims, on the extensive mobilisation of the Muslim community. Hence, it would be wrong to think of the non-fully-religious Muslims as only token or 'symbolic' Muslims.[22]

I have given some account of what terms like 'equality', 'inclusion' and 'recognition' mean in contemporary discourses, but what do they mean in practical terms? What kinds of specific policy demands are being made by or on behalf of religious groups when these kinds of terms are being deployed? I suggest that these demands have three dimensions, which get progressively 'thicker' and are progressively less acceptable to radical secularists.

1. No religious discrimination

The very basic demand is that religious people, no less than people defined by 'race' or gender, should not suffer discrimination in job and other opportunities. So, for example, a person who is trying to dress in accordance with their religion or who projects a religious identity, such as a Muslim woman wearing a headscarf (*hijab*), should not be discriminated against in employment. At the moment in Britain there is no legal ban on such discrimination, and the government has not said that the case for it is not proven. The legal system leaves Muslims particularly vulnerable because while discrimination against *yarmulke*-wearing Jews and turban-wearing Sikhs is deemed to be unlawful *racial* discrimination, Muslims, unlike these other faith communities, are not deemed to be a racial or ethnic group. Nor are they protected by the legislation against religious discrimination that does exist in the UK, for that, being explicitly designed to protect Catholics, only covers Northern Ireland. The best that Muslims are able to achieve is to prove that the discrimination against them was indirectly against their ethnic characteristics, that they suffered an indirect

22. J. Rex, 'National Identity in the Democratic Multi-Cultural State', *Sociological Research Online*, 1 (2) para. 4.13, http://www.socresonline.org.uk/socresonline/1/2/1.html (1996).

discrimination in virtue of being, say, a Pakistani or an Iraqi. While, it is indeed the case that the discrimination against Muslims is indeed mixed up with forms of colour-racism and cultural-racism,[23] the charge of indirect discrimination is a much weaker offence in law, carrying with it no compensatory requirements for the victim. Moreover, some Muslims are white and so do not enjoy this second-class protection and many Muslim activists argue that religious freedom, being a fundamental right, should not be legally and politically dependent on dubious concepts of race and ethnicity.[24] Campaigning for religious discrimination legislation in Britain has an importance for Muslims greater than for other minority faiths. The same applies to the demand for a law in Britain (again, it already exists in Northern Ireland) to curb and punish incitement against religious hatred to parallel the law against incitement to racial hatred (which extends to certain forms of anti-Jewish literature).[25] After some years of arguing that there was no evidence of religious discrimination, the hand of the British government has been forced by the European Union's Article 13 of the Amsterdam Treaty (1999) including religious discrimination in the list of the forms of discrimination that all member states are expected to eliminate. The UK government has recently announced its intention to implement a European Commission directive to outlaw religious discrimination in employment in 2003.[26] A Muslim organisation concerned with these issues is the Forum Against Islamophobia and Racism (FAIR), set up in 2000, 'for the purpose of raising awareness of and combating Islamophobia and racism, monitoring specific incidents of Islamophobia and racism, working towards eliminating religious and racial discrimination, campaigning and lobbying on issues relevant to Muslim and other multi-ethnic communities in Britain' (publicity materials).

2. Parity with native religions

Many minority faith advocates interpret equality to mean that minority religions should get at least some of the support from the state that older established religions do. Muslims have led the way on this argument too, and have

23. T. Modood, 'Difference, Cultural Racism and Anti-racism' in P. Werbner and T. Modood (eds.), *Debating Cultural Identity* (London: Zed Books, 1997).

24. UKACIA, *supra* note 6.

25. CRE (Commission for Racial Equality), *Free Speech: Report of a Seminar* (London, 1990); T. Modood, 'Muslims, Incitement to Hatred and the Law' in J. Horton (ed.), *Liberalism, Multiculturalism and Toleration* (London: Macmillan, 1993); reproduced in UKACIA (UK Action Committee on Islamic Affairs), *Muslims and the Law in Multi-faith Britain: Need for Reform* (London: UK Action Committee on Islamic Affairs, 1993).

26. Cabinet Office *et al*, *Towards Equality and Diversity, Implementing the Employment and Race Directives* (UK Government, 2001).

made two particular issues politically contentious, namely, the state funding of schools and the law of blasphemy. After some political battle, the government has recently agreed to fund four Muslim schools, as well as a Sikh and a Seventh Day Adventist school, on the same basis enjoyed by thousands of Anglican and Catholic schools and some Methodist and Jewish schools (in England and Wales, over a third of state-maintained primary and a sixth of secondary schools are run by a religious group but all have to deliver a centrally determined national curriculum). Some secularists are unhappy about this. They say they accept the argument for parity but believe this should be achieved by the state withdrawing its funding from all religious schools.[27] Most Muslims reject this form of equality in which the privileged lose something but the under-privileged gain nothing[28] (except perhaps the resentment of the newly dispossessed). More specifically, the issue between 'equalising upwards' and 'equalising downwards' here is about the legitimacy of religion as a public institutional presence.

Muslims failed to get the courts to interpret the existing statute on blasphemy to cover offences beyond what Christians hold sacred, but some political support exists for an incitement to religious hatred offence, mirroring the existing incitement to racial hatred offence. The government, indeed, inserted such a clause in the post-September 11 new security legislation, in order to conciliate Muslims, who, amongst others, were strongly opposed to the new powers of surveillance, arrest and detention that were being proposed. As it happened, most of the latter was made law, but the incitement to religious hatred offence was defeated in Parliament.

3. Positive Inclusion of Religious Groups

The demand here is that religion in general, or at least the category of 'Muslim' in particular, should be a category by which the inclusiveness of social institutions should be judged in the same way that anti-racists use 'black' and feminists use 'female'. So that, for example, employers should have to demonstrate that they don't discriminate against Muslims by explicit monitoring backed up by appropriate policies, targets, managerial responsibilities, work environments, staff training, advertisements, outreach and so on.[29]

27. It has even been argued – though in the name of integration rather than multiculturalism – that this should be done expressly to prevent state-funded Muslim schools.

28. For a further discussion of this theme see the chapter in this book by Michael Ipgrave.

29. FAIR (Forum Against Islamophobia and Racism), *A Response To The Government Consultation Paper, 'Towards Equality and Diversity: Implementing the Employment and Race Directives'* (London, March 2002); CBMI (Commission on British Muslims and Islamophobia), *Response To the Commission on Racial Equality's Code of Practice* (London, February 2002).

Similarly, local authorities should provide appropriately sensitive policies and staff, especially in relation to (non-Muslim) schools, social and health services and, say, fund Muslim community centres or Muslim youth workers in addition to the existing Asian and Caribbean community centres and the existing Asian and Black youth workers.[30] Or, to take another case—an organisation like the BBC currently believes it is of political importance to review and improve its personnel practices and its output of programmes, including its on-screen 'representation' of the British population, by reference to making provision for and winning the confidence of, say, women, ethnic groups and young people. Why should it not also use religious groups as a criterion of inclusivity and have to demonstrate that it is doing the same for viewers and staff defined by religious community membership? In short, Muslims should be treated as a legitimate group in their own right (not because they are, say, Asians), whose presence in British society has to be explicitly reflected in all walks of life and in all institutions; and whether or not they are so included becomes one of the criteria for judging Britain as an egalitarian, inclusive, multicultural society. A potentially significant victory along these lines was made when the government agreed to include a religion question in the 2001 Census. This was the first time this question had been included in the Census since 1851 and was largely unpopular outside the politically active religionists, amongst whom Muslims were foremost, but had the potential to pave the way for widespread 'religious monitoring' in the way that the inclusion of an ethnic question in 1991 had led to the routinisation of 'ethnic monitoring'.

A Panicky Retreat to a Liberal Public-Private Distinction

If the emergence of a politics of difference out of and alongside a liberal assimilationist equality created a dissonance, as indeed it did, the emergence of a British Muslim identity out of and alongside ethno-racial identities has created an even greater dissonance. Philosophically speaking, it should create a lesser dissonance for it seems to me that a move from the idea of equality as sameness to equality as difference is a more profound conceptual movement than the creation of a new identity in a field already crowded with minority identities. But this is to naively ignore the hegemonic power of secularism in British political culture, especially on the centre-left. While black and related ethno-racial identities were welcomed by, indeed were intrinsic to the rain-

30. Muslim Parliament of Great Britain, *supra* note 7; UKACIA, *supra* note 6.

bow coalition of identity politics, this coalition is deeply unhappy with Muslim consciousness. While for some this rejection is specific to Islam, for many the ostensible reason is that it is a religious identity. What is most interesting is that in this latter objection, if it is taken at its face value, the difference theorists, activists and paid professionals revert to is a public-private distinction that they have spent two or three decades demolishing. The unacceptability, the bad odour, of Muslim identity is no doubt partly to do with the conservative views on gender and sexuality professed by Muslim spokespersons, not to mention issues to do with freedom of expression as they arose in the Rushdie affair.[31] But these are objections to specific views, as such they can be argued with on a point-by-point basis[32]—they aren't objections to an identity. The fundamental stated objection to Muslim identity is that it is a politicised religious identity.

The nature of the objection is that religion belongs to the private sphere and is not a legitimate basis for a political identity. This is a classical liberal distinction though it has never been followed in a pure form except, in different ways, perhaps in France and the USA. It is of course incompatible with the politics-of-difference perspective on the essentially contested nature of the public-private distinction described above. It is also a distinction that does not fit with contemporary British society, in which there is an 'established' church, the Supreme Governor of which occupies that post by virtue of being the Monarch and head of state. Hence in the last few years many liberal and radical multiculturalists have declared that they think it is time to 'disestablish' the Church of England.[33] Most extraordinarily, it is said that the inclusion of religious minorities, like Muslims, into the British polity requires not just the abolition of the Church of England's constitutional privileges but the severance of any relationship between the state, local or central, and religion. One explicit implication of this would be the phasing out of state funding for denominational schools, of which there are thousands (two Muslim primary schools having joined these ranks for the first time in December 1997). Initially, there were few members of religious minorities joining this discussion and so the secular multiculturalists were taken to be speaking for the marginal religious minorities. More recently, spokespersons of a number of

31. Modood, *supra* note 25.

32. Though it is noticeable that Muslim homophobia gets far more condemnation than say, black homophobia, and Muslim sensitivities against offensive literature get far less sympathetic treatment than those of radical feminists against pornography, and Jews against holocaust revisionism, not to mention legal restraints against incitements to racial hatred. See Modood, *supra* note 25.

33. G. Saghal and N. Yuval-Davis, *Refusing Holy Orders: Women and Fundamentalism in Britain* (London: Virago Press, 1992).

non-Christian religious minorities have argued for the importance of maintaining a symbolic and substantive link between religion and the state.[34] In fact, somewhat surprisingly, besides arguing for various benefits for the minority religions and the importance of religious discrimination legislation to complement that on racial discrimination, they have not challenged the Anglican privileges or even the conception that Britain is/ought to be a Christian country.[35]

It is once more worth emphasising that the panic that the rise of Muslim assertiveness has caused among secular multiculturalists has resulted in knee-jerk reactions and inconsistencies.[36] By forcing the debate about religion and politics into the polar options of establishment-disestablishment, they have obscured other options such as replacing the Anglican/Christian link with the state by a pluralised religions-state link, or by developing other forms of institutionalisation which would give political and administrative expression to a multi-faith society. Nor have they suggested any lay or secular forms of representation for Muslims and related groups. In fact, the latter would be just as or more consistent with the ethos of Sunni Islam. Most mosques in Britain are run by local lay committees and the *mullah* or *imam* is a usually a minor functionary. At the national level too, very few of those who aspire to be Muslim spokespersons and representatives have religious authority and are not expected to have it by fellow Muslims. So the argument ought to be more about the recognition and support of communities rather than necessarily about ecclesiastical or spiritual representation in political institutions.

These debates would indeed be more consistent with the notions of group 'recognition' and of publicity that currently inform much multiculturalist thinking. Instead, by suggesting that if a religious denomination is not 'established' then it effectively is a matter of private religious observance and conscience and has no place among public, political identities multicultural disestablishmentarians are applying different standards of publicity to religion than they apply to ethnic and other identities. We thus have a mixed-up situation where secular multiculturalists argue that the sex lives of individuals—traditionally a core area of liberal privacy—is a legitimate feature of political identities and public discourse and seem to generally welcome the sexualisation of culture, if not the prurient interest in the sexual activity of public char-

34. Modood, *supra* note 23.

35. *Ibid.*

36. Women Against Fundamentalism (WAF), 'Founding Statement', *Women Against Fundamentalism Journal* (1992); Saghal and Yuval-Davis, *supra* note 33.

acters, while on the other hand religion—a key source of communal identity in traditional, non-liberal societies—is to be regarded as a private matter, perhaps as a uniquely private matter. Most specifically, Muslim identity is seen as the illegitimate child of British multiculturalism.

Indeed, the Rushdie Affair made evident that the group in British society most politically opposed to (politicised) Muslims weren't Christians, or even right-wing nationalists but the secular, liberal intelligentsia.[37] While hostile press reporting and inflammatory headlines about black people are more characteristic of the tabloids than the broadsheets, with the latter usually castigating such journalism, Muslims are frequently criticised in the op/ed pages of the broadsheets in a way that few, if any, other minority groups are. Muslims often remark that if in such articles the word 'Muslims' were substituted for 'Jews' or 'blacks', the newspapers in question would be attacked as racist and indeed risk legal proceedings.[38] The large Fourth Survey found that nominal Christians and those without a religion were more likely to say they were prejudiced against Muslims than those Christians who said their religion was of importance to them.[39] Just as the hostility against Jews, in various times and places, has been a varying blend of anti-Judaism (hostility to a religion) and anti-semitism (hostility to a racialised group), so it is difficult to gauge to what extent contemporary British Islamophobia is 'religious' and to what extent 'racial'. It is generally becoming acknowledged that of all groups Asians face the greatest hostility today, and Asians themselves feel this is because of hostility directed to Muslims.[40] These matters are not at all easy to disentangle, they have hardly been researched at all and anti-Muslim racism is only just beginning to be acknowledged by anti-racists. One has also to acknowledge that there must be analytical space for forthright criticism of aspects of Muslim doctrines, ideologies and practice without it being dismissed as Islamophobia—this being exactly the parallel problem of distinguishing anti-Zionism and anti-semitism.

37. The feeling is mutual: it is not Christian hegemony but radical secularism and sexual liberalism that Muslims, in private and public, fulminate against.

38. *Cf.* Runnymede Trust, *Islamophobia: A Challenge To Us All* (London: The Runnymede Trust, 1997).

39. Modood *et al*, *supra* note 5 p. 134.

40. Modood *et al*, *supra* note 5.

Conclusion

In conclusion, I will merely say that the emergence of Muslim political agency has thrown British multiculturalism into theoretical and practical disarray. This is worrying because on any objective reading there cannot be, what one might call, a race relations settlement in Britain without the Muslims as nearly half of all non-whites are Muslims. On the other hand, Muslims cannot prosper without political allies and without the goodwill of the educated classes, both of which are denied to them at the moment. What may be of international and comparative interest here is that, as far as I know, in no other country at the moment is this debate taking place in quite this way. Britain thus can be contrasted to France, where the Muslim presence has stimulated a neo-republican anti-multiculturalist consensus.[41] In Britain, multiculturalism continues to make political headway while, paradoxically, the opposition between rival versions of multiculturalism deepens.[42]

41. T. Modood and P. Werbner (eds.), *The Politics of Multiculturalism in the New Europe: Racism, Identity and Community* (London: Zed Books, 1997); A. Favell, *Philosophies of Integration: Immigration and the Idea of Citizenship in France and Britain* (Basingstoke: Macmillan, 1998).

42. T. Modood, 'Anti-Essentialism, Multiculturalism and the 'Recognition' of Religious Minorities', *Journal of Political Philosophy*, 6 (4) December, pp. 378-399 (1998); reproduced in W. Kymlicka and W. Norman (eds.), *Citizenship in Diverse Societies* (Oxford: Oxford University Press); Modood, *supra* note 11.

Appendix

UN Declaration on the Elimination of All Forms of Intolerance and of Discrimination Based on Religion or Belief

Resolution Adopted by the General Assembly at its 73rd plenary meeting on 25 November 1981 on the Report of the Third Committee (A/36/684)] 36/55.

Considering that one of the basic principles of the Charter of the United Nations is that of the dignity and equality inherent in all human beings, and that all Member States have pledged themselves to take joint and separate action in co-operation with the Organization to promote and encourage universal respect for the observance of human rights and fundamental freedoms for all, without distinction as to race, sex, language or religion, Considering that the Universal Declaration on Human Rights [General Assembly Resolution 217A (III)] and the International Covenants on Human Rights [General Assembly Resolution 2200A (XXI)] proclaim the principles of non-discrimination and equality before the law and the right to freedom of thought, conscience, religion and belief,

Considering that the disregard and infringement of human rights and fundamental freedoms, in particular of the right to freedom of thought, conscience, religion or whatever belief, have brought, directly or indirectly, wars and great suffering to mankind, especially where they serve as a means of foreign interference in the internal affairs of other States and amount to kindling hatred between peoples and nations,

Considering that religion or belief, for anyone who professes either, is one of the fundamental elements in his conception of life and that freedom of religion or belief should be fully respected and guaranteed, Considering that it is essential to promote understanding, tolerance and respect in matters relating to freedom of religion and belief to ensure that the use of religion or belief for ends inconsistent with the Charter, other relevant instruments of the United Nations and the purposes and principles of the present Declaration is inadmissable,

Convinced that freedom of religion and belief should also contribute to the attainment of the goals of world peace, social justice and friendship among peoples and to the elimination of ideologies or practices of colonialism and racial discrimination,

Noting with satisfaction the adoption of several, and the coming force of some, conventions, under the aegis of the United Nations and of the specialized agencies, for the elimination of various forms of discrimination, Concerned by manifestations of intolerance and by the existence of discrimination in matters of religion or belief still in evidence in some areas of the world,

Resolved to adopt all necessary measures for the speedy elimination of such intolerance in all its forms and manifestations and to prevent and combat discrimination on the grounds of religion of belief,

Proclaims this Declaration on the Elimination of All Forms of Intolerance and of Discrimination Based on Religion or Belief:

Article I

1. Everyone shall have the right to freedom of thought, conscience and religion. This right shall include freedom to have a religion or whatever belief of his choice, and freedom, either individually or in community with others, and in public or private, to manifest his religion or belief in worship, observance, practice and teaching.
2. No one shall be subject to coercion which would impair his freedom to have a religion or belief of his choice.

3. Freedom to manifest one's religion or beliefs may be subject only to such limitations as are prescribed by law and are necessary to protect public safety, order, health or morals or the fundamental rights and freedoms of others.

Article 2

1. No one shall be subject to discrimination by any State, institution, group of persons or person on the grounds of religion or other beliefs.
2. For the purposes of the present Declaration, the expression "intolerance and discrimination based on religion or belief" means any distinction, exclusion, restriction or preference based on religion or belief and having as its purpose or as its effect nullification or impairment of the recognition, enjoyment or exercise of human rights and fundamental freedoms on an equal basis.

Article 3

Discrimination between human beings on the grounds of religion or belief constitutes an affront to human dignity and a disavowal of the principles of the Charter of the United Nations, and shall be condemned as a violation of the human rights and fundamental freedoms proclaimed in the Universal Declaration on Human Rights and enunciated in detail in the International Covenants on Human Rights, and as an obstacle to friendly and peaceful relations between nations.

Article 4

1. All States shall take effective measures to prevent and eliminate discrimination on the grounds of religion or belief in the recognition, exercise and enjoyment of human rights and fundamental freedoms in all fields of civil, economic, political, social and cultural life.
2. All States shall make all efforts to enact or rescind legislation where necessary to prohibit any such discrimination, and take all appropriate measures to combat intolerance on the grounds of religion or other beliefs in this matter.

Article 5

1. The parents or, as the case may be, the legal guardians of the child have the right to organize the life within the family in accordance with their religion or belief and bearing in mind the moral education in which they believe the child should be brought up.
2. Every child shall enjoy the right to have access to education in the matter of religion or belief in accordance with the wishes of his parents or legal guardians, the best interests of the child being the guiding principle.

3. The child shall be protected from any form of discrimination on the grounds of religion or belief. He shall be brought up in a spirit of understanding, tolerance, friendship among peoples, peace and universal brotherhood, respect for freedom of religion or belief of others, and in full consciousness that his energy and talents should be devoted to the service of his fellow men.
4. In the case of a child who is not under the care either of his parents or of legal guardians, due account shall be taken of their expressed wishes or of any other proof of their wishes in the matter of religion or belief, the best interests of the child being the guiding principle.
5. Practices of a religion or beliefs in which a child is brought up must not be injurious to his physical or mental health or to his full development, taking into account article 1, paragraph 3, of the present Declaration.

Article 6

In accordance with article 1 of the present Declaration, and subject to the provisions of article 1, paragraph 3, the right to freedom of thought, conscience, religion or belief shall include, inter alia, the following freedoms:

(a) To worship or assemble in connexion with a religion or belief, and to establish and maintain places for these purposes;
(b) To establish and maintain appropriate charitable or humanitarian institutions;
(c) To make, acquire and use to an adequate extent the necessary articles and materials related to the rites or customs of a religion or belief;
(d) To write, issue and disseminate relevant publications in these areas;
(e) To teach a religion or belief in places suitable for these purposes;
(f) To solicit and receive voluntary financial and other contributions from individuals and institutions;
(g) To train, appoint, elect or designate by succession appropriate leaders called for by the requirements and standards of any religion or belief;
(h) To observe days of rest and to celebrate holidays and ceremonies in accordance with the precepts of one's religion or belief;
(i) To establish and maintain communications with individuals and communities in matters of religion and belief at the national and international levels.

Article 7

The rights and freedoms set forth in the present Declaration shall be accorded in national legislations in such a manner that everyone shall be able to avail himself of such rights and freedoms in practice.

Article 8

Nothing in the present Declaration shall be construed as restricting or derogating from any right defined in the Universal Declaration on Human Rights and the International Covenants on Human Rights.

Bibliography

Books and Journal Articles

A

Adhar, R. (ed.), *Law and Religion* (Aldershot: Ashgate, 2000).

Ahsan, M.M., and A.R. Kidwai (eds.), *Sacrilege Versus Civility: Muslim Perspectives on the Salman Rushdie Affair* (Leicester: Islamic Foundation, 1991).

Alderman, G., *Modern British Jewry* (Oxford: Clarendon, 2nd ed, 1998).

Allen, C., and J. Nielsen, *Summary Report on Islamophobia in the EU after 11 September 2001* (Vienna: European Monitoring Centre on Racism and Xenophobia, May 2002).

al-Ghazali, M., *Huquq al-Insan Bayn Ta'alim al-Islam Wa- I'lan Al-Umam al-Muttahidah* (Human Rights between Islamic Principles and the United Nations' Declaration) (Cairo: al-Maktabah al-Tidjariyyah, 1963).

al-Mota'al al-Saidi, A., *al-Hurriyyah al-Diniyyah Fi al-Islam* (Religious Freedom in Islam), (Cairo: al-Fikr al-Arabi House, undated).

al-Qadir Awada, A., *al-Tashri al-Djina'i al-Islami* (Islamic Criminal Legislation) Vol. 1 (Beirut: al-Kitab al-Arabi House, undated).

Alsayyad, N. and M. Castells (eds.), *Muslim Europe or Euro-Islam: Politics, Culture and Citizenship in the Age of Globalisation* (New York: Lexington Books, 2002).

Alston, P., and J. Crawford (eds.), *The Future of UN Human Rights Treaty Monitoring* (Cambridge: Cambridge University Press, 2000).

An-Na'im, A.A., (ed.), *Human Rights in Cross-Cultural Perspectives, A Quest for Consensus* (Philadelphia: University of Pennsylvania Press, 1992).

An-Na'im, A.A., 'The Islamic Law of Apostasy and Its Modern Applicability: A Case from the Sudan', *Religion* 16, p. 214 (1986).

An-Na'im, A.A., 'The Legal Protection of Human Rights in Africa: Doing More with Less' (Unpublished. Forthcoming).

An-Na'im, A. A., *Towards an Islamic Reformation: Civil Liberties, Human Rights and International Law* (Syracuse, NY: Syracuse University Press, 1990).

An-Na'im, A. A., J.D. Gort, H. Jansen, H.M. Vroom (eds.), *Human Rights and Religious Values, An Uneasy Relationship?* (Michigan: William B. Eerdmans Publishing Company, 1995).

Appignanesi, L., and S. Maitland (eds.), *The Rushdie File* (London: Fourth Estate, 1989).

Arendt, H., *On Revolution* (New York: Viking Press, 1963).

Avis, P., *Church, State and Establishment* (London: SPCK, 2000).

B

Bacal, A., *Ethnicity in the Social Sciences: A View and Review of the Literature on Ethnicity* Reprint Paper on Ethnic Relations, No. 3 (Coventry: Centre for Research in Ethnic Relations, University of Warwick, 1991).

Badham, P., (ed.), *Religion, State and Society in Modern Britain* (Lampeter: Edwin Mellen Press, 1989).

Bainton, M., (ed.), *Anthropological Approaches to the Study of Religion* (London: Tavistock, 1990).

Barot, R., (ed.), *Religion and Ethnicity: Minorities and Social Change in the Metropolis* (Kampen: Kok Pharos, 1993).

Bebbington, D., *The Nonconformist Conscience: Chapel and Politics, 1870-1914* (London: George Allen and Unwin, 1982).

Becker, J.W., and R. Vink, *Secularisation in the Netherlands, 1966-1991: changing opinions, changing behaviour* (The Hague: SCP, 1994).

Becker, R., 'Spiritual care on the rocks', *The European Journal of Palliative Care*, Vol. 8, No.4, (2001).

Beckford, J., and S. Gilliat, *Religion in Prison: Equal Rites in a Multi-Faith Society* (Cambridge: Cambridge University Press, 1998).

Benhabib, S., *Situating the Self* (New York: Routledge, 1992).

Berman, D., *A History of Atheism in Britain: From Hobbes to Russell* (London: Croon Helm, 1988).

Bharania, M., 'Who's afraid of Protocol Twelve', *New Law Journal*, 19 January 2001.

Bloom, I., J. P. Martin and W.L. Proudfoot (eds.), *Religious Diversity and Human Rights* (New York: Columbia University Press, 1996).

Boerefijn, I., *The Reporting Procedure under the Covenant on Civil and Political Rights: Practice and Procedure of the Human Rights Committee* (Antwerp, Groningen, Oxford: Intersentia-Hart Publishers, 1999).

Boven, T. van, 'Advances and Obstacles in Building Understanding and Respect Between People of Diverse Religions and Beliefs', *Human Rights Quarterly* Vol. 13, (1991).

Boven, Th.C. van, *De volkenrechtelijke bescherming van de godsdienstvrijheid* (Assen: Van Gorcum, 1967).

Boven, T. van, C. Flinterman, F. Grünfeld and I. Westendorp (eds.), *Seminar on the Right to Restitution, Compensation and Rehabilitation for Victims of Gross Violation of Human Rights and Fundamental Freedoms, Maastricht, 11-15 March 1992* (Utrecht: Studie-en Informatiecentrum Mensenrechten, and Maastricht: University of Limburg Human Rights Project Group, 1992).

Bovenkerk, F., 'Crime and the Multi-ethnic Society: A View from Europe' in *Crime, Law and Social Change* (19).

Boyle, K., and J. Sheen (eds.), *Freedom of Religion and Belief, A World Report* (London: Routledge, 1997).

British Council of Churches, *The New Black Presence in Britain: A Christian Scrutiny* (London: British Council of Churches, 1978).

Brody, R., and D. Weisbrodt, 'Major Developments in the 1989 Session on the United Nations Commission on Human Rights', *Human Rights Quarterly*, Vol. 11, (1989).

Bruce, S., *Religion and Modernisation: Sociologists and Historians Debate the Secularisation Thesis* (Oxford: Oxford University Press, 1992).

C

Cabinet Office *et al*, *Towards Equality and Diversity, Implementing the Employment and Race Directives* (UK Government, 2001).

Cable, V., *The World's New Fissures: Identities in Crisis* (London: Demos, 1994).

Calhoun, G., (ed.), *Habermas and the Public Sphere* (Cambridge, Mass.: MIT Press, 1992).

Cantle, T., *Community Cohesion: A Report of the Independent Review Team Chaired by Ted Cantle* (London: The Home Office, 2001).

Cashmore, E., *The Rastafarians*, Report (Oxford: The Minority Rights Group, 1984).

Cassese, A., (ed.), *UN Law/Fundamental Rights, Two Topics in International Law* (Alphen aan den Rijn, The Netherlands: Sijthoff & Noordhoff, 1979).

CBMI (Commission on British Muslims and Islamophobia), *Response To the Commission on Racial Equality's Code of Practice* (London, February 2002).

CCCS (Centre for Contemporary Cultural Studies), *The Empire Strikes Back* (London: Hutchinson, 1982).

Christian Institute, the, *European Threat to Religious Freedom* (The Christian Institute, 2000).

Cohn-Sherbok, D., (ed.), *The Canterbury Papers: Essays on Religion and Society* (London: Bellew, 1990).

Cohn-Sherbok, D., and D. McClellan (eds.), *Religion in Public Life* (London: Macmillan, 1992).

Comerford, R., M. Cullen and J. Hill, *Religion, Conflict and Coexistence in Ireland* (London: Gill and Macmillan, 1990).

Council of Europe, *Preliminary Conclusions: Seminar on Religion and the Integration of Immigrants* (Strasbourg, 1999).

Crasnow, R., 'Religious freedom and equal treatment', *New Law Journal*, Vol. 152, 5 April 2002.

CRE (Commission for Racial Equality), *Free Speech: Report of a Seminar* (London, 1990).

D

Daniels, N., *Islam and the West: The Making of an Image, 1000-1300 AD, Volume I* (Edinburgh: Edinburgh University Press, 1960).

Daniels, N., *Islam and the West: Islam, Europe and Empire, Volume II* (Edinburgh: Edinburgh University Press, 1967).

Davidson, S., *Human Rights* (Buckingham: Open University Press, 1993).

Davie, G., *Religion in Britain Since 1945: Believing Without Belonging* (London: Blackwell, 1994).

Davies, J., *A History of Wales* (London: Penguin, Eng. ed, 1994).

Davies, N., *The Isles: A History* (London: Macmillan, 2000).

Denham, J., *Building Cohesive Communities: A Report of the Ministerial Group on Public Order and Building Cohesive Communities* (London: The Home Office, 2001).

Denzinger, H., and A. Schönmetzer, *Enchiridion Symbolorum Definitionum et Declarationum de Rebus Fidei et Morum* (Barcelona: Herder, 36th ed, 1975).

Devine, T.M., *Scotland's Shame: Bigotry and Sectarianism in Modern Scotland* (Edinburgh: Mainstream, 2000).

Donald, J., and A. Rattansi (eds.), *'Race', Culture and Difference* (London: Sage, 1992).

Donnelly, J., 'Human rights, a new standard of civilization?', *International Affairs* Vol. 74, No. 1, (January 1998).

Donnelly, J., *International Human Rights*, 2nd ed., (Boulder: Westview Press, 1998).

Duran, K., 'The Centrifugal Forces of Religion in Sudanese Politics', *Orient*, Vol. 26, No. 4 (December 1985).

Durkheim, E., *The Elementary Forms of Religious Life* (New York: The Free Press, 1947).

E

Eberle, C.J., *Religious Conviction in Liberal Politics* (Cambridge: Cambridge University Press, 2002).

Edge, P., and G. Harvey (eds.), *Law and religion in Contemporary Society: Communities, Individualism and the State* (Aldershot: Ashgate, 2000).

Eijl, C. van, L. Heerma van Voss and P. de Rooij, *Sociaal Nederland, Contouren van de twintigste eeuw* (Amsterdam: Aksant, 2002).

Eltayeb, M.S.M., *A Human Rights Approach to Combating Religious Persecution: Cases from Pakistan, Saudi Arabia and Sudan* (Antwerpen, Groningen, Oxford: Hart Intersentia, 2001).

Esposito, J. L., 'Sudan Islamic Experiment', *Muslim World*, Vol. 76 (1986).

Evans, C., *Freedom of Religion under the European Convention on Human Rights* (Oxford: Oxford University Press, 2001).

Evans, M.D., *Religious Liberty and International Law in Europe* (Cambridge: Cambridge University Press, 1997)

Ewing, K.D., 'The Human Rights Act and Labour Law' Vol. 27 *Industrial Law Journal*, (1998).

F

FAIR (Forum Against Islamophobia and Racism), *A Response To The Government Consultation Paper, 'Towards Equality and Diversity: Implementing the Employment and Race Directives'* (London, March 2002).

Favell, A., *Philosophies of Integration: Immigration and the Idea of Citizenship in France and Britain* (Basingstoke: Macmillans, 1998).

Flannery, A. OP: *Vatican Council II: The Conciliar and Post-Conciliar Documents* (Dublin: Dominican Publications, 1975).

Flood, P.J., *The Effectiveness of UN Human Rights Instruments* (Westport: Praeger, 1998).

Fortuyn, P., *De Islamisering van onze cultuur: Nederlandse identiteit als fundament* (Uithoorn: Karakter Uitgevers BV, 2002).

Fortuyn, P., *Tegen de islamisering van onze cultuur, Nederlandse identiteit als fundament* (Uithoorn: Karakter Uitgevers, 1997).

Fuss, D., *Essentially Speaking* (New York: Routledge, 1989).

G

Gaustad, E.S., *Liberty of Conscience: Roger Williams in America* (Valley Forge, PA: Judson, 1999).

Ghandhi, P.R., *The Human Rights Committee and the Right of Individual Communication: Law and Practice* (Aldershot: Ashgate, 1998).

Gilbert, A., The Making of Post-Christian Britain: a History of the Secularisation of Modern Society (London: Longman, 1980).

Gill, R., *Social Context of Theology: A Methodological Enquiry* (London: Mowbrays, 1975).

Gilliat, S., *Higher Education and Student Religious Identity* (Department of Sociology, University of Exeter, Exeter, in association with the Inter Faith Network for the United Kingdom, London, 1999).

Gilroy, P., *There Ain't No Black in the Union Jack* (London: Routledge, 1987).

Goodrick-Clarke, N., *Black Sun: Aryan Cults, Esoteric Nazism and the Politics of Identity* (New York University Press, 2002).

Gordon, C.N., 'Islamic Legal Revolution: The Case of Sudan', *International Lawyer* Vol. 19, (1985)

Goulbourne, H., *Ethnicity and Nationalism in Post-imperial Britain* (Cambridge: Cambridge University Press, 1991).

Goulbourne, H., 'Varieties of Pluralism: the notion of a pluralist, post-imperial Britain', *New Community*, 17 (2), January (1991).

Gregory, D., 'The role of religion in the secular workplace', *Notre Dame Journal of Law, Ethics and Public Policy* Vol.4, (1990).

Group of Consultants on Cultural Aspects of Equality of Opportunities for Immigrants, *Study* (Strasbourg: Council of Europe, 1996).

H

Habermas, J., *The Theory of Communicative Competence, vol. 1: Reason and the Rationalisation of Society* (Boston: Beacon, 1983).

Habermas, J., *The Theory of Communicative Competence vol. 2: Lifeworld and System* (Boston: Beacon, 1987).

Halliday, F., *Islam and the Myth of Confrontation* (London: I.B. Tauris, 1995).

Hammer, L.S., *The International Human Right to Freedom of Conscience* (Aldershot: Ashgate, 2001).

Harris, D., M. O'Boyle and C. Warbrick, *Law of the European Convention on Human Rights*, (London: Butterworths, 1995).

Harris D., and S. Joseph (eds.), *The International Covenant on Civil and Political Rights* (Oxford: Clarendon, 1995).

Hart, D.A., *One Faith? Non-realism and the World of Faiths* (London: Mowbray, 1995).

Hastings, A., *Church and State: The English Experience* (Exeter: Exeter University Press, 1991).

Haynes, J., *Religion in Global Politics* (London: Longman, 1998).

Helweg, A.W., *Sikhs in England: The Development of a Migrant Community (2nd edition)* (Delhi: Oxford University Press, 1986).

Hepple, B., M. Coussey and T. Choudhury, *Equality a New Framework – Report of the independent review of the enforcement of UK anti-discrimination legislation* (Oxford: Hart, 2000).

Hickey, J., *Religion and the Northern Ireland Problem* (Dublin: Gill and Macmillan, 1984).

Hill, M., *A Sociological Yearbook of Religion* No. 4, (London: SCM Press, 1971).

Holt, J.C., *Magna Carta* (Cambridge: Cambridge University Press, 1976).

Horton, J., (ed.), *Liberalism, Multiculturalism and Toleration* (London: Macmillan, 1993).

R.E. Howard, *Human Rights and the Search for Community* (Boulder: Westview Press, 1995).

F. Hussain, *The Anti-Islamic Tradition in the West* (Leicester: Muslim Community Studies Institute, 1990).

R. Hutton, *The Triumph of the Moon: A History of Modern Pagan Witchcraft* (Oxford: Oxford University Press, 1999).

I

Independent Review of the Enforcement of U.K. Anti-Discrimination Legislation, *Equality Bill* (University of Cambridge Faculty of Law, 10 July 2002).

J

James, A., *Sikh Children in Britain* (Oxford: Oxford University Press, 1974).

Janis, M.W., (ed.), *The Influence of Religion on the development of International Law* (Dordrecht: Martinus Nijhoff, 1991).

Janis, M.W., and C. Evans (eds.), *Religion and International Law* (The Hague: Martinus Nijhoff, 1999).

Jong, C.D. de, *The Freedom of Thought, Conscience and Religion or Belief in the United Nations (1946-1992)* (Antwerp, Groningen, Oxford: Intersentia-Hart Publishers, 2000).

JUSTICE, *Towards Equality and Diversity: Implementing the Employment and Race Directives – responding to the Government's Consultation Paper* (JUSTICE, March 2002).

K

Kabbani, R., *Letter to Christendom* (London: Virago, 1989).

Krishnaswami, A., *Study of Discrimination in the Matter of Religious Rights and Practices*, UN Doc.E/CN.4/Sub.2/200/Rev.1, 1960. Reprinted in the *NYU Journal of International Law and Politics* Vol. 11, p. 227 (1978).

Knott, K., *Religion and Identity in the Study of Ethnic Minority Religions in Britain*, Community Religions Project Research Papers, ns. 2, (Leeds: University of Leeds, 1986).

Küng, H., *Christianity and the World Religions, Paths of Dialogue with Islam, Hinduism, and Buddhism* (Glasgow: Collins, 1985).

Künnemann, R., 'A Coherent Approach to Human Rights', *Human Rights Quarterly, A Comparative and International Journal of the Social Sciences, Humanities, and Law* Vol. 17, No. 2 (May 1995).

Kymlicka, W., and W. Norman (eds.), *Citizenship in Diverse Societies* (Oxford: Oxford University Press).

L

Lamont, S., *Church and State: Uneasy Alliances* (London: Bodley Head, 1989).

Larsen, T., *Friends of Religious Equality: Nonconformist Politics in Mid-Victorian England* (Woodbridge: The Boydell Press, 1999).

Law Commission, The, *Offences Against Religion and Public Worship*, Law Commission Report No. 145 (London: HMSO, 1985).

Lerner, N., 'Proselytism, Change of Religion and Adherence to International Human Rights', *Emory International Law Review* Vol. 12, (1998).

Lerner, N., *Religion, Beliefs and International Human Rights* (MaryKnoll, NY: Orbis Book, 2001).

Luthra, M., *Britain's Black Population: Social Change, Public Policy and Agenda* (Aldershot: Ashgate, 1997).

M

Macphereson, W., *Sir William Macpherson's Inquiry into the Matters Arising from the Death of Stephen Lawrence on 22nd April 1993 to date, in order Particularly to Identify the Lessons to be Learned for the Investigation and Prosecution of Racially Motivated Crimes*, 24 February 1999, (London: The Stationery Office, 1999)

Marty, M.E., and J. Moore, *Education, Religion and the Common Good: Advancing a Distinctly American Conversation about Religion's Role in our Shared Life* (New York: Jossey-Bass, 2000).

Mayer, A.E., *Islam and Human Rights: Tradition and Politics* (Boulder, Colorado: Westview Press, 1991).

McCrudden, C., D. Smith, C. Brown, *Racial Justice At Work* (London: PSI, 1991).

Medina, C., *The Battle of Human Rights: Gross, Systematic Violations and the Inter-American System* (Dordrecht: Martinus Nijhoff Publishers, 1988).

Meron, T., (ed.), *Human Rights in International Law: Legal Policy Issues* (Oxford: Clarendon Press, 1984).

Meron, T., *Human Rights Law-making in the United Nations, A Critique of Instruments and Processes*, (Oxford: Clarendon Press, 1986).

Moreno, P.C., (ed.), *Handbook on Religious Liberty Around the World* (Charlottesville: The Rutherford Institute, 1996).

Modood, T., 'Anti-Essentialism, Multiculturalism and the 'Recognition' of Religious Minorities', *Journal of Political Philosophy*, 6 (4) December, pp. 378-399 (1998).

Modood, T., *et al*, *Britain's Ethnic Minorities: Diversity and Disadvantage* (London: Policy Studies Institute, 1997).

Modood, T., 'British Asian Muslims and the Rushdie affair', *Political Quarterly* Vol. 61, no. 2, (1990).

Modood, T., 'British Multiculturalism: Some Rival Positions and Thoughts on the Way Forward', seminar paper to the *Commission on the Future of Multi-ethnic Britain*, London, July (1998).

Modood, T., 'Catching up with Jesse Jackson: being oppressed and being somebody', *New Community*, 17 (1), October (1990).

Modood, T., (ed.), *Church, State and Religious Minorities* (London: PSI, 1997).

Modood, T., *Not Easy Being British: Colour, Culture and Citizenship* (London: Runnymede Trust, 1992).

Modood, T., *et al*, *Ethnic Minorities in Britain* (London: PSI, 1997).

Modood, T., 'Political blackness and British Asians', *Sociology* Vol. 28, no. 3 (1994).

Modood, T., and P. Werbner (eds.), *The Politics of Multiculturalism in the New Europe: Racism, Identity and Community* (London: Zed Books, 1997).

Monsma, S.V., and J.C. Soper (eds.), *Equal Treatment of Religion in a Pluralistic Society* (Grand Rapids, MI: Eerdmans, 1998).

Monsma, S.V., and J.C. Soper, *The Challenge of Pluralism: Church and State in Five Democracies* (Lanham, MY: Rowman & Littlefield, 1997).

Montgomery, J.W., *Human Rights & Human Dignity* (Michigan: Probe Ministries International, Zondervan Publishing House, 1986).

Moon, G., (ed.), *Race Discrimination. Developing and Using a New Legal Framework* (Oxford: Hart, 2000).

Muslim Parliament of Great Britain, *Race Relations and Muslims in Great Britain: A Discussion Paper* (London: The Muslim Parliament, 1992).

N

Naber, J.M.M. (ed.), *Freedom of religion: a precious human right, A survey of advantages and drawbacks* (Assen: Van Gorcum, 2000).

Nye, M., 'Hare Krishna and Sanatan Dharm in Britain: The Campaign for Bhaktivedanta Manor' *Journal of Contemporary Religion* Vol. XXI, No. 1, (1996).

O

O'Dair, R., and A. Lewis, *Law and Religion* (Oxford: Oxford University Press, 2001).

P

Paige, G.D., C. Satha-Anand (Qadar Muheideen) and S. Gilliatt (eds.), *Islam and Nonviolence* (Honolulu: Center for Global Nonviolence Planning Project, 1993).

Partsch, K.J., (ed.), *Des Menschen Recht Zwischen Freiheit Und Verantworting* (Berlin: Duncker & Humblot, 1989).

Pennings, P., *Verzuiling en Ontzuiling: de lokale verschillen: opbouw, instandhouding en neergang van plaatselijke zuilen in verschillende delen van Nederland na 1880* (Kampen: Kok Agora, 1991).

Pateman, C., *The Sexual Contract* (Stanford: University of Stanford Press, 1988).

Peters, R., and G.J. de Vries, 'Apostasy in Islam', *Die Welt des Islams* Vol. XVII (1976-1977).

Phillipson, G., 'The Human Rights Act, 'Horizontal Effect' and the Common Law: A Bang or a Whimper?' Vol. 62 *MLR* (1999).

Poulter, S., *Asian Traditions and English Law* (London: Runnymede Trust, 1990).

R

Rahman, S.A., *Punishment of Apostasy in Islam* (Lahore: Institute of Islamic Culture, 1972).

Rath, J., R. Penninx, C. Groenendijk and A. Meijer, *Europe and its Islam: the Netherlands, Belgium and Britain react to an emerging religious community* (Leiden: Brill, 2001).

Rex, J., and R. Moore, *Race, Community and Conflict* (Oxford: Oxford University Press, 1967).

Rex, J., 'National Identity in the Democratic Multi-Cultural State', *Sociological Research Online*, 1 (2), http://www.socresonline.org.uk/socresonline/1/2/1.html (1996).

Richardson, J., and M. Introvigne, ''Brainwashing Theories' in European Parliamentary and Administrative Reports on 'Cults' and 'Sects'', *The Journal for the Scientific Study of Religion* No. 2, Vol. 4, (2001).

Robilliard, St. J., *Religion and The Law: Religious Liberty in Modern English Law* (Manchester: Manchester University Press, 1984).

Runnymede Trust, *A Very Light Sleeper: The Persistence and Dangers of Antisemitism* (London: Runnymede Trust, 1994).

Runnymede Trust, *Islamophobia: A Challenge for Us All* (London: Runnymede Trust, 1997).

Rushdie, S., 'The New Empire Within Britain', *New Society*, 9 December (1982).

S

Saghal, G., and N. Yuval-Davis, *Refusing Holy Orders: Women and Fundamentalism in Britain* (London: Virago Press, 1992).

Salbstein, M., *The Emancipation of the Jews in Britain: The Question of the Admission of the Jews to Parliament, 1828-1860* (London & Toronto: Associated University Press, 1982).

Schie, P.G.C. van, (ed.), *Tussen polarisatie en paars: de 100-jarige verhouding tussen liberalen en socialisten in Nederland* (Kampen: Kok Agora, 1995).

Sivanandan, A., 'RAT and the Degradation of the Black Struggle', *Race and Class*, XXVI (4) (1985).

Smith, W.C., *The Meaning and End of Religion* (London: SPCK, 1978).

Stenton, F., *Anglo-Saxon England* (Oxford: Oxford University Press, 3rd ed, 1986).

Sullivan, D.J., 'Advancing the Freedom of Religion or Belief through the UN Declaration on the Elimination of Religious Intolerance' *The American Journal of International Law* 82 (1988).

Sullivan, D., 'Gender Equality and Religious Freedom: Toward a Framework for Conflict Resolution', *New York University Journal of International Law and Politics*, Vol. 24, (1992).

Sutherland, S., and P. Clarke (eds.), *The World's Religions, The Study of Religion, Traditional and New Religion*, 2nd ed., (London: Routledge, 1991).

Swidler, L., (ed.), *Religious Liberty and Human Rights in Nations and in Religions*, (Philadelphia: Ecumenical Press and New York: Hippocrene Books, 1986).

T

Tahzib, B., *Freedom of Religion or Belief: Ensuring Effective International Protection* (The Hague: Martinus Nijhoff, 1996).

Taverdi, K., *A History of Armenians in Britain* (London: Centre for Armenian information and Advice, 1988).

Thierstien, J., and Y.R. Kamalipour (eds.), *Religion, Law and Freedom: A Global Perspective* (Westport: Praeger Publishing, 2000).

Tier, A.M., 'Islamization of the Sudan Laws and Constitution: Its Allure and Its Impracticability', *Verfassung und Recht in Uebersee* Vol 25, Issue 2, (1990).

U

UKACIA (UK Action Committee on Islamic Affairs), *Muslims and the Law in Multi-faith Britain: Need for Reform* (London: UK Action Committee on Islamic Affairs, 1993).

V

Vogel, S.H. de, 'Clergy Morale: the ups and downs', *Christian Century*, 1149, (17 December 1986).

Vyver, J.D. van der, 'Religious Fundamentalism and Human Rights', *Journal of International Affairs* Vol. 5, No. 1, p. 38 (Summer 1996).

Vyver, J.D. van der, and J. Witte Jr, (eds.), *Religious Human Rights in Global Perspective, Legal Perspectives*, (The Hague: Martinus Nijhoff Publishers, 1996).

W

Wade, W., 'Horizons of Horizontality', Vol. 116 *LQR* (2000).

Wadham, J., and H. Mountfield, *Blackstone's Guide to the Human Rights Act 1998* (London: Blackstone, 1999).

Warberg, G.R., 'The Sharia Law in Sudan: Implementation and Repercussion, 1983-1989', *The Middle-East Journal*, Vol. 44, No. 4, (Autumn 1990).

Brody, R., and D. Weisbrodt, 'Major Developments in the 1989 Session on the United Nations Commission on Human Rights', *Human Rights Quarterly*, Vol. 11, (1989).

Weller, P., 'The Inter Faith Network for the United Kingdom' in *The Anglo-Indian Historical Review: A Journal of History* Vol. XX, No. 1, pp. 20-26 (1994).

Weller, P., A. Feldman, K. Purdam *et al*, *Religious Discrimination in England and Wales* (London: Home Office Research Study 220, 2001).

Weller, P., K. Purdam et al, *Religious Discrimination in England and Wales: Interim Report* (Derby: University of Derby, 2000).

Werbner, P., and T. Modood (eds.), *Debating Cultural Identity* (London: Zed Books, 1997).

Witte, J. Jr, 'Law, Religion, and Human Rights', *Columbia Human Rights Law Review* Vol. 28, No. 1, (Fall 1996).

Witte, J., and J.D. van der Vyver (eds.), *Religious Human Rights in Global Perspective: Religious Perspectives* pp. 392-393 (The Hague: Martinus Nijhoff Publishers, 1996).

Wolffe, J., (ed.), *The Growth of Religious Diversity: Britain From 1945. A Reader* (Sevenoaks: Hodder and Stoughton, 1993).

Wright, N., *Public Truth or Private Option? Gospel and Religious Liberty in a Multi-Faith Society in the Light of the Resurrection* (Joppa Group Occasional Paper, 1999).

Y

Young, I., *Justice and the Politics of Difference* (Princeton University Press, 1990).

Index